AENGUS FINUCANE

IN THE HEART OF CONCERN

BY DEIRDRE PURCELL

NEW ISLAND

Aengus Finucane: In the Heart of Concern
First published in 2014
by New Island Books
16 Priory Hall Office Park
Stillorgan
County Dublin
Republic of Ireland

www.newisland.ie

The Author acknowledges that this Work has been commissioned by Concern Worldwide, a company limited by guarantee registered in Ireland (company number 39647) which has been granted charitable status (charity number CHY 5745) and has its registered offices at 52/55 Lower Camden Street, Dublin 2, and published by New Island Books, registered in Ireland (Company Number 186067) whose registered office is at 16 Stillorgan Office Park, Stillorgan, Co. Dublin.

PRINT ISBN: 978-1-84840-386-4
EPUB ISBN: 978-1-84840-387-1
MOBI ISBN: 978-1-84840-388-8

British Library Cataloguing Data.
A CIP catalogue record for this book is available from the British Library.

Typeset by JVR Creative, India
Cover design by Mariel Deegan
Printed by ScandBook AB, Sweden

This book is dedicated, with humility, to the founders, fundraisers, donors (whose generosity makes the work possible), staff and volunteers of Concern, who, along with their families and supporters, have fulfilled and continue to fulfil the organisation's vision, as articulated by Father Aengus Finucane, to lift millions of the poorest of the poor out of destitution, starvation, violence, exploitation, neglect and despair.

CHRONOLOGY OF KEY EVENTS

1932 Birth of Aengus Cornelius Finucane, Limerick.

1936 Sexton Street School, County Limerick.

1944 Novitiate, Kilshane Seminary, County Tipperary.

1959 Ordination as Holy Ghost Father (Spiritan).

1959–1968 Pastoral parish mission work in Nigeria.

1967 Outbreak of civil war in Biafra/Nigeria.

1968–1970 Biafra airlift at ULI airport.

1968 (March) Africa Concern founded by Father Raymond Kennedy, John O'Loughlin Kennedy and Kay Kennedy.

1971 First Concern Volunteers go to Calcutta.

1972 Concern volunteers go to Bangladesh.

1972–1978 Aengus Finucane appointed as director of Bangladesh.

1981 Aengus Finucane becomes CEO of Concern.

1988 Concern office opens in Belfast.

1991 Concern office opens in London.

1994 Concern office opens in New York.

1997 Aengus Finucane retires, becomes honorary president of Concern US.

1999 Concern office opens in Chicago.

2008 Aengus Finucane's final trip overseas (Haiti).

2009 Aengus dies.

Do as much as you can,
as well as you can,
for as many as you can,
for as long as you can.

— Father Aengus Finucane, C.S.Sp

'Aengus reflected the best of who we are as a nation, embodying and promoting a spirit of humanity, dignity and equality. His courage, leadership and drive to reach the poorest changed the way we think about and work with those most in need. If I'm asked about his legacy, I would point to the fact that he not only saved but transformed the lives of millions of people across the developing world.'

– Dominic MacSorley, CEO of Concern

INTRODUCTION

'We have a strong inclination to do evil,
and you have to fight like hell to do any good.'

— Aengus Finucane

How do you define Aengus Finucane? Far from easily.
On the surface the task might seem simple enough because there are so many visible and obvious facets: Spiritan (Holy Ghost) priest, CEO of Concern in Ireland and latterly honorary president of Concern US, native and Freeman of Limerick City, recipient of many awards and honorary doctorates and an influence on governments and on other non-governmental agencies in the area of development and aid. A people person who was the charismatic focus of a huge circle of intensely loyal friends.

Party-giver. Storyteller. Family man in its widest sense. A big-picture guy. But above all, a passionate — and compassionate — friend of the poorest of the poor in any country, or on any continent inflicted with famine, war, natural disaster or any emergency situation that could benefit from his attention and that of the organisation he loved and cherished from the bottom of his huge, brave heart.

As well as his considerable height, he carried the kind of weight and girth that would do credit to the front row of his beloved Munster rugby team, making him seem taller still. 'A giant' was a description not infrequently applied to him and he was most definitely an imposing physical presence. Sonorous too. In times gone by, Holy Ghost seminarians were, we're told, trained to project their sermonising voices by dint of standing at one end of a football field to address a tutor at the other end. In the course of that schooling, Aengus's voice, naturally a resonant bass, became, according to one informant, 'even boomier.'

When Father Aengus Cornelius Finucane entered a room, his entrance was noted. When he held court at one of his parties, the focus was on him. When he addressed a gathering, made a case to a Prime Minister or importuned a new Concern donor, his audience paid attention.

His reputation had perhaps preceded him in the case of one potential donor at least, because during their first meeting in a New York restaurant this man reported that he did all the talking deliberately so as not to let Aengus get a word in. Predictably, perhaps, the man subsequently caved, became a staunch, lifelong pal and proponent of his new friend's organisation and is now chairman of Concern US. He is Tom Moran, whose day job is president and CEO of the highly successful insurance company Mutual of America, and is one of the scores of people interviewed for this book.

Aengus was always a prolific correspondent, report-writer and chronicler of events during his working life. Even before joining Africa Concern, so named on its founding in March 1968, as a Holy Ghost Father serving in his Nigerian parish, he constantly wrote home. Throughout a subsequent lifetime with Concern, alongside this evocative correspondence, he sent an additional flow of memos and reports to headquarters, in which, employing distinctive and flowing penmanship, he would outline achievements and failures, obstacles overcome or ways round them, along with suggestions for future innovations.

His brother, Father Jack Finucane, had followed into the Holy Ghosts, to Nigeria and then into Concern, himself serving there with great distinction until he retired. After his older brother's passing, he gathered together all these documents, including the personal letters and musings and with the help of family members, spent months categorising and filing them for future reference.

Finally, however, the number of archive boxes proved to be so large he could not house them all, so he gave them into the care of Concern headquarters in Camden Street.

Where, in error, their contents were shredded.

The tragedy is small in comparison to the life-and-death situations both brothers encountered daily in their work in what was then described as the Third World. Although very different in personality, inclinations and habits, sometimes bickering and disagreeing as brothers do, Aengus and Jack had been deeply devoted not just to their cause in service of social justice and to the poorest of the poor but to each other, so for Jack, already devastated by his brother's passing, the destruction of this archive served further to deepen his grief.

And so, with very few papers having survived the shredder – and many of these quite repetitive – the method chosen to write this book was by interview, recording the voices of people who knew Aengus, loved him, or in some cases, differed strongly with him but respected him just the same. Here are reactions and recollections of huge events, plus personal assessments and anecdotes about this singular cleric from a wide circle of people he loved, worked with and occasionally exasperated, including family, friends, donors and fellow priests.

In this new archive, there are also the voices of outsiders who encountered him and his brother within and outside the fields of Concern, including those of the current and former presidents of Ireland, Michael D. Higgins and Mary Robinson, the latter famously having gone to Somalia at Aengus's direct invitation during the worst phase of the conflict there.

The most vivid accounts of the organisation, and of the Finucane brothers, comes from Concern volunteers who, as the backbone of early operations, lived and worked closely with one or both of the Finucanes. Many were in their (very) early twenties when they travelled shiny-eyed to places they and their parents had to look up in school atlases; they knew they were bound for strenuous work in areas of poverty-ridden squalor but went anyway.

A word here about the way these recordings have been used – and a caveat. Every one of the interviews is fascinating in its own right: Concern – and Aengus – sure knew how to attract and recruit dedicated and innovative individuals. What has been intriguing is not just each individual's assessment of Aengus, but the way in which, with a few exceptions, views about his character and ability concurred, even when the holders had clashed with him about certain issues or styles of management.

Equally striking was to hear details about their reasons for joining, the attitude changes and fast-tracked maturity engendered by stints abroad in such taxing environments. They came to Concern as professionals – nurses, administrators, accountants, agronomists – but very quickly flowered to become astonishingly able and independent innovators and advocates, even entrepreneurs.

With their stories, these interviewees, a few of whom are undeniably mavericks, show what a broad church Concern was in Aengus's time, and still is. Their tales illustrate the power of his influence: he could stimulate a diverse spectrum of characters to play to the highest level of ability.

When talking about Aengus (or Jack, or Concern in general), some of the experiences related by outsiders, for instance broadcaster Mike Murphy and journalists Donal Byrne and Tom McSweeney, are included to show how difficult the circumstances in which these aid workers and their leaders operated really were, even from the time when they got out of their beds every morning.

Aengus achieved what he did through inspired and visionary thinking, leadership and doggedness about reaching goals. He saw the world, not as his oyster as many global businessmen do, but as an imperfect network of nations presiding over regimes of unequal opportunities for multitudes of their citizens, who, due to blatant injustice or poverty, were forced to live out their lives at sub-human level. It was his mission, he believed, to rebalance these inequities inasmuch as he could do so. He led the charge, but knew that he could not win the battles he chose on his own. He did it with carefully selected teams, and strong back-up from his organisation.

One caveat about these interviews as research-resource: details can be misremembered as time passes, and there have been some radically different versions of the same event, necessitating a stab at judging which was the more, or *most* authentic. (The writer, Tony Farmar, who has written a comprehensive history of Concern's development during its first thirty years, *Believing in Action*, came up against the same conundrum.)

At this remove, many of the legends that have grown up around Aengus, still referred to, erroneously, by many as 'one of the founders of Concern', are a little hazy. He loved the Irish language (especially *Nuacht* on TG4), and would understand perfectly if some of these variations on what happened to him might fall under the headline of the traditional Gaelic: *Dúirt bean liom go ndúirt bean léi (go ndúirt bean eile gur inis bean di …).* (A woman told me that a woman told her (that another woman said that she was told by a woman…)). In other words, we're talking about multiple and exponential hearsay.

Aengus was a 'Titan', said many interviewees, but that description encapsulates only a small part of the story. Although no pushover, it has emerged that he was tender with greenhorn volunteers. When remembering him, volunteers and colleagues said again and again that a major talent of his was the ability to discern latent aptitudes and talent in those who had not yet discovered these in themselves. Known to have a pithy catchphrase for all eventualities, in the context of spotting hidden talent, his 'Give me the makings', i.e. *give me malleable but previously undetected traits,* covered this particular skill.

He exhibited it right from the beginning when faced with youngsters entrusted to his care in the early foreign fields, such as Bangladesh, where he arrived just after the lethal war that sundered East from West Pakistan in the early 1970s. These women and men, middle-aged now, all talked of an action-driven personality, of foresight, goodness and a generous nature. He was ultra-discreet with confidences, apparently being of major assistance when approached for relationship counselling.

A peacemaker and mediator according to most, he could be wrathful and critical when his very high standards, both personal and work-related, were in his opinion breached. These squalls passed quickly,.

People mentioned his bluntness, but also his tact when the need arose. For instance, when he discerned interpersonal spikiness within Concern's communal living quarters, he would quietly separate the antagonists by moving them around between venues in such a way that those being moved felt they were going somewhere better, and those who remained believed this as well. A few remarked drily that he created inner circles, mostly composed of women, whom he favoured above others. This, it was emphasised, never compromised the work, or their retrospective esteem for him.

While Aengus often received and held confidences from others, he seldom revealed any depth of personal information about himself. Yes, he would chat freely – and long into the night – about his origins and family, about work and work colleagues, about his beloved Limerick, Munster rugby teams, hurling, Gaelic football, history, politics and his days in Bangladesh. He had no problem relating tales about his formative days as a priest-turned-aid worker in Biafra. Yet despite lengthy probing of dozens and dozens of observers, family members, fellow-workers and friends, all of whom wanted to be as helpful as they could, the innermost worries or difficulties of Father Aengus Finucane have remained somewhat opaque. Yet during the transcription of the recordings, sometimes an unexpected little phrase or a small: 'I wonder if…?' piece of speculation, or maybe even a sudden, startling insight turned out to be crucial in creating a three dimensional image, the thoughtfulness and depth of this big personality who liked to present himself as convivial and open.

All interviewees were asked individually if they missed him. Many answered immediately and affectionately in the affirmative. Many more took a moment to think about how to answer, and then, almost with wonder, as though the idea had just occurred to them, responded with: 'But I think he's still here!' Indeed, many spoke about him in the present tense.

On the surface, with his appetites for company, get-togethers, late nights and good whiskey, Aengus could glibly be seen as a sybarite. When asked to balance all this praise and love for him with something a little more gritty, the riposte was invariably: 'He'd never go to bed!' It is clear, though, that underneath was a profound spirituality. Several of the ex-volunteers have spoken of the serenity they experienced, and he exuded, when he celebrated Mass at the kitchen tables of Concern houses in Bangladesh and other fields – even on the breakfast table in his apartment in the Seabury complex near the seafront in Dublin's Sandymount. Jack, now retired from Concern, and a redoubtable presence in his own right, was and remains every bit as passionate as his brother about the work of Concern. Like Aengus, in his prime he was highly energetic and born to lead, but is as unlike his sociable and extrovert brother as it is possible to be for those born of the same parents. Definitely not a party animal, he is reserved, seeming almost aloof until you get to know him.

'Give Jack a problem,' said one interviewee, and 'he thinks, comes up with a solution, and sometimes these are ingenious.' As a team playing for Concern, and as brothers within a family where loyalty was the prime virtue, they were very, very close.

Five years the younger, after ordination as a Holy Ghost Father, Jack too was sent by his superiors to Nigeria, where there were already hundreds of his confrères ministering in the parishes. He was quickly elevated to the rank of Parish Priest of

Umuahia not too far from where his brother was situated. They worked hard, and according to one of Aengus's friends who was also there at the time, like Father Jack in Brian Friel's *Dancing at Lughnasa*, this was to be where their working lives would be until retirement or death.

But the state of Biafra then seceded from Nigeria in 1967. Nigeria retaliated by mounting a complete naval blockade, cutting off supplies of food, medicines and all other essentials. As a result, the Biafrans very quickly succumbed to famine and disease.

Along with members of their order and other missionaries, the brothers came together under an umbrella group of aid organisations to participate in a daring and dangerous way of providing supplies: a night-time airlift into an airstrip at a place called Uli from a warehouse on the island of Sao Tome 300 kilometres away. This was funded partially by Africa Concern, founded and run from Dublin by yet another Holy Ghost priest, Raymond Kennedy (at the time at home in Ireland on vacation from his mission post in Nigeria), his brother, John O'Louglin Kennedy, and the latter's wife, Kay.

This airlift has been well documented, especially via a TV documentary in the *Radharc* series for RTÉ: 'Night Flight to Uli', in which Holy Ghost priest, Father Tony Byrne, who was supervising the airlift from the island, told viewers ironically that on his day of ordination he had not expected to find himself buying planes and running an airline. The aircraft had originally been leased, but because the cost of insurance premiums for such dangerous missions became exorbitant, purchasing became the only option. The Biafra experience, and the parts played in it by both Aengus and Jack, are in themselves worth a chapter of this book and so it is planned.

Until he retired, Aengus was Concern's public face, although many say that in a lot of ways, towards the end, the organisation outgrew him, not least during a period of enforced absence from the helm because of several bouts of ill-health.

Even before he left, Concern had begun to expand and develop rapidly in tandem with its client nations, and to keep pace with the burgeoning expansion of theory and debate in the developmental aid sector along with its affiliate, Concern US, to which our hero rebounded in short order and with renewed ebullience, as honorary president.

This expansion and consolidation continues. Now highly professionalised, Concern works more and more with partner bodies, and although there are volunteers both in the UK and US, these days it depends hardly at all on overseas volunteerism. Unlike its founders and early activists, it does not rely at all on the Holy Ghost Fathers, from whom it grew.

Aengus's best known 'action-first' mantra, and the one that graces his memorial card, is:

> *Do as much as you can,*
> *as well as you can,*
> *for as many as you can,*
> *for as long as you can.*

While Aengus accepted that the core business of Concern was always about the poorest of the poor – and frequently reminded everyone of this – he did begin to worry, said many interviewees, that process and development theory was trumping the needs of individuals and families, particularly women and children. 'People first, always people' was his cry. When presented with some new project or report, he would often respond: 'What's in it for the poor person?'

Even the tiny minority who criticised what they saw as his principal-teacher management style never lost admiration for his sincerity and ardour for his cause, as well as his effectiveness, both as an administrator in the field and in parting donors from their money.

To be fair, funding had risen during that expansion to multiples of millions. Staff and contract employees entering the organisation were coming in not merely with the necessary qualifications, but with specialist master's degrees and even PhDs in development aid and related subjects. Donors were demanding more feedback, and even becoming picky with how their money was spent, while large sources of funding from governments, institutional donors, NGO partnerships and charitable foundations brought with them their own demands for process and accountability. In addition, a professional fundraising operation, with professional oversight, alongside the older methods such as the annual Concern Fast, was being promoted with vigour and was proving to be lucrative.

Jack is now around the same age as Aengus was when he died, and the question remains as to how long the Finucanes' influence will persist. At the time of writing, three chief executives: David Begg, Tom Arnold and Dominic MacSorley, all highly and vocationally motivated, each with an individual modus operandi, have taken office in Camden Street. With the exception of a few now in management, all of the volunteers Aengus knew and loved – and who loved him in return – have gone into other organisations, or have simply retired. Some have taken a seat on Concern's governing body, the council. All are mortal. When asked to furnish an instinctive answer as to the single most striking quality in Aengus Finucane, David Andrews, the former Irish Minister for Foreign Affairs, did not have to think for long. He knew Aengus quite well, and saw him in action, for instance during the conflict in Somalia when he travelled there with Mary Robinson. He also dealt with the priest at home when Aengus was in full, passionate advocacy as he sought funding for his cause.

Andrews's response to the 'striking quality' question was immediate: 'Leadership. He was a natural leader. A big man in every sense, yes, a real leader.'

Concern's ethos, as defined by its founders, was simple: to help the starving children of Biafra. Similarly, when Aengus took over as CEO, the core of Concern's service was to lift the poorest, most forgotten people out of destitution and into living standards conducive to human dignity. That ethos still holds. And while the two CEOs who immediately succeeded him (Begg and Arnold) may have placed different emphases on ways to fulfil this mandate, both, in interviews for this book, said they had always kept this baseline at the forefront of their minds.

Dominic MacSorley is most definitely his own man with his own vision. Much of that original philosophy survives him as he sits behind Aengus's big desk, under Aengus's map of the world, where a handmade, rickety globe of the world presented to Aengus in 1983 by Dominic in a refugee camp on the Thai–Cambodia border is on prominent display.

He is careful, however, not just to look to the past, but also to glean the best of it, marrying its lessons with current thinking.

The word 'colossus' was used a lot when journalists, both in Ireland and abroad, eulogised Aengus. Obituaries in newspapers around the world concentrated on his crusade for the poor and downtrodden. This from the *Los Angeles Times*, for instance: 'His credo, oft-repeated when stumping for donors, was that other saying of his: "We have a strong inclination to do evil, and you have to fight like hell to do any good." '

He lived and breathed Concern, to the extent that some members of his extended family complained that around the dinner table in Limerick, when Aengus was present, there were many abortive attempts to rebel against the continuous, almost boring talk about the organisation. His brother Jack said that in latter years, when the two of them met socially, for instance for a lunch together, they would agree as they sat down that for once there would be no talk about Concern. 'And within two seconds, we'd be talking about Concern.'

By all accounts, Aengus kept his personal emotions under tight control. Joseph Cahalan, CEO of Concern US, remembers seeing him 'tear up' only once. In Chicago, the local fundraising arm of the organisation holds an annual Women of Concern luncheon, established to boost the coffers and to honour a particular woman, but also to raise awareness of the organisation. Cahalan was sitting with Aengus at this event some years ago when he saw a tall, elegant black woman, who was not familiar to him, coming across the room. 'She was six feet one or two, wearing a white silk suit, and it was clear she was approaching our table.'

The woman introduced herself as a paediatrician, educated as such in Yale, married to a banker. She had heard about this lunch, and that Father Aengus was going to be attending. She said she knew then that she had to attend too because she had last met him when she was an 11-year-old refugee. She lived and worked as she did now, she said: 'All as a result of Concern.' It was at that point, added Cahalan, 'Aengus began to cry.'

Multiplied by many millions, that woman's survival – and her flourishing – represents Aengus's legacy, a legacy copper-fastened by another individual case, seen and heard by Dolores Connolly, one of the Chicago Women of Concern.

A number of years ago she accepted an invitation to join a panel discussion about the UN's eight Millennium Development Goals, two of which aim to halve extreme poverty rates and provide universal primary education by 2015. This panel discussion was to be held in front of an audience of future business leaders, MBA students at the prestigious Notre Dame University in Indiana.

Dolores accepted the invitation:

> I mention Concern, and I'm interrupted. At the back of the room, this huge guy gets up. 'Can you say again what organisation? Are you talking about Concern from Biafra? Are you talking about those two brothers? I've heard stories about these two guys. They were trying to starve us out, and these guys would light fires in the night and they would

airdrop this food and my father and my grandfather would have to go out and get it off the runway. These guys were legendary in my village! And there were two of them ...'.

He wouldn't stop talking. He took over the whole meeting....

Job done for Concern. Aengus's legacy confirmed.

– Deirdre Purcell, Mornington, 2014.

1

'Stand up and let your brother sit down!'

– Delia Byrnes Finucane (Aengus's mother)

Aengus's sibling, Sister Patsy Finucane of the Mercy Congregation, speaks about her brother's obsession with his life's work:

> Really and truly, you'd have a pain in our house – every meal, every function. I used to get irritated with him perpetually talking about Concern, and he'd look at me and say: 'Are you not interested then?'
> 'I am, but there's a limit.'

Aengus and Jack (and Jim, Jack's twin, a banker) were three of seven siblings, three girls, four boys, brought up in a house on the Shelbourne road in Limerick. Mary, a public health nurse, is the eldest, Joe, the youngest, was in finance. Biddy, who passed away in 2003, was a homemaker.

Jim, Joe and Biddy have had fourteen children between them, and they too have become absorbed into the immediate clan so that, according to Sarah Finucane, one of Aengus's devoted nieces, quite regularly there could be nineteen people, many times even more, around the

Finucane table for Sunday dinner. 'And don't talk to me about Christmas ...'.

Despite, inevitably, the occasional internal spat, this is such a close-knit family, so fiercely loyal to each other that they can be imagined as a tightly packed quadrilateral phalanx, facing the four points of the compass, impermeable to invasion as they stand shoulder to shoulder and back to back. That, at any rate, is the initial impression.

Born on 26 April 1932, Aengus attended the Christian brothers' school in Sexton Street, in that era when missionary priests and nuns of all cloths toured the classrooms, proselytising for vocations. Redemptorists, Dominicans, Medical Missionaries of Mary and others of many hues, including the Holy Ghost Fathers, bustled into dingy, grey classrooms and stood in front of dusty blackboards to talk not just about spiritual callings and service of the Creator through the particular ethos of their orders and congregations, but about altruism and the fulfilment of a life well lived. They spun tales of living in hot lands, far from the grim, dismal economy and drizzle of 1950s Ireland. They dazzled boys and girls from poor backgrounds with offers of an education, a career, a chance to be independent of the crushing rigidity of the class-ridden mono-culture then prevailing in Ireland. Crucially, they plucked chords in the hearts of young, idealistic and impressionable boys and girls impatient to be free, by offering adventure, planting the idea of doing God's work in exotic locations.

In those times, if you couldn't get into 'teacher training', the next best thing was a job for life in the civil service, with 'establishment' after five years and success in your oral Irish exam.

Forever after, you pushed a pen around a brown desk between four brown walls, squatting in some former colonial mansion in Dublin that had been honeycombed into cubicle-like offices. Maybe you got into an insurance company; or maybe a bank, if you were really lucky and had a relative who was 'well got'. You went 'home' for the weekends where you met your future spouse at Macra[1] functions or in the palaces of dreams – the barn-like dancehalls situated at rural crossroads. If you stayed in Dublin during those weekends, you danced and hunted the opposite sex in the Teachers' Club, the National, Crystal or Ierne Ballrooms.

Meanwhile, the steady stream of answers to those calls 'to enter' had as much to do with escape and adventure as they had with accepting a vocation from the Divine. For many young men and girls, the faraway lands described by these vigorous and charming priests and nuns had up to then been pictured only in carefully curated stamp collections. In cramped, shared bedrooms all over the country, heads-together children negotiated over gorgeously vivid illustrations of butterflies, unusual animals and rare flowers in glowing colour: 'One of my Nyasalands and one Swaziland and one of my Philippines for that one of your Singapores?'

What is more, these calls for vocations came at a time when, for the majority, a university education was an unattainable luxury.

But here, as rain splashed into puddles in yards outside the windows of their classroom, was confirmation, directly from the mouths of Holy Mother Church, that you could achieve the distinction of having letters after your name and respect in your town, village or townland. And even more exciting was the prospect of exploration of lands filled with beautiful colours under a constant yellow sun, all the while conquering souls for God.

During the first five or six decades of the twentieth century in Ireland, these aspects of becoming a priest or nun in a missionary order are absolutely recognised and acknowledged

---

1 *Macra na Feirme*, founded in 1944 and literally 'sons' or 'stalwarts' of the farm (or countryside) is a voluntary rural organisation running a nationwide network of clubs for young people between the ages of 17 and 35. Activities include sport, agriculture, travel, performing arts, community involvement and public speaking.

by contemporaries who entered with Aengus, and by Jack, too, who joined his brother five years later in the huge training seminaries of Kilshane and Kimmage.

In interview, when asked directly whether it was more important to him and to Aengus to go abroad to the missions or to become a priest, Jack responded instantly:

> To us it was the same thing.
>
> (You could have been a diocesan priest?)
>
> Didn't want to. From the very beginning I wanted to go to Africa. That was what attracted me to be a missionary priest.
>
> (Why was that?)
>
> We were influenced by the people who went before us. Limerick had quite a number of Holy Ghost priests, and these people came home on holidays. You'd meet them and mix with them, you heard their stories. That frontier approach – that's what attracted. I had two cousins who were Dominicans, but I wasn't interested in their lifestyle. They weren't on the real missions, as we thought. We were going, as we thought, to the real missions. To Darkest Africa.

As it happened, one of these clerical-storytellers, to whom both Finucanes avidly listened, was Limerickman Bishop Joseph Whelan of the diocese of Owerri in the Nigerian state of Biafra. He was revered by his fellow Shannonside citizens for his missionary and humanitarian work. In those early days, none of the three, bishop or two future Holy Ghosts, could have known that they were to work together in the Biafran civil war and famine in the late 1960s, or that in the minds of the Irish public this catastrophe was to become associated for the rest of their lives with the Finucanes.

At this point, it might be interesting to look ahead a little by quoting some of the words given in interview by Donal

Byrne, now a senior editor in the RTÉ newsroom, but who was at the time of the 1984 Ethiopian famine, a reporter with *The Irish Times*. With a party of journalists he travelled to Ethiopia with Concern to cover the 1984 famine, where he had his first taste of the fieldwork practices of the Finucanes, their staff and volunteers.

That famine had crashed memorably onto our TV screens, firstly via the work of Mike Wooldridge, the BBC's East Africa correspondent, and shortly afterwards, to astonishing global effect, via Michael Buerk, whose reportage, along with the pictures of his cameraman, Mohamed Amin, spurred a worldwide response.

It wasn't Donal Byrne's first trip to cover a disaster; he had been abroad with other charitable organisations. And he had never been less than clear-eyed about 'the missions'. Like us all, he had dropped pennies into collection boxes and had received an acknowledgment when the head of a small 'black baby' fixed to a spring on the top of the alms box wobbled his or her head in delighted gratitude at receiving such largesse.

This was to be Byrne's first close encounter with Concern in general and with the Finucanes in particular, in this case Jack. He also encountered Aengus subsequently, and with what is now called, popularly the 'helicopter view' here is some of what he said:

> What was called 'the missions' way back in the past always had some vague and quite questionable mean-ings for me. But when you were dealing with those Finucane guys – this is a very personal view – you could see they had decided that this was their voca-tion. It seemed to me that they were almost defrocked in the literal sense and that nothing was going to get in the way of that vocation. That's how strong they were, what allowed them to manage politically, both

nationally in Ireland and with governments in the strangest kinds of places with the strangest administrations. It was the first time I'd seen, at first-hand and close-up, what it meant to be a missionary in a modern context.

To Donal, this was an indication of how the Church had, at some point, 'divided silently. (*Yes I have a vocation, but my vocation is not to be sitting in a parochial house in Glenealy; my work is to go to the four points of the globe.*)'

I'm equally convinced that if these nuns and priests weren't doing what they were doing abroad, they'd be gone out of the Church; they wouldn't be part of any conventional set-up.

He believes that what was remarkable about the Finucanes is that they were 'mavericks to begin with', but that a lot of such individualists are useless in a crisis:

These were people who could handle a crisis with natural ability, talent, leadership and a natural diplomacy. I don't think Jack, inasmuch as I knew him, would have the tolerance for sitting in endless meetings about how, in six months' time, we might be able to do something. Crisis was what drove him. You could see it in him physically: the challenge was there, he was up to it.

It's only since I began to think about what I might offer as my own thoughts that I began to think of Jack as a priest. Aengus too, although he wore his collar more and was more evidently a cleric at meetings and so forth. The collar helped him on occasions, and I think he knew it. When you're selling something to Irish people, and you are there as a trusted man of the cloth, this caring, compassionate figure, wearing a clerical collar does help.

Again he goes back to that era, putting a context on the work of aid and charity organisations:

> It's only when I saw the scale of what was on the ground [in Ethiopia] and what had to be dealt with, I began to understand what was in play here. Their experience, for instance. They could do huge work with limited resources, and could affect and improve the lives of a large, large number of people and do it effectively and speedily.
>
> And although I didn't know them well enough to presume, my impression was that beneath this drive and determination was a spiritual motivation. If you were offered an enormous salary to do what they were doing, I don't think you'd last a month.

There will be more from Donal Byrne presently.

The males in the Finucane family grew up to be big men; their grandfather was a blacksmith in Kilrush; he and his wife had nine sons. One of them, John, (known as Jack; to avoid confusion, let's call him 'Jack Senior') became the father of Mary, Aengus, Patsy, Jack, Jim, Biddy and Joe, and was the only one of the nine who made 70 years of age.

Tom had what was generally known during that era as a 'good job' in the Department of Finance in Dublin.

As a group, the Finucanes are modest about their achievements. Tom Finucane, one of Jack Senior's brothers, was head of the exchequer section of the Department of Finance. Professor Paul Finucane, one of Aengus's and Jack's nephews, is the foundation head of the graduate entry medical school at the University of Limerick. His brother Jim Finucane, another professor, is a noted endocrinologist at Beaumont Hospital. You get the picture. This was, and is, a high-achieving family.

Jack Senior, a committed Republican who was twice interned, worked for the London Steamboat Company, but finished his working life as company secretary at J. J. O'Toole's, a firm of paper merchants, where until he retired he lived a simple life, cycling home for his dinner in the middle of the day.

A deeply devout Catholic, he took just two foreign trips in his lifetime: one to Lourdes, one to Rome, instead preferring to holiday with his family in Kilkee. He was a quiet man, and 'contented' by all accounts, including Patsy's, who is interviewed while sitting in her small flat on the south side of Dublin. Allegedly retired from a life spent in education, she is busier than ever with pastoral and other work, including Ki massage, reflexology and counselling.

(Had their mother identified Aengus for a vocation?)

No, but our grandmother, Grandma Finucane, never doubted but that he would be a priest. It was a custom in that part of County Clare that the eldest became a priest.

She goes on to relate an extraordinary story she heard many times growing up. Aengus, she believes, knew it too because it involved him:

... and we did talk about it. I have a very vivid memory of one particular morning. Dad used to try to go to Kilrush to visit his mother once every six weeks, and when war came he had to go down by boat – the flour boat – from Limerick docks to Cappa pier.

This morning, Mum was getting us ready for school, we used to line up in the kitchen to have our hair brushed and so on. Dad came in and he was carrying his case. 'I think I'll go to Kilrush today.'

Mother stopped what she was doing. 'What are you talking about? You were in Kilrush three weeks ago.'

And he said: 'Yes, but I always said that if I got this urge, I'd answer it. I'll go down to the docks after work, and if I can get on a boat, I'll go. So if I'm not back, you'll know I've gone.'

This, remember, was 1940s Ireland, where personal telephones were only for doctors, parish priests and bank managers.

So he went to Kilrush. It was November, as far as I remember. When he got to his mother's house, she opened the door: 'Jack, what are you doing? You're not due at all!'

Anyhow, he stayed that first night, and when the second night came, decided to go and visit his aunt, his mother's sister, who lived nearby. On leaving, he said to his mother: 'You go to bed now, and I'll bring you up hot milk when I get back.' And when he got back, she was dead in the bed.

Clare people have this extraordinary devotion to the dead, and Dad always used to pray to his own father that his mother wouldn't die alone.

She did, as it happened, but the crux of this story is that her son was there to take from her hand the envelope she was clutching. 'In it was money for Aengus's ordination.'

In Sister Patsy's opinion, Aengus himself never doubted but that he was destined for the Church, and not just because of those exciting talks given in his classroom by the vocation-seeking clerics. 'He was very religious as a child, very prayerful.' Even when still a boy, alongside his passion for the hurling and football he played for his club, Treaty Sarsfields, he became involved in the Penny Dinners service run by the local conference of the St Vincent de Paul.

Again and again, interviewees of all hues, and not just Patsy or the other members of Aengus's close family, made sure to emphasise that one of his most transparent traits was that, whatever the cause, when he was in, *he was in*. 'We used to get a pain in the face with Penny Dinners, because if Aengus was involved in Penny Dinners we were all involved in Penny Dinners,' says Patsy.

Liam Burke and John Leahy, friends and fellow Limerick men, both agree with this drive Aengus exhibited from a very early age and have seen it first-hand.

Burke, whose father had a small shop near where the Finucanes lived, now runs a photographic agency, Press 22, in the city. He became a friend of Aengus's in the early 1980s when he travelled to various disaster areas in Concern countries of operation to capture images. He has supplied the organisation with these, free of charge, ever since. His iconic image of a boy carrying his little brother, (captioned 'He's not heavy, he's my brother') was snapped in Ethiopia and was widely used by the organisation for many years to illustrate promotional and fundraising material.

Burke admired Aengus, not just personally, but for his ethos. They had long discussions about the poor. 'I think Concern is the only organisation I know that wants to put itself out of business. That was Aengus's philosophy.'

> I remember being in the shop as a small boy and seeing children in their bare feet coming to take the rotten fruit and vegetables, and ham that was rank. This was the early 1960s, so this is how I know that *Angela's Ashes* [a famous memoir of a poverty-stricken Limerick child-hood by Frank McCourt, later filmed] was authentic. When he was young, Aengus would have seen this, and probably worse than this, a lot earlier. I think it made a lasting impression on him.

Incidentally, when in his later years he went to New York as honorary president of Concern US, Aengus met McCourt, who lived there and the two became firm friends.

John Leahy is a Limerick motor dealer. He was taken into the Finucane family circle by his friend Joe, Aengus's brother. He says that Frank McCourt's book did not exaggerate the abject poverty in certain areas of the city in the late 1930s and 1940s, even into the 1950s and early 1960s. He characterises Aengus's boyhood work with the Penny Dinners as being a characteristic effort to do something about lifting the poor with 'not a hand-out but a hand-up'; a phrase that resonated with him throughout his life and work.

Long before Aengus got to his work, however, there was the little matter of ten long years of priestly training.

From all of the siblings and very close friends, it is clear that during the Finucanes' growing up it was their mother who held sway, setting the rules and running her household. Aengus, being the eldest son, being such a 'good' boy, so devout, religious and charitable, did she favour him? Spoil him?

According to Patsy:

> I was never conscious of favouritism, and there was nothing in the way we were treated to indicate that. Mum would say: 'They were all different, but I loved them all.' It's only looking back, I would think she probably did favour Aengus. He was very appealing, a very charming child, could get around anyone.

That quality of charm was taken with Aengus into adulthood. Patsy illustrates it with a story from much later, when all seven siblings were adults:

> I was in the dining room, in the most comfortable chair in the house by the fire. It had always been called 'Dad's chair'. And I was sitting in it, and Biddy was sitting in Mum's chair, when Aengus came into the room.
>
> He could stand like a helpless child in the middle of the room looking around – *Oh dear! Where am I going to sit?'* On this occasion, he was standing thus

when his mother bustled in: Patsy! Stand up and let your brother sit down!'

Patsy: 'Excuse me?'

Aengus: 'You heard your mother speaking!'

And while everybody else would be running around, there he'd be, sitting in the best chair all evening!'

2

'Terminus ad quem …
The goal was to get ordained and get to Africa'

– Father Mick Reynolds

Aengus Finucane was born energetic, channelling a lot of his early drive not just into Penny Dinners but physically into participation in sport. A fervent supporter of Munster rugby, (and Shannonside rugby club in particular) he was present in Thomond Park when the provincial team famously defeated the New Zealand All Blacks. According to informants ever after, in Cardiff, Twickenham, anywhere he could catch a match involving Ireland or his own team, when asked by neighbouring spectators where he was from, he never answered 'Ireland', or even 'Limerick', it was always 'Munster'.

While still young and on the Gaelic pitch for Treaty Sarsfields, Aengus's contribution to the team was not his finesse but his burly, charging presence. (In his turn, Jack played for the same club, ascending to selection by the Limerick Minor team in both disciplines.) At CBS in Sexton Street, the Christian Brothers count J. P. McManus, entrepreneur, philanthropist and racehorse owner, along with Aengus, as two of their star graduates. (And actually, on the joint accession to the rolls of Freemen of Limerick City, McManus presented Aengus and Jack with two magnificent silver horse sculptures, one each.)

By universal agreement of contemporaries and family, his time at the school inculcated in Aengus Cornelius Finucane a lifelong devotion to the Christian Brothers, evidenced by his whip-like defence of them as a group when they were attacked in print, in media or verbally in discourse as some members have been for proven abuse of the children in their care. He would reluctantly acknowledge that, yes, there did exist the odd vicious, sadistic member of that organisation – while continuing to have difficulty with the incontrovertible evidence of the perversion of a few. In general, however, to the day he died he held fast to the fact, also unarguable, that without the Brothers, for decades the state's education of its young males would have been unconscionably lacking.

In later life, when in New York as honorary president of Concern US, most of the time he stoutly resisted all offers of hospitality and sponsorship of his accommodation at comfortable hotels in favour of a tiny, cell-like room in the Brothers' house. On one occasion when she was in New York and visiting him, he brought Sarah, one of his devoted nieces, proudly to see it. Her reaction? 'Jesus, Uncle Aengus! This would drive anyone to drink.'

'Sure I'm gone out of here at 8.00 in the morning,' he was taken aback, 'and God knows what time I'd be home. And all I need is a bed ...'.

His bed from the time he left Sexton Street was, after his summer holidays, in the seminary of the Holy Ghost Fathers where he was to train for the priesthood for ten years.

Founded in Paris in 1703, the Congregation of the Holy Spirit, *Congregatio Sancti Spiritus*, abbreviated to 'C.S.Sp.' as a suffix to the names of its members, was set up by a young law student, Claude Poullart des Places, who gave up his chance at a career to dedicate his life to the service of the poor. He died at the age of 30 and, according to his wishes, was buried in a paupers' grave.

To read the order's history is to understand how deeply Aengus and Jack Finucane and their colleagues are imbued with the early mission of the founder: no outcast, criminal, slave, beggar, destitute, prostitute or person of lower caste is to be judged or is beyond the reach of love and ministry.

Now an international organisation, since its foundation the Holy Ghost Fathers have lived and worked in missionary parishes and schools all over the world. Many died in harness, as it were, succumbing to tropical diseases for which they were ill-prepared.

Up to the 1960s, Nigeria, and in particular the east of that country, had been the main destination for graduates from the Irish seminary in Kimmage. These Irish priests and their co-workers, the Holy Rosary Sisters, brought education and spread Roman Catholicism throughout that vast land by dint of a method that was quite simple: they took full advantage of the desire for education.

The Nigerian people, the Igbo tribe in particular, but most other tribes too, were desperate for learning. As a result, they were more than willing to convert to Catholicism, which was a requirement for access to the mission schools. 'They flocked in,' according to one of Aengus's longest serving clerical friends, Father Mick Reynolds. 'This was proselytising, pure and simple; it's now treated with disdain in many quarters. It's out of fashion.'

Father Reynolds and Father Dick Quinn, the second of Aengus's close friends from those seminary days, were two of the fifty-five who entered the Holy Ghost Fathers' training centre in 1959; forty-nine finished, including these three. As an indication of how times have changed, in 2014 there is just one seminarian going through Kimmage.

Jack's seminary experience, five years behind his brother's, was post-Vatican Two and although this may have coloured his thinking, according to him, the regime in Kimmage during his time there differed little from that of Aengus.

The closeness and value of the friendship between Aengus Finucane, Dick Quinn and Mick Reynolds survived until Aengus died. It survived the seminary experience, despite the best efforts of their superiors. With what has to be the biggest understatement within these pages, Father Quinn says: 'We were not encouraged to become friends':

> Mick and Aengus and myself always got on together within the constraints, but you never got an opportunity to talk one-to-one to anybody. There was silence all day anyhow except for certain periods after lunch and after the evening meal. Then we went for a walk around the estate, which was very big. We went in threes.
>
> The walk on a Tuesday – which was our recreation – was also in threes. The rule, in Latin, was: *Nunquam Duo, Semper Tres* – never two, always three. These walks started in the courtyard, with everyone milling around, until the first three names were called out, who then went off, hats and umbrellas at the ready – you had to have your hat on all the time – then the next three, then the next, and so on.

It has to be emphasised that during this era the Holy Ghost seminaries were not the only houses where this kind of regime was imposed. To varying degrees, it was at that time, apparently, the norm in all religious institutions.

For instance, in the 1950s, and well into the 1960s, Catholic seminarians and clergy were not allowed to attend theatres or cinemas. This being Ireland, they found an 'Irish solution': they watched the performances by standing in the wings, their view partially obscured by the ugly, unpainted backs of the canvas flats, with cross-hatched supporting lumber. Wearing full clerical garb, they peered through gaps in that scenery and got in the way of assistant stage managers, prompters, stagehands, and even the actors making entrances and exits, particularly any unfortunate who rushed off to make a quick change.

Actors were always aware of these off-stage hovering presences: of spectrally glowing clerical collars too big for thin necks, perhaps a glint of spectacles in the overspill of stage lights.

Dick Quinn, who loves opera and cinema and to whom culture is and was an essential part of life, keenly felt this particular stricture. He managed to watch 'one or two' performances of the d'Oyley Carte Opera Company, or at least the tops of the performers' bobbing heads, from a perch in the Gaiety Theatre fly tower, a dangerous place for the inexperienced, not only because of the height, but because of its lacing of wires, ropes, pulleys and battens flying up and down as the scenes changed below.

The real absurdity, though, occurred at one stage when he was teaching Leaving Cert English to a class at St Mary's in Rathmines. Shakespeare's *Julius Caesar* was on the curriculum that year, and coincidentally the film based on the play and starring Marlon Brando came to town. 'The whole school went out in buses to see it in the Ambassador Cinema, but I wasn't allowed to go.'

One thing is clear: they all hated the weekly Chapter of Faults, a mass meeting where each student seminarian was expected to snitch on his fellows about transgressions of even the most minor rules.

'It was a stupid exercise,' says Mick Reynolds. 'It had no meaning because everyone had to partake, and your turn came, and you were finding the most anodyne stuff: "Mr Finucane broke silence"; "Mr Quinn was looking around in chapel …".'

Yes, they were all 'Mister', no first names allowed. Stuck for accusations on one occasion when asked to rat on 'Mister Finucane', Mick Reynolds cast around a bit and could only come up with: 'He was a bit noisy.'

They were strictly forbidden to see each other during summer or other holidays when they were released back to their families, but this tenet, at least, was widely flouted, with no one willing to rat on others' seaside swims with families not their own, or summer evening tennis matches with (perish the thought!) cousins who were *girls*. And had *friends who were not related*....

In accumulation, these practices, these instruments of control, seemed designed to create dissent, suspicion and alienation amongst the troops, keeping them unsettled and therefore subservient.

'You went through it for the *terminus ad quem*,' say both priests, Reynolds and Quinn. The goal was to get to Africa.'

'It was conditioning,' Jack agrees. 'We knew that, but in order to get ordained and get to Africa, these were the hoops you had to go through.'

Some of this stuff, however, was bizarre by any standards. According to Jack, 'I failed Latin in my Leaving Cert, and when I went to Kimmage there was one professor teaching us ontology and cosmology who taught these subjects through Latin.'

Ontology is the philosophical study of the nature of being; cosmology is the study of the origin and evolution of the universe. (For the Holy Ghost student, study of the latter included creation by the deity.) 'So here we were,' Jack continues, 'going through this exercise on a daily basis, and we didn't understand a word of it, not a *word*, for two years.'

How did he manage to get through the exams in these subjects?

They were oral, through Latin. You learned phrases off, and if you heard a certain phrase in a certain question, you gave a certain answer. All part of the conditioning.

The most inhumane aspect of the seminary regime, though, was the treatment of those who couldn't hack it. Dick Quinn again:

If anyone kicked over the traces they'd be politely asked to go. I'm not aware of anyone who kicked up and who stayed.

But when someone either decided to go or was asked to go, he was sworn to secrecy. Not allowed to tell anyone. We'd all go off to prayers at 6.00 in the evening, then straight to evening meal, and when we came back, the person had cleared his room and was gone. No goodbyes. Never came back. Just vanished.

Both priests, Father Dick Byrne and Mick Reynolds, talk about
the utter liberation of graduation, ordination and then setting
off for the missions. This next scene is widely reported by the
clerics themselves, by the Finucane family and by many friends
and acquaintances who heard the bones of the story from
Aengus and others involved.

Each new group of Holy Ghost Fathers left for Africa
initially by boat from the quays at Dublin's North Wall. Having
cast off, they gathered on the aft deck to watch Ireland recede
into the mist. All agree on that.

Memories of what happened next diverge. Depending on
whose is the most reliable, it occurred when the boat passed
the Kish Lighthouse, or when it cleared the twelve-mile limit
and entered international waters, or when those on deck could
no longer see the twin chimneys of the Poolbeg power plant
on the Great South Wall. But they all remember that on a
signal they all, in concert, took off their black hats and threw
them overboard. This expression of newfound freedom, if not
its exact timing, has been permanently etched into communal
memory.

During their separate interviews, both Mick Reynolds
and Dick Quinn said something identical, later spontaneously
echoed by Jack: 'We entered at 18 and left at 18, even though we
were actually 28.' And then, said Jack, 'when we got to Africa, we
grew up very, very fast.'

It is difficult to credit now, but these young priests of
their era were sent off with no training in Kimmage about
anthropology, differing tribal traditions or religions, or what
exactly to expect from the people they met when they got to
their assigned Nigerian parishes.

Mick Reynolds adds:

It was training for spiritual life, not for day-to-day
practical life in Africa. You had no clue as to what it
was going to be like, and we went through ten years in
Kimmage without any preparation for the missions as

such. No one even told us that the first essential of the missionary is to be alive!

Those first French missionaries who went out there were all dead in six months – trying to live with the people.

The American Peace Corps came out around the time we were there in Nigeria. They were more or less told to have nothing to do with the missionaries, so a lot of them tried to identify with the people. They got scurvy and all that, and they went home again.

Good food, good housing, good medical attention, good holidays – all very important. People will say, and they do: 'But how can you live like that amongst these very poor people with your big house and good food? Why don't you identify?'

Was there ever a feeling of superiority because of the long years of education? All those degrees?

I suppose so, and there would have been a couple who would have been arrogant in the way they treated the Africans.

Anyhow, off they all went, Aengus and his companions, hatless to Nigeria, heavy with education, full of good cheer and better intentions. Their arrival, however, taught them instantly how unprepared they had been.

In short order, they had to adjust to the climate, the lack of home comforts and the different foods. This they managed to do, as it was to be expected. Sheltered as they had been from the ways of the world throughout their rigid and heavily supervised schooling, however, the most striking and rapid adjustment had to be made when, almost at once, they were confronted with the sight of squads of bare-breasted women with their entirely naked children.

In addition to obvious language difficulties, they also had to contend with snakes and assorted large, biting insects. What was more, many found themselves isolated quite quickly, miles from their former colleagues and now responsible for innumerable people clamouring for attention in remote parishes spanning hundreds, perhaps thousands of square miles, and in which frequently – and quite literally in some cases – communication could take place only via jungle drums.

These young men, who threw their hats – and shackles – so exuberantly into the Irish Sea because their adventure was beginning, did indeed have to grow up very, very fast.

3

'The Igbo were a dynamic people, and if you introduced any self-help initiative you had to run to stay ahead of the stampede as they moved forward.'

– Aengus Finucane

'People don't want you to 'identify'; they want you to lift them up!'

– Father Mick Reynolds

Aengus was welcomed to Nigeria by his brother Jim, who was already in the country working for Barclays Bank, and who, incidentally, furnishes a vivid snapshot of one way in which Irish missionaries, including the Holy Ghost Fathers, offered a nationwide hospitality network.

Suppose Jim had to take a journey from Lagos to Kano, a distance of 1,400 miles, or 2,253 kilometres. He would start out early in the morning, bump along all day through the bush regions in his trusty VW:

> ... and then at about four o'clock in the afternoon, I'd start looking and there it would be, a little signpost saying something like: Catholic Mission, 2 miles.
>
> You'd roll up and ask: 'Any chance of a kip for the night?'

And it was off again early in the morning to the next stage of the journey. It could have been any order, Holy Ghosts, Kiltegan, it didn't matter. They'd all take you in and give you the bed. Meanwhile, 'the boys' washed the dust off your car ready for the morning.

That throwaway reference to 'the boys' brings up another conundrum faced immediately by these young priests.

It doesn't sit easily with most Irish people to have servants, 'boys' or otherwise. The Irish middle-class habit of getting up early to clean the house and having it nice and tidy before the professional cleaner comes in is still endemic within a certain generation, especially amongst women. In Bangladesh, for instance, this writer, mortified to find a local man ironing her clothes, protested – and got short shrift. Ironing was this man's job. A valuable one, not just for him and his family, but for the Concern people themselves, who didn't have to face doing the laundry when they arrived back, exhausted, from a long and intense day's work.

Paula Donaldson, one of those early volunteers in Bangladesh with Aengus and Jack, learned quickly that there were no comparisons to be made between the values of different types of work: manual, clerical, professional or so-called menial. She quotes another of the Aengus Finucane adages: 'Nobody is born a slave or a servant.'

Whether you were earning a few cents fashioning rush table mats alongside other women on a Concern handcraft programme in Dhaka, were a street sweeper in Calcutta, a person selling a bundle of wire on the side of the road in post-earthquake Haiti or a businessman at the height of a stellar career made no difference to your personhood.

'Aengus gave us a good grounding in equality matters.'

As for those early days in Nigeria when these infant missionaries found themselves suddenly having the opportunity – and authority – to change the lives of hundreds and thousands of people desperate to 'get on', Jack illustrates their charges' obsession with education. While teaching in a school in his new parish, he found almost immediately that the students did not need supervision, even during study periods when he was absent. Should any of them act the maggot, their fellow students brought them immediately to heel. During teaching hours there was no point using banishment from a classroom as punishment for misbehaviour:

> The student who had been sent out would simply walk around the building and stand forlornly at the window of the room, looking back in at you, trying to catch the lesson so he wouldn't miss anything and fall behind.

In one of the small number of personal documents that survived that shredder, Aengus Finucane wrote:

> I was fortunate that my first assignment in Africa was with the Igbo people in eastern Nigeria. They were a dynamic people, and if you introduced any self-help initiative you had to run to stay ahead of the stampede as they moved forward.

And so, long before he became a guru to so many, young Father Aengus Finucane's beat was in the state of Biafra. Mick Reynolds, who started the journey to Nigeria with him on that hat-shedding boat, was not so far away, by Nigerian standards, in Umuahia. Dick Quinn, the third of these Musketeers, joined them in the area much later because he had been assigned to do a five-year degree, meaning that rather than the standard term he spent thirteen years being trained before he was ready to travel out. Now 82, eight days older than Aengus would be if he had lived, he paints a good picture of what daily life was like for them:

> Most of us were on our own in the bush within twelve months. You either learn in the first year or you don't,

and if you don't, you don't, but even if you do learn that
first year, you just keep repeating it. I used to say they
haven't been thirty years in Nigeria; they've been one
year multiplied by thirty. I firmly believe that.

'It was terribly hot all the time,' Father Quinn goes on, 'which
exacerbated the daily struggle simply to eat properly and sleep
at night.'

During their long days on duty as pastors, they celebrated a
daily Mass, and three on Sundays, complete with long sermons.
In later life, Aengus tended to be verbose when he got near a
speaker's platform, but always explained this away by saying that
in Nigeria, Mass-goers had in a lot of cases travelled many miles
to hear his sermons, and always made it clear that they wanted
full value for making the journey.

As well as these pastoral duties, the three friends, Aengus,
Mick Reynolds and Dick Quinn – and later Jack – were all
running schools and according to Quinn, their schedules and
those of the hundreds of other Holy Ghosts in the adjacent
parishes, were broadly similar to his own.

On a First Friday he would say his morning Mass, conduct
his morning classes and then, although his was not a very big
parish, have to hear 300 to 400 confessions. This posed its own
difficulties, with most of the penitents confessing in the Igbo
language; a language in which his skills were poor to non-
existent. 'So it was a formulaic thing. They came and said what
they were going to say, which we understood, more or less, and
then we gave absolution.'

Was there a huge element of mental strain in being catapulted
into such work, living on one's own in a remote bush station
with such enormous responsibility? For instance, had he ever
experienced an impulse, portrayed so strongly in Brian Friel's
Dancing at Lughnasa, in which the Father Jack character, home
from the African missions, has clearly 'gone native'?

Father Quinn's response to that question is as telling and as
clever as he is: 'I empathise greatly with that character.'

He tells then of how these young priests, although busy, very often felt cut-off and lonely.

> My father dropped dead on a Saturday, and they hoped I'd get home for the funeral so they put it off until the Tuesday, but I didn't get word until the following Saturday.
>
> And then I spent three days trying to phone my mother, I had to travel several hundred miles, I could get through to Lagos but I couldn't get through from Lagos to Dublin.

This type of personal detail seems to make the shredding of Aengus's archive even more of a calamity since we will never really know first-hand how he felt personally about these early days. As it turns out, however, Father Quinn questions the widespread view of what was lost with those papers:

> I am quite certain that he would have had not a single thought about himself in those papers. There would have been lots of stuff about what he said and what he did and where he went, maybe copies of speeches he had made, but there would have been nothing – *nothing* – about his inner state. I'm quite certain about that.
>
> We'd all have been the same. In our congregation we didn't have either the language or education to exchange deep thoughts. I have nothing in my papers about what I think about anything. *Anything.* And I'm quite certain that any of us of that time would be the same. That whole caring-and-sharing thing – we didn't even know how to do it.
>
> And when you went there and got into ministry in Africa, plunged into the work, it was so bizarre and busy, you didn't have the opportunity to spend time divining what other people thought or felt. Certainly not how you yourself felt. That was always put off, and

I think the first time any of us had a chance to think about ourselves, our reactions, our feelings, was after Biafra.

Was there ever any counselling offered after the Biafran war experience?

'Never heard of it. If Aengus or Mick had it, they never told me, so I'm quite certain that they didn't.' He harks back to their training. 'Priestly formation was the phrase used – it was actually priestly deformation, because at the time it was, like, if you have a problem, I've the solution. Cracked stuff.'

Later in life, when they did get time to think about themselves, did it occur to them that the training might actually have been psychologically damaging?

For most of them, he doesn't think that this penny ever dropped, at least 'not in that language. It was just that we did know there had been too much about control, and felt it wasn't right.'

Privately, Dick Quinn never accepted a particular director's view of the vow of obedience.

Yes, obedience means that you must do what your superior tells you. The director's view, though, was that: 'You must do what your superior tells you – but you must also accept objectively that what he told you is objectively right.' No matter how stupid it was.

On top of all his other duties and pursuits during those years in Nigeria, Aengus served as chaplain to those confined to death row in Enugu prison and often reminisced about his pastoral visits to one man in particular, a very serious transgressor. He would tell this man all about heaven and forgiveness and the goodness and mercy of God, who delivered Dismas (the Good Thief, crucified alongside Jesus) because he had repented.

The day came when the priest got a call from the prison governor. The authorities had set an execution date, and the governor would be obliged if this could be conveyed to the condemned man. He, the governor, felt that if he were to be the one to impart the news, the reaction amongst the prison population would be extreme. The place would explode.

Not relishing his task, Aengus nevertheless went in and told the man what the story was.

'Fair enough', said this man, or words to that effect.
[Aengus, taken aback]: 'I did think you might react differently?'
'Why would I?'
'Well, it's a big event.'
'Yes, Father, but don't I know I'm going to heaven?'
'Why would you think you know that?'
'Isn't that what you've been telling me for the last few months?'

And so pastoral life went on until, on 29 July 1966, following clashes between Northern Muslims and some ethnic tribes, including the Igbo, General Johnson Aguiyi-Ironsi, military head of state, was assassinated by elements in his own army, which then took power.

Peace talks between this new military government and the regional government of Eastern Nigeria, held in Ghana in 1967, broke down, and on 30 May 1967 the army's General Emeka Odumegwu-Ojukwu announced that the regional council of the peoples of Eastern Nigeria had decided that the new independent state of Biafra should secede from Nigeria.

It had now done so, declared the general, who was taking it on himself to become the head of state of the newest republic on the planet. Nigeria reacted with all its military might, including a complete naval blockade.

4

'The crisis in Biafra changed the nature of the work of many priests
and missionaries from educators and managers to full-time aid workers.
Amongst these people were two young brothers: Fathers Aengus and
Jack Finucane. With little training and even less time, they and many
other Holy Ghost priests in Biafra began turning schools into refugee
camps and set up food distributions and emergency hospitals, working
tirelessly to alleviate the suffering of hundreds of thousands caught up
in the conflict.'

– Gerry Reynolds[2]

Unlike many of the bloody disputes affecting various countries
in Africa to this day, many of which flit in and out of the
ever-present twenty-four-hour news cycle depending on where
editors decide their spotlights should shine, the Biafran conflict
caught the attention of the world when the extent of the Nigerian
blockade of foods, medicines, fuel and other necessities began to
be recognised elsewhere, including in Ireland. Widespread famine
was threatening, and was a reality in some areas.

Speaking in Chicago in October 2006, Aengus reminded
his listeners that more than 800 million people suffer from

---

2 (Writing in *The Irish Times Supplement*, published to celebrate the fortieth
anniversary of Concern in 2008.)

hunger and malnutrition 'in our world of plenty, waste and excess,' and that in sub-Saharan Africa the statistics were even more staggering: in most cases 60 to 70 per cent of national populations live on less than one US dollar a day.

> While it may be too simplistic to assume that what is wasted in one part of the world can be used to feed people in another, there have to be ways better to orga-nise the food chain so as to recoup and redirect some of the billions of dollars being lost. We should seek to increase our own level of awareness of what we person-ally consign to garbage and help raise the awareness of people around us.

That was in 2006. Despite economic growth in many African and Eastern nations in this more recent era, plus the sincere international efforts towards achieving the UN's Millennium Development Goals, were he now to speak publicly, his horror and passionate indignation can barely be imagined as he enumerates the difficulties faced by millions upon millions of men, women and children trapped in countries ravaged by ethnically and religiously based genocides, disease, starvation, ignorance, cruelty and sheer neglect.

So, if only in self-interest, he might say, those of us sitting comfortably on the larded parts of the planet should wake up and pay attention, because citizens of even the poorest nations now have access, in however haphazard a manner, to unceasing flows of information via social media and news channels with global reach. Thus made aware of the basic inequality in the distribution of resources, they will not for much longer meekly accept their fate. And of course it is now clear that many factions have already decided not to do so.

In the late 1960s Biafra was very quickly isolated, its territory shrinking by the day as the Nigerian military made inroads. The Holy Ghost Fathers had to make rapid adjustments to their pastoral plans and ways of life. They adapted. Faced with the decision either to maintain their physical parishes, in which many churches had already been bombed to rubble or to retreat with congregations fleeing from the advancing Nigerians, the decision was a no-brainer for them and they became, virtually overnight, aid workers, keeping pace with their people. With supplies already perilously low, they set up field hospitals and feeding centres, while sending, by any means possible, urgent pleas for help to the outside world.

The pleas were heard by Father Raymond Kennedy, a Holy Ghost Father himself, who had been stationed in the diocese of Owerri. Coincidentally, he was in Ireland at the time, and having received the distress call decided that he couldn't sit on his hands.

His brother, John O'Loughlin Kennedy, and John's wife, Kay, were already involved in charitable work, for instance with Viatores Christi, an organisation which, since 1960, has operated in the faith-based development sector worldwide. All three, therefore, had lots of Nigerian and other useful contacts, and just before Christmas 1967 they announced an awareness-raising press conference in the Shelbourne hotel in order to raise funds for a 'mercy flight' filled with supplies for starving Biafran children.

Raymond Kennedy's superiors, as well as the Irish political authorities, were alarmed. Anecdotally, according to Jim Finucane who knew Nigeria – and business in Nigeria – very well, one of the reasons for opposition by Irish officialdom had to do with trade interests. Clerical worry, on the other hand, was about safety, not just of their members under siege, but also for those still serving in greater Nigeria and working, as Nigeria might now see it, in opposition. According to Aengus's own words in an article he wrote afterwards: 'There were 2,500 Irish missionaries overall in Nigeria at the outbreak of the war.'

Back home, that 'awareness' press conference, while not deliberately nobbled by official opposition, was compromised because of it, and the turnout was poor, although the trio did manage to send one 'mercy flight' to Biafra.

Raymond, John and Kay were not, however, to be put off by official snubs or jitters, and went home to work hard on their contacts, including teachers, others who had worked in Nigeria and even the wives of those still there. Fortuitously, two Nigerian emissaries sent by the Bishop of Onitsha to Ireland and Europe to publicise the plight of the Biafran people were already available, and they, along with all the others, were invited to a meeting in John and Kay's house on Northumberland Road.

By the end of that meeting, they had agreed to call themselves 'Africa Concern', and to meet every Tuesday to continue with their fundraising strategy. They employed the use of good (voluntary) PR and advertising people who, cleverly, were pushing an open door with Irish people, for whom combining the words, 'famine', 'starving' and 'dying children' always leads to huge response. The funds did come in, slowly at first, but quite soon by the sackload, to the extent that, overwhelmed, the trio had to borrow three further recruits – people who had experience with The Irish Sweepstakes. These three set about instituting proper accounting procedures.

The plan was to use the money as quickly as possible, and to bypass the naval blockade on Biafra by flying the aid into Biafra's heartland from some airfield as close as possible nearby.

They also decided quite quickly that, rather than having to book very expensive cargo space on commercial sea-freighters, they would acquire their own ship. Helped by a large donation from the Dutch charity Mensen in Nood, by August of 1968 they had sourced one suitable to their needs. Refitted, fully loaded with foods, medicines and clothing, the 600-ton vessel was relaunched under a new name, the *Colmcille*, and set sail for the island of Sao Tome, arriving there on 26 September.

Independently of these efforts to send aid to the starving by the fledgling Africa Concern, another group was set up in March 1968 by Vincent Grogan, then the Supreme Knight of the Knights of Columbanus, who solicited donations from their own members. Very quickly, however, the Knights expanded their efforts and created an inter-denominational group, The Nigeria/Biafra Refugee Fund, which in turn conjoined with Africa Concern under the banner of the Joint Africa Famine Appeal.

Alongside Raymond Kennedy and his Holy Ghost colleagues and supporters who were running this appeal were now the Supreme Knight; the Reverend Ivan Biggs, who was a Methodist minister; Judge Kingsmill Moore, a senior Freemason; Vivian Simpson, a Belfast MP; Mary Guckian, headmistress of a school in Derry; Val Jagoe, who set up a branch in Cork, and Donal Nevin, an influential trade unionist from Dublin. When the Biafran crisis was over, many of these people stayed with Concern, as it eventually became, including Judge Kingsmill Moore and the Reverend Biggs.

Dominic MacSorley, Concern's current CEO, is in awe of this start-up:

> ... their extraordinary vision. Nothing like it had actu-
> ally even been tried before in Ireland. That they actually
> had the courage and foresight to buy a ship – that kind
> of outside-the-box thinking survives, and hopefully
> will survive, in Concern to this day.

From such modest and visionary beginnings, the organisation's growth accelerated, its progress very well documented, particularly in Tony Farmar's book, *Believing in Action*. In it, Farmar documents a lovely little anecdote about those early days, recounted by Kay O'Loughlin, one which exemplifies the cleverness with which this nascent Concern raised funds for its first cause.

It was decided to operate one Biafran campaign as a quasi-competition between Irish counties. What was publicised was that John O'Loughlin Kennedy, who at the time was a senior economist with Garret FitzGerald's Economist Unit, had set fundraising targets for each county, the results of which would be published.

The idea caught on, and O'Loughlin made sure that each local newspaper was regularly informed as to how exactly its county was doing. This, of course, led to counties exceeding their targets. (The people of Cork felt they had been insulted by the miserliness of the figure that had been set for them, and as a result oversubscribed it by six times.) One donor, however, who had lived in Dublin for thirty years, nailed his colours firmly to his home county. He sent in his subscription with a note: 'This is to go down to the credit of Roscommon. Not Dublin.'

In itself, the Uli airlift evinced all the ingredients of an action movie in which the theme was bravery for a cause. The opening sequence might look something like this:

A black night in darkest African jungle.

Through the cacophony of sound from nocturnal creatures can be heard the propeller beat of a distant aircraft approaching....

Out of the dense foliage, running human silhouettes appear. They spread out, lighting two parallel rows of kerosene lamps. In the dim yellow glow, a narrow airstrip is slowly revealed. Alongside it as the shot zooms out, and only dimly visible, stands a convoy of trucks and cars.

Pan up to a small plane, descending, almost touching the treetops, fuselage glinting in the flare of the kerosene lanterns.

Pull wider to reveal that above the small plane is the sinister outline of a Nigerian bomber....

Like many of their priest-colleagues, Aengus and Jack became totally caught up in aid distribution, which centred around deliveries through that air operation at Uli airport, a grand name for what was in reality a (slightly) widened roadway carved from the jungle: 'A nice wide road, but a damn narrow runway,' according to one of the pilots who shuttled in from the island of Sao Tome, sometimes three times a night.

The late Canadian journalist Hugh McCullum has written admiringly about the operation in the online publication *AfricaFiles*, concentrating his piece on his compatriot airmen, who, piloting either a 'lumbering' DC-6 or a 'temperamental' Super Constellation, flew in, 'skimming blind over the trees at 2,000 feet to avoid the guns and fighters of the enemy.' These crews referred jauntily to their airline, which bore the logo of JCA (Joint Church Aid) as the 'Jesus Christ Airline'.

Insouciance did not endure. Four crew members were killed when one of the Super Constellations crashed on landing. Over the course of these deliveries, McCullum wrote, twenty-five people lost their lives directly as a result of these flights.

The Spiritans ran their own segment of this operation, at first using the services of BIAS (Belgian International Air Services.) Then, however, Holy Ghost Father Tony Byrne, who with fellow Holy Ghost Billy Butler had been running the show on Sao Tome, acquired their own planes and moved operations to Libreville in Gabon.

This amalgamated charity relief operation delivered 60,000 tons of aid over 5,314 air movements involving a wide conglomeration of organisations, many of them faith-based, including Caritas and the World Council of Churches. And there, in the darkness of Uli every night, was Aengus with his local colleagues, waiting to receive the supplies and to distribute them.

There have been many allegations over the years that, as well as aid supplies, the holds of some of these aircraft were also loaded with arms, and that the Holy Ghost Fathers were involved in gunrunning. Even now, forty-six years later, when the Finucanes' names are mentioned in conversation in this country the response can be: 'Oh yeah? Weren't they the priests gunrunning in Biafra?'

This should be laid to rest once and for all. Jack and others involved (including Aengus in his lifetime) flatly deny this. Not on their watch, they say, and there is no evidence whatsoever to gainsay them.

That being said, leaving the Spiritans out of it, there is a grey area. It is impossible to refute the charge that there *could* have been some mercenary groups who took advantage of the crisis. There is no evidence one way or the other. In *Believing in Action*, Tony Farmar deals in depth with this, including the unease felt back home by an Irish government anxious to maintain good relations with Nigeria. Spiritan leaders worried too. Unlike the Irish bishops who had jurisdiction over Diocesan clergy, they had no such control over these independent Holy Ghost Fathers, who reported to local bishops in the jurisdiction in which they happened to operate.

Farmar quotes from a contemporaneous letter written by Raymond Kennedy, who seems obliquely to hint that he, for one, accepted that it was possible that some contraband could have been brought in without the knowledge of his priestly colleagues:

> We have nothing like enough money to do the job. Therefore we must collaborate with people who are not very nice. [...] However, being a small organisation which cannot fund all its activities unaided, we are compelled to receive help from any quarter that is not too embarrassing.

British intelligence reports released under the thirty-year rule have revealed the allegation that both Britain and Russia, alarmed that their own interests might be damaged should the Biafrans prevail, were sending arms to Lagos. France, similarly, was flying them from Côte d'Ivoire and Gabon, in both of which they had an interest. But the Finucanes, and all charities concerned, vehemently insist that, as far as they could humanly discover, none of them, either directly or indirectly, via collusion, or even with a nod and a wink, brought arms into the new Republic.

Jack Finucane's recounting of these events at Uli ('Bravery? What bravery?') is unique in its understatement of his own role in this remarkable operation:

In 1968 it began to get very serious and very close, and the Nigerians began to close in. I remember leaving my parish after the first explosions came over the roof, and you realised that you were in serious danger. That happened twice. I was appointed kind of as a coordinator of relief supplies to the area coming in at night, and that continued until 1970. And in January 1971 the war ended.

End of story. Direct quote. On tape.

Here is what actually happened. Aengus worked at the Uli airstrip, where, within the maximum of a twenty-minute window given by the pilots before they took off again, he supervised the unloading of cargo and its transfer onto the waiting trucks, not shirking its manhandling.

Meanwhile, Jack operated as 'a kind of coordinator' to the aid programme at the distribution point twelve miles away. This meant helping to unload ten tons of aid off the truck convoy when it arrived, identifying and organising it within a storage warehouse – a half-built church – and then loading it again into some of his fleet of ninety-seven trucks, making sure each load was specific to the needs of particular field hospitals, clinics and feeding stations before dispatching it.

It was at Uli that one of the legends about Aengus Finucane was born. As always with legends, there are several versions. Let's go with the one chosen by Farmar, as noted coolly and with attention to detail by the historians of the Joint Church Aid Airlift official report:

> A man jumped out of a car and held up the last lorry in a convoy at gunpoint. An indignant Gus Finucane jumped out of a Peugeot 404 Estate, threw himself at the bandit and embraced him in a nineteen-stone rugby tackle. The bandit's accomplices started their car

and abandoned their friend, who was handed over to
the authorities.

One of the more controversial aspects of this air operation
was the evacuation of vulnerable children, who were packed
into the emptied planes for the return journey to Gabon and
Cameroon so they could be rehabilitated and receive medical
treatment.

In the Biafran situation, more than 4,000 children were evacuated
to Cameroon and Gabon, while 40,000 were accommodated in
institutions throughout the war zone. Five years after hostilities
ceased, as a result of a vigorous reunification programme by the
Nigerian authorities, fewer than a hundred of these children had
still not been reunited. One of the main factors in the success of this
reunification programme was the commitment and caring practices
in the institutions in which the children had been placed. Aengus
had been in charge of one of those institutions in Gabon.

During the war between Biafra and Nigeria, although
estimates vary, it is now assumed that despite the best efforts
of those international charities and all the missionaries and
aid workers present in Biafra, almost half a million children
died. The blockade held and the Nigerians, with far superior
weaponry and numbers of boots on the ground, squeezed the
territory tighter and tighter until there was no option but to
surrender, and the war ended with Biafra's reabsorption into
Nigeria.

The fallout for the Finucanes and the other missionaries
was that they were now 'illegals': 'We had Biafran stamps in our
passports, and now that we were back in Nigeria we had entered
that country illegally,' according to Jack.

They were rounded up, 'all together, including the Rosary
Sisters, about twenty of us,' arrested, charged with illegal entry
and the importation of arms and brought to Port Harcourt for
arraignment.

Before their court case came on they were in detention for three weeks, 'a sort of house arrest really. But with guards and so on ...'. Then, during their court case, each was sentenced to six months in prison: 'You went up, the charges were read out, you were found guilty, "six months." '

Wasn't he afraid of going to gaol? 'No. We were never afraid for some reason. We'd no experience of this. Gaol,' adds Jack Finucane with his usual economy of speech, 'worked out very well,' despite the fact that 'eight or nine of us' were in a cell, measuring, he guesses, about nine square metres.

> One chap was a scripture scholar, so we would pass the morning with scripture. Somebody else was a very good bridge player, so he would teach anyone who wanted to learn. Another guy was very good at athletics, and he would take a PT class, so we weren't just sitting down looking at each other; we were active.

What wasn't so pleasant, however, was that they all got sick. Then: 'as far as I can remember, after I would think about ten days,' they were thrown out of the country, driven by truck to Port Harcourt Airport, flown to Lagos, and then next morning to Geneva. And then back to Kimmage. The Holy Ghost authorities were aghast. Hundreds of men, now unemployed, descending on the order and looking for jobs.

5

'I had the loveliest man [Father Aengus Finucane] here this morning
to interview you. But you weren't here, so he interviewed me …'.

– Nellie Meagher (mother of Brigid, potential volunteer)

In his later years, even when still in his prime with Concern,
Aengus would grow misty-eyed whenever Bangladesh was
mentioned, and always referred to that posting, from 1972–1978,
as his 'golden' time. Mind you, he could have said 'golden era',
'golden days', 'golden years' – whatever. Within memories, as we
know, details can be flexible but the essence remains consistent:
those years were for him the best of the best.

This had actually surprised him, because up to the time he
went there, Africa, particularly Nigeria, held that big heart of his
in a loving grip, and he hadn't planned on taking on any field in
the subcontinent.

A large number of the volunteers who flocked around
him socially when he entertained and held get-togethers in
his Sandymount apartment were of the group that served with
him in Bangladesh. As will become apparent, he wore one
Bangladeshi programme as a crown of particular pride, both on
his own head and that of Concern.

According to various people who had worked with him
in Africa, he had not been all that keen on going east when

asked to do so by the organisation. Largely, it was said, because he had not been enamoured of the Asian merchant class he had encountered while bartering for supplies in the cities and towns of Nigeria. 'He didn't like the way they treated their African staff,' according to one.

Even so, as the nascent state of Bangladesh was at the time seen as the place of greatest need, he agreed to go there (having worked for a while in St Mary's College in Rathmines), and by the time he arrived to take up his post, the new state was already becoming a huge focus for his organisation, and as a theatre of operations was destined to expand exponentially. From the mid to late period of his stewardship, a very large volunteer force, plus staff, ran all kinds of programmes, concentrating mainly, but not exclusively, on women.

Meanwhile, in December 1972, Jack, having been thrown out of Nigeria following Biafra's re-absorption, was in California finishing a degree in Education. He received a phone call (not from Aengus) asking him to set up a catering school in Dhaka. Concern had received a gift of kitchen equipment from Raymond Kennedy's brother, who was living in California.

So he travelled out to Bangladesh to join his brother, with a day job supervising a brand new Food Services Institute. 'We were training chefs and waiters.' Although he hired a real chef, he himself became 'a sort of Head Chef,' presiding over a huge American fridge and:

> ... these massive urns with a turning wheel on the side that could take a full bag of rice. It worked. We trained lads for two or three years, and they had no problem getting jobs afterwards in hotels, embassies or in the homes of local expats.

Meanwhile, under the widespread initiatives of Jack's brother, destitute women from the Bihari ghettos were trained to embroider and crochet tablemats, tablecloths, wedding trousseaux, cotton calendars, rush baskets and coasters. Initially the products were for sale locally to expatriates, including the Finucane brothers themselves and the Concern volunteers, who, when going home, carried caseloads of the stuff. The pieces were so finely wrought, however, that diplomats based in Dhaka started to buy them, and eventually there was a real industry there, with Concern running warehouses and outlets in Bangladesh, and a network of shops in Ireland, with exports being handled via agencies in Calcutta. The work for women fitted into Aengus's fundamental vision and mission. Without his insistent encouragement and his making it practically possible, it would not have been as wildly successful as it was.

Each and every one of Concern's volunteers interviewed is worth a full chapter in this book, and many could give enough material for a standalone volume. Whatever can be fitted in between these covers can be only a sideways swipe at many individually fascinating personalities, and can cover just a fraction of what they achieved, especially when given free rein to follow their own initiatives under Aengus's far-seeing eye, to say nothing of a succession of enlightened field and country directors, including Jack. If some seem to get more prominence than others, it is purely for reasons of space and inevitable repetition. But every person interviewed has added tiles to the mosaic of Aengus's profile and the accounts of Concern's work.

Most made light of their own efforts, giving credit to the ethos for which they signed up and the inspired leadership they encountered. After their stints as volunteers, some renewed their contracts, some were offered paid jobs and stayed, some came home but went overseas again, some went into other areas of Concern.

Even if they left the organisation altogether, many chose to stay in aid development work, and it is a source of pride to the organisation that, of the many who went on to take high office in huge international organisations like the World Food Programme or various UN agencies, Concern has always been seen as a good calling card.

These are fascinating people, exhibiting drive, courage, insight, entrepreneurship, altruism and individuality, laced with a desire for adventure. Not only that, they also shared an ambition to leave a beneficial footprint after they left their stations, and it was clear that, had they chosen other career paths, many could – and would – have risen to the top.

Take Ursula Sharpe. Having served with Concern she is now a Medical Missionary of Mary, who went to Uganda for the MMMs after her own profession as a nun in that order. Very quickly, she detected that the Aids epidemic was about to explode exponentially in that country, and against all conventional Catholic teachings of the time took specific action: 'If you weren't teaching about condom use and how to put them on and all that, it wouldn't have been moral – we wouldn't have been behaving morally.' As a result of her work rate and determination, she was listened to by the UN, who (eventually) replicated her initiatives.

Or take Moira Conroy (Brehony), who, as this author saw, could transform a dusty plain into a fully functioning refugee camp with sanitation, clinics and feeding stations in less time than it takes to get off a trolley in an Irish hospital corridor. After twenty-three years working tirelessly in some of the most abandoned and war-torn places on the globe, she now lives in Tanzania and works as a lay missionary for the MMMs. Despite having been robbed, tied up and beaten almost senseless in Nairobi in 2013, having recovered physically she went back to work in Arusha, living under the shadow of Kilimanjaro and continuing her work for those less fortunate than she feels she is herself.

Like the Jewish volunteer from Rhode Island, Irwin Shorr (of whom, more later), all, by common consent, were changed utterly by being subsumed for a time into the ethos of the Concern family, which was headed, spiritually and literally, by Aengus and Jack Finucane.

And of course there is always Ciunas Bunworth. With a background in catering, she rose through the ranks to field and country directorates in various Concern theatres. Before joining the organisation and going to Bangladesh as her first posting, she was 'living the good life, a good car, going to the races, eating out and having the great social life of someone in their mid-twenties.' But she heard a radio commercial asking for people to go to Bangladesh with Concern. 'Father Aengus Finucane was on it, saying: "We need people. There are a lot of people to feed." '

Feeding ... Catering ... 'I could do something about that, I thought, and I answered the ad to ease a sort of slight social niggle that I should contribute.' For one defined – and short – period:

> Definitely it was *bye bye, Ireland, I'm going to Bangladesh for eighteen months.* Then it was going to be *bye bye, Bangladesh, I'm going home to Ireland to earn money and pick up my life again.* I'm 65 and am now retiring from Concern.

She stayed, despite first impressions of the Concern house in Dhaka: 'There were all these plastic chairs. You sat on one of them and you stuck.'

Many of these early volunteers had their initial experience of aid work, and in some cases their first experience of living abroad, when they were sent out of Ireland by Concern, some to places of which they had never even heard. Bangladesh was one of those places.

And Brigid Ryan (Meagher) is one of the people who was sent to Bangladesh in the early days of that field. While none is typical of all, she does in some ways exemplify the type of personality attracted to such work. It is noteworthy that a very high proportion of Irish volunteers came from very large families; Brigid is the fifth of nine children.

She is a sturdy human dynamo and chatterbox from a farming and butchering background. On leaving school she decided to become a nun, but her family wouldn't hear of it. So, to bide time until she was of an age to make her own decisions, she signed up for teacher training in Domestic Science.

She arrived for our interview in the Johnstown House Hotel in Enfield along with her pal Father Ciaran Kitching, a diocesan priest and teacher, who himself served with Concern in Bangladesh and in Ethiopia, and whose enduring legacy to the organisation is the Concern Debates, a knockout competition held annually since 1984 in which pupils from 120 schools in Ireland take to the arena and present their (researched) views on development issues. The debates are consciousness-raising – and a good marketing thrust for Concern – but by participating, students (more than 45,000 so far) and teachers hone their researching skills and, it is hoped, will also become lifelong advocates on issues relating to poverty, social justice and human rights.

It was cold that day in Enfield, and the management very kindly organised hot tea for us, as well as electric heaters, around which the three of us huddled in the hotel's small library.

Just before graduation, with the becoming-a-nun idea on the back-burner, Brigid got an offer of a permanent and pensionable job as a domestic science teacher in the local convent school in Cahir. (No way was she taking that, Mammy! She'd end up as an old maid! There were a lot of them around the place.)

She was going home from her (non-permanent teaching job) to have her dinner one afternoon around Easter 1973 when, just like Ciunas Bunworth, she heard the ad on the radio with Father Aengus Finucane saying that there were a lot of people to feed and that they were looking for nurses and doctors. There was no mention of teachers, but she called Concern anyway, and was told that Father Aengus Finucane would call her back.

He didn't.

So anyway I came home again one dinnertime some weeks later and Mammy said: 'I had the loveliest man here this morning to interview you. But you weren't here so he interviewed me…'.

[Ciaran Kitching intervenes] It was something they did. The Holy Ghosts did interview the mothers. They said they always learned more about a person by going into a house for one minute in one room, talking to people, seeing if they were comfortable in their own place.

She always knew, Brigid says, that life had been very good to her, and her vocation was now to work with the underdogs. 'I loved the idea of a challenge. And all right I wasn't a doctor or nurse, but I could always feed people. I was a homemaker, a good cook.'

Prior to her departure, however, she discovered when being briefed that the task of 'feeding people' was already under control: Bread for the World, a German NGO, was funding the Concern feeding programmes. 'But we'd love if you'd come out and set up a scheme that gave employment opportunities for women.'

Jack was field director at the time, and met her at the airport. 'He was the programmer and organiser; Aengus was the dreamer and visionary. They were a marvellous team.' She then adds, airily:

> Chalk and cheese personalities of course. Jack was always the kind person. I was afraid of Aengus. He'd say, 'No, you can't be a cook. Your job here is not to cook; you'd be taking a job away from the cooks. You do what I tell you to do and that's your job.'
>
> I was never afraid of anything. My husband later was always saying: 'No more Bright Ideas, Brigid,' but the thing is, Aengus didn't mind the bright ideas. That's what I was there to do: to work for the women and to spend the German money!

Assigned an on-site interpreter (and general helpmate) named Islam, she arrived in Saidpur to work with the Biharis – the population who had sided with West Pakistan during the war, now marooned, generally despised by the indigenous population and living crammed into huge jute barns around the fringes of the city:

> ... They were like hay barns, with holes in the corrugated iron, and they'd have their dividers made with jute sacks and bamboo canes, Bunsen burners running with cow dung....
>
> Brid Leahy was the one with me, and we were told that it was up to us: the two of us could do anything with the women as long as it hadn't anything to do with sewing machines. That was the man's task in a Muslim society.

The first thing she noticed when she settled in to her 'nice concrete house' in Saidpur was the mortality rate of small children:

> Babies were breastfed, and that was wonderful, but then the women were pregnant again and the new baby was put to the breast and the older child got nothing and died. There was no weaning.

The nurses were working on changing that, and 'you'd get upset over dead babies, but the general attitude was just: *please God, things will improve.*' As she was prospecting around the place to find some way of employing the women, she noticed something:

> ... the rickshaw-wallahs were wearing these gorgeous sort of crochet vests, and the women came to me all washed and polished in these gorgeous saris, but underneath they had these lovely petticoats – pillow-case lace – all beautifully embroidered, but worn and overbleached.

Crochet ... embroidery ... bingo!

Having started her women's programmes in those jute warehouses-cum-accommodation blocks, the next thing she noticed was that her women were 'all chesty' from the smoke and the grime. 'I decided we were getting out of these holes.'

'Across a few fields' she discovered a big old warehouse with fresh air and a courtyard. And once installed in those 'big airy sheds', the women worked so hard she couldn't keep up with their productivity and expansionist tendencies, and no matter how many trips she made to Calcutta for fresh materials, demand always outstripped supply.

> Before long I realised how gifted they were. When we ran out of carbon paper for the embroidery class, next thing I see this one pulling out her petticoat and with a spoon and cooking oil, putting the new material on the embroidery on her petticoat, and there she was, tracing away on the design on it with a metal spoon.
>
> I ran out of crochet hooks because of the demand, and next thing I found this hook that wasn't one of ours, and wasn't it a bicycle spoke that one of these women had filed into shape! They were so eager to come to class they'd be bringing their daughters, and pretending they weren't their daughters.

Then, with unconscious poignancy, she adds:

> They were used to good quality, you see. Their men had been the backbone of the civil service in Bihar before the war. They reminded me of the Mayo or Kerry people, backbone of ours.

This girl-woman, who had never before been abroad except in her imagination, was now, within months of arrival, responsible for a burgeoning industry, eventually employing over 1,000 women. As ever, when he empowered females, Aengus had been handsomely rewarded.

Amidst this positivity, however, and she is a supremely positive person, there were several occasions when Brigid was reminded, brutally, of the ethos that pertained – one that could be very different to that in which she had been brought up.

One day, with one of the volunteer nurses, Noreen, she was travelling from Saidpur to the local hospital at Dinalpur with a very sick little boy and his mother when, with some distance still to go, the child deteriorated. They pulled into the side of the road, where the nurse performed a successful tracheotomy.

> When we arrived at the hospital, Noreen ran immediately to the doctors, who were English-trained. Noreen was beautiful with long blonde hair, the doctors' dream, and they surrounded her to chat, offering her cups of tea and refreshments, but she persisted. She didn't want tea or attention; she wanted them to bring the little boy to the theatre immediately.

Of course they would, they promised. And so, delighted with the outcome, the two Concern women departed again for Saidpur, leaving the mother behind to feed and look after the child, and to sleep under his bed, as was the practice for relatives.

That night the gates of their compound rattled, and when they went out to investigate they found the distraught mother: 'crying and crying. As soon as we left, they never bothered with the little boy; just left him to die.'

Professional begging got to her too, but worst of all for her was the night when the night guard came in and said, 'Sister, you're needed.'

> It was dark, and the hurricane lamps were out. He said: 'A man has been caught raiding our warehouse, and we have him hanging from a tree now, and we just need your permission to hang him.'

I couldn't give that permission, I told him, but he persisted. I sent for Islam.

> 'Islam, I can't give permission for this. Just tell them to cut him down and let him off.'
> 'But Sister, if you let him go he can say he was beaten up by these locals because they're Biharis, and that he's a Bangladeshi.'
> 'Tell me, then, what the hell I can do?'
> 'Get out the typewriter ...'.

They typed a notice: 'I WAS FOUND BREAKING INTO THE WAREHOUSE OF CONCERN ON THIS DATE'. They had to get the man's thumbprint to sign the declaration, and had to get it before he was cut down. 'So that took hours. And meanwhile, everyone who passed ripped into him. Eventually, though, he was cut down.'

'We were only 23, but we were all strong women, when I look back.' And of course she, like most, gives credit for this liberation of strength to Aengus.

Later, in the early 1980s, the broadcaster Mike Murphy visited both Bangladesh and Calcutta with his daughter, Carol, who was only 15.

> I'd been doing the Concern fast, and other bits and pieces for Concern. I'd admired it from a distance. Jack was the host, and we hit it off really well. Every evening we'd sit and chat about anything and everything. He explained about begging: you're not giving alms; you're doing prac-tical things to help them become self-sufficient.

He was struck by the 'tenacity of those two Finucane brothers in sticking to the concept they had created for themselves. Their family background must have been great. They were two fine men, two big, strong men, capable, compassionate, intelligent, but living what had to be a lonely life.

63

Daytime trips revealed the extent of the problems faced by both the Finucanes and all who worked in the Bangladesh field:

> We went out in a boat to where vagrants had been rounded up and moved onto tiny islands in the river – which would be inundated the next time the monsoons came, and the authorities' response to that would be, 'so what?'
>
> On the river, at a corner where rubbish would gather, we saw dead babies. Upriver, women had had them, knew they couldn't support them, so put them in the river to let them float away.
>
> But although we saw awful, terrible things, we were mightily impressed with what Concern was doing. What those Finucanes and those young people were doing.

In Calcutta, he and Carol learned about the pavement people:

> They had a tarpaulin, stretching from the railings to the edge of the pavement, about six feet. There'd be another tarp next store. Entire families were born, lived and died in that one little area of pavement and for the privilege, paid protection money to gangsters.

They also went to visit a hospice run by Mother Teresa's organisation, and were impressed 'that they were looking after these people.' Nevertheless, Mike had:

> ... an uncomfortable feeling that they were more concerned about gaining extra souls for heaven, helping them on their way, rather than curing them. They were baptising them before they died and so on.
>
> Yes, they were being made more comfortable than if they were lying out on the street, but I did

feel they were counting scalps for the Lord more than anything else. Turning people into Catholics, giving them Extreme Unction and then: 'Good luck, we won't detain you any longer!

6

*'He was politically incorrect — that's what I adored about Aengus.
You did a thing because it was the right thing to do. You weren't
talking projects or budgets; you were talking about human beings on
the bottom rung of the ladder. That was the ethos of Concern, and he
wanted to keep it like that.'*

— Jacqueline Duffy (former Press Officer, Concern)

In Bangladesh there is a place called Dulla, about an hour
outside the town of Mymensingh, which itself is about
120 miles due north of Dhaka. It is not all that far from the
Brahmaputra River.

To get to it, you take a dirt road from Mymensingh, travelling
alongside a railway track for quite some time. At a certain point,
you turn right across this railway track, and very soon you see
ahead of you a huge house, obviously the former mansion of a
zamindar (landlord), U-shaped, built of faded red brick, fronted
with a long cement verandah running the length of the ground
floor. The house sits behind a huge maidan, literally an open field,
just like the traditional, verdant English 'village green'. All around
is the equally lush green of the rice paddies. There are no gates.

At this time, 1975, the paintwork is peeling, and although
the windows can be closed off at night with massive wooden
shutters, there is no glass. Off to the left you can see a village, but

it's hazy and you can pick out very little detail. You can, however, just make out what is being sold on the counters of the dukans, the little stalls along the fringes of the railway.

If you drive around towards the back of the house you will see a set of outbuildings, obviously inhabited, and a large, stagnant pond, where women wash clothes and sometimes men fish.

These are the sights that confront two young Concern volunteers, Dorothy Devlin and Sheila O'Leary, who, based in Mymensingh, have been driven there, at his request, by one of the drivers attached to their compound. He is clearly nervous. They are not sure why, but he is a trusted colleague who came to them and said that there was something they should see.

Inured as they now are to difficult situations, when they get inside what they find horrifies them so deeply that they rush to Dhaka to tell Aengus. Incarcerated there are, they estimate, 2,500 women, at least. Silent women. Rows and rows of them, packed so tightly that they can barely move, looking back at these white intruders with indifference. 'It was that silence,' they said afterwards, 'that's what got to us.'

The women, it turned out, were officially vagrants, captured during one of the 'routine' round-ups operated by the Department of Social Welfare to cleanse the streets of Dhaka. Based on Victorian Poor Laws still extant at the time in Bangladesh, if you had no visible means of support you were subject to arrest, brought briefly before a magistrate, and if you couldn't prove that a husband or other relative, usually male, could be found to claim you and prove his support, you were beaten onto the back of a truck and packed off into one of these vagrants' homes.

Dulla was populated by destitutes, prostitutes, beggars, widows, women who were pregnant outside marriage whose families had shunned them, and women whose husbands had simply abandoned them. 'In Bangladesh, men tended to deal with poverty by walking away from it. It was not uncommon,' says Philip O'Brien, the Concern accountant in Dhaka at the time, later Bangladesh country director.

His memory of Dulla is fresh because he has written a thesis on his experiences with the poor of that nation, and just before being interviewed for this book had given a separate, more personal interview in connection with his elevation to the presidency of the International Montessori Association. During that interview he was asked to name both the most influential person in his life and the most influential incident. His answers were, respectively, Father Aengus Finucane and their work in the Vagrant Home in Dulla.

'We already knew about the Vagrant Home in Mirpur,' he says, 'because it was very close to the Women's Training Centre we were running.'

Broadcaster Mike Murphy, on that Concern-facilitated visit to Calcutta and Bangladesh, visited the Mirpur facility. As he speaks on the patio of his home in Dublin, the memory of that visit is so vivid that, for the time it takes to recount it, it is clear that this fresh, sunny day has been occluded by the steamy, crowded confines of that home. One episode he experienced there traumatised and obviously still haunts him.

> I witnessed women being brought to the prison in a truck for begging. I saw a couple of wardens using big sticks to beat the women on and off the trucks. Then we went inside, and saw these male wardens putting on a good show for us: how happy these women are here. Then they brought out this woman prisoner to dance for us.
>
> She danced.
>
> All the male wardens gathered with us to watch her. I realised halfway through we were being used, conned – these guys were getting their jollies....

His immediate reaction was: *I've got to get out of here.* But then, even more upsetting: *If I do that, do I ruin this young woman's position within the prison?*

Then one of the warders said to me: 'She's dancing for you! We would like you to take her out of the prison – take her out and look after her!'

Completely flummoxed, he looked across at his Concern escort and knew immediately by the expression on her face that she was saying *absolutely no*.

Not that I had been going to say 'yes', although I didn't know. I was completely floored by the dilemma from a moral point of view: my being here means I've walked this poor woman into something....

He and his escort did manage politely to extricate themselves:

... but when we left I asked if I should have said yes, and she said absolutely not, that Concern had worked very, very hard to get a moral watchdog-type position in that place on the basis that conditions, and the position of those poor women, would be far worse if it wasn't there.

For Aengus, Philip O'Brien and Concern in general, the existence of the home at Dulla came as a revelation. If it had not been for that brave and caring driver, it might never have been discovered by any agency. 'It was really, really rural,' according to O'Brien. 'Out in the middle of nowhere.'

But when its existence was revealed, he was immediately asked by Aengus to go up and take a look, but to tread carefully, however, because the authorities were very sensitive about the issue of how they dealt with vagrants, especially in the eyes of westerners, of whom there were now myriads in the country, operating in trade, diplomacy and in the aid and development sector.

Aengus himself, says O'Brien, was known in the aid agency business:

... as having a laser-sharp focus on dealing with his brief, the betterment of the poorest, always conscious about how easy it would have been to slide up the social scale and work with people a little above the bottom rung, who had at least some resources. So we were always working with women who had literally nothing.

People like Rab Chowdhury were helpful. (Abdur Rab Chowdhury was a senior lawyer and government minister, initially cultivated by Aengus for his influence, but who then became a very good friend, not just to him but to Concern.)

But in the matter of the vagrant homes, I don't think he got any support from the other aid agencies. Cole Dodge of Oxfam, maybe – he was a personal friend.

The authorities were suspicious as to why on earth a small Irish expatriate NGO would be showing interest in such worthless people. There was also internal opposition within the organisation.

In much the same way that later on there would be internal arguments about decisions to feed *génocidaires* in Rwanda, there were serious disputes in Concern itself about going into these vagrants' homes. Some of the volunteers in Dhaka, for instance, were opposed to the move on the political basis that by doing so Concern was aiding and abetting a nefarious state practice.

The same arguments were waged around the head of Jack Finucane when he stuck to his own principles during the 'resettlement programme' in Ethiopia after the 1984 famine, where people were ripped wholesale from their home villages and, almost without warning, transported to the south of the country, where the land was better, but nothing else was, especially infrastructure. They were strangers in a strange land, with little knowledge or experience of how to manage there.

Jack's attitude was: 'These are people who are where they are now through no fault of their own. It was nothing that they did.'

70

And so, against the tide of much opinion, he brought Concern in there to help. 'If we don't, what are these people, dumped here by their government, going to do?'

Once confronted with the reality of the overcrowding and conditions in Dulla, it was another done deal for Concern as far as Aengus was concerned. 'Aengus got us there in the end,' says O'Brien.

During his initial visit he too had noticed the silence, despite the hundreds and hundreds of children rounded up and incarcerated with their mothers. For a country that spilled over with colour – the deep greens of the rice fields, gorgeous saris of women, garishness of rickshaws, buses and signage – the inside of this Dulla house was particularly drab. The women were dressed identically in institutional garb, stone-coloured, Department of Social Welfare-issue cotton saris trimmed with a narrow red border. Taken together with the dowdy décor, the effect was deadening.

From a western perspective, one might wonder why, in such an open place with no gates or fences, no one made any attempt to escape. The answer is pretty obvious when the plight of these women is taken into account. Where would they go? To whom? To what?

'Most people in there had not one single possession,' says O'Brien. The regime from the guards was undoubtedly brutal, and their lathis, (heavy iron-bound bamboo sticks) were always at the ready.

Once installed, the women were subjected to sexual assaults. Despite all of this, however, at least they and their children were fed, and they had a roof over their heads during the monsoon rains. Some of them even had the luxury of a mat on which to lie for sleep, providing that floor space could be found.

While Philip O'Brien does remember 'one or two complaints of rape,' by and large apathy was the norm. 'And those women were very careful not to be seen talking to the white man.'

Just as they had during the negotiations to get into the home at Mirpur, discussions began about Dulla. The authorities made it clear from the outset that they were not going to stop rounding up the street people and arresting them, but in preparation for a positive outcome to the talks, Philip, now in charge of the efforts to provide services within Dulla, no matter how minimal they eventually proved to be, moved to Mymensingh.

During the parlay with the Department of Social Welfare, Concern made it clear that the organisation could not deal with the numbers incarcerated in Dulla and could handle a maximum of just 600, emphasising that even that was a stretch. While it was a very big house, it had not been constructed to accommodate what was essentially now an open prison for thousands. The guards, all male, were accommodated separately in the converted outhouses in the grounds behind the house proper.

Finally, Aengus succeeded in getting permission for access, and when the organisation was eventually allowed in, O'Brien found that, miraculously, nearly 2,000 women and their children had vanished into the ether, leaving just the core 600 that had been requested.

Concern people set to, just as they had in Mirpur, constructing and repairing, providing latrines and washing facilities and 'a bit of training. We set up a weaving programme and there was intense competition to get into it.'

Most importantly, they acted as a presence in the place. Bearing witness in the hope that some of the abuses they had good reason to suspect had been pertaining, might lessen.

One such abuse happened to a 7-year-old girl who got lost in Dhaka. Separated from her mother, she was swept up in one of the periodic round-ups and brought to a vagrants' home, where she was raped by the manager, who then returned her to the streets. As 'damaged goods', she would not be taken back into her family, even if she could find them, and would find it very difficult to marry.

Another girl, when working in a garment factory at 10 years old, was assaulted by her supervisor, and she too was from then on shunned by her family and had to live on the streets, where her only possibility of material survival was sex work. In doing so, she left herself open to being arrested.

Because of practices such as this, despite many being 'cultural' in nature, in 2004, Concern started a project with 3,800 of these sex workers and 1,200 of their children, providing antenatal care, vaccinations, education in the prevention of HIV and Aids, schooling for the children and, in an area where the organisation excels, training these women in skills that offered the possibility of a livelihood in a trade other than selling their bodies. In the course of this training, it also gave them information about their human, legal and social rights, and tried to make them politically aware.

Not all the women took on all of this successfully; some returned to the streets, saying that while they knew that it was dangerous, violent, and that they risked incarceration in a vagrants' home, at the very least it gave them some control of a small portion of their income.

Many westerners (such as the present author) who go to Bangladesh and similar places find the widespread, almost cultural, fatalism with which setbacks and disasters seem to be absorbed very difficult to comprehend. On the one hand this apparent stoicism has to be admirable, but on the other, it seems passive, even tragically so, in situations where action might prove to be beneficial. While the Bangladeshi people are undoubtedly resilient in the face of what are, to most of us, catastrophic conditions, there are times when this resilience fails.

Not often, however. Philip O'Brien remembers going to Chittagong after a very serious cyclone, when a huge swathe of housing and countryside was razed. Having arrived into the middle of this devastation he noticed a big tree, which had miraculously withstood the storm. In its trunk, lengthways, was embedded a long piece of corrugated iron, which was all that remained of someone's dwelling. 'And there was a man there, attempting by brute force to wrestle the piece of corrugated iron out of that tree, giving up, then starting again.'

On one of his later visits to the children of the Dulla vagrants' home, so eerily silent, Philip brought net-loads of footballs with him, and when he opened the boot of his car and kicked them all over the nearby 'maidan', the effect was electrifying. Children instantly spilled out from nowhere, excited children who made a huge racket, kicking and shouting, playing, behaving like children.

Children in Bangladesh didn't always get the chance to play like this, as was attested by O'Brien's first journey, which involved travelling from a 'ghat', the dock from which a ferry was boarded. 'I saw all the women holding out their children, wanting to sell them.'

Horror at the selling of children is always the western reaction, 'but when you think about it, they are trying to save their babies by looking for someone who might take them and be kind to them.' Once their milk had dried up or had been transferred to the newest child, there was no way for these women to feed, clothe or bring up the one who was now being offered to an obviously well-off stranger. These women literally had nothing, except the knowledge that inevitably there would be more babies to come.

However, even forewarned and armed with this information, these tiny kids with backward-facing legs, hands or feet, who sat at the ferry ghats seeking alms, were very difficult to behold.

Although he had been initially hesitant to transfer his affection from Africa to Southeast Asia, and despite having to face situations like this and sometimes even worse on a daily basis, when asked in later life what had been his favourite field of endeavour for Concern, as we know, Aengus Finucane unswervingly replied, 'Bangladesh.'

He was perhaps most proud of several stand-out accomplishments. One was his successful persuasion of the authorities to diversify into growing wheat along with the universal rice. Another was the success of his micro-finance programmes where women were given small-business loans, and if anything an even bigger success resulted from the slow but persistent work that allowed Concern into those vagrant homes to give some succour to the people who were at the core of the organisation's mission: the outcasts – the poorest of the poor.

Not every volunteer sailed through his or her stint in a posting like Bangladesh without psychological and emotional difficulties.

As it happens, Cleo O'Reilly ('Aengus and I clicked right from the beginning') was one of those for whom the initial adjustment was severe. She went to Bangladesh as a volunteer in the Women's Career Training Institute, 'teaching typing and all that,' to qualify Bangladeshi women and girls to be secretaries. This was a country where, in the state sector, being a secretary was a male job.

At the time, however, the authorities were making incremental efforts to modernise and become a fully secular society:

> ... and the sheik [Sheik Mujib Rahman, the president, later assassinated with most of his family in August 1975] had made spaces in the government services for these girls to be employed. The ones I trained were going out to companies like the state airlines and banks.

While this training was mostly successful, Cleo – a Dub, vital, energetic and quirky – was one of those who found it very difficult to deal with the mass apathy and fatalism she found amongst the population in general.

> I felt from the beginning that the whole drive for people to get up and go had left them because everything was against them: the climate, the floods, the crowds. You'd go to Calcutta and the poverty was just as bad, but there was something different about the population. In Bangladesh they just seemed to accept their fate. Africans have a different attitude: they always believe something will turn up.

A second difficulty for Cleo O'Reilly was that she found it extremely painful to deal with the way local people reacted to and treated each other. At one point she and another volunteer, Eithna Caffrey, had been sent by Aengus to Saidpur.

> We were living in a convent and we were surrounded by these wailing people all night long. The nuns would open the gate and beat people off and drag in the worst. There were people with spinal TB, and they'd crawl along to try to get a bit of help, but they weren't starving so they weren't allowed in. I just couldn't deal with it. I remember bawling, and my husband said to me: 'You might as well go home; you're no use to anybody here.'

Her husband, Vincent O'Reilly, was another Concern worker. But he then switched to the UN, and the two of them with their two children subsequently became citizens of th   ʳˡᵈ and saw a great deal of it. Those Concern grappling h embedded into Cleo's heart, however, and like never lost touch with Aengus, or indeed with On one occasion, she found herself 'driving Dara [her first baby] and 2,000 [Concern] bʋ be done. And the Concern volunteers woul our house. That's the Concern way: you jus

At the institute, Cleo worked with th Mary Humphreys, and a Bangladeshi woʌ senior. 'She was a fantastic lady with a degree froʌ of Lebanon, but because she was a Bangladeshi womaʌ wasn't allowed to meet directly with officials. I was the one who had to go,' apropos of which she conveyed the most wonderful image. Dressed by Mary Humphreys, 'like the Ayatollah's wife in a long skirt,' with her long blonde hair 'stuffed into a turban', she and Miss Humphreys would set off on Mary Humphreys's Honda 50, zigzagging and zooming through the swarms of rickshaws and other vehicles towards official meetings. She smiles affectionately at the memory. 'Yeah, Mary Humphreys ...'.

Miss Humphreys is, quite literally, 'old school', and at her suggestion her interview was conducted in one of the lovely drawing rooms of the RDS, where she is a member. Now retired, she was a long-term employee of Concern, and put many many volunteers through her capable hands.

Before joining the organisation, however, she started her working career as a school principal in a girls' school in Nigeria, 'before Biafra and all that. I go far back. They [the Holy Ghost Fathers] were looking for voluntary teachers to go to Africa,' and so, B.A. H.Dip in hand, she went along for an interview.

> Father Michael Doheny interviewed me, and I went down to one of their missions there: a girls' boarding school. I stayed until we completed our first West African Leaving Cert. I handed over to a Nigerian lady then, but then of course the Biafran war broke out.

Miss Humphreys is one of those who adds her personal colour to the intriguing tapestry of diversity in the personalities and backgrounds of those who populate Concern. Not only is she from a robust, middle-class background, she is Irish republican royalty, if that is not an oxymoron. (It is, but it describes her well.)

With a father who was nephew to The O'Rahilly (shot dead in the GPO during the 1916 Rising), and a grand-aunt very famous in *Cumann na mBan,* her fighting spirit is undiminished in its loyalty to the founding fathers of Concern, the Kennedy O'Loughlins.

She first met Aengus in his early Nigerian days. 'We shook hands. A lovely person, very charming, but of course that's not a word they like being used about a priest. I was very impressed. Concern was beginning a little after I came back and joined.' Which posting had she enjoyed most?

> Field director in Yemen – the whole Yemen experience, great political and academic discussions around the table. New programmes in health and engineering....

Actually, I enjoyed whatever work I was doing, three months in Ethiopia, for instance.

But it was all so very interesting and different. Job satisfaction out of all of them. You're working so hard at everything and they're all making different demands, so you couldn't say that anything in particular was a golden time.

She does admit, though, that she particularly enjoyed 'zipping up and down the west coast of Africa, surveying where Concern might be of help.'

The Women's Career Training institute in Bangladesh, where she had worked with Cleo O'Reilly, had originally been set up by the state to train war widows, with Aengus, as always looking out for women in need, very happy to conjoin Concern:

... because of course there was no welfare or support in Bangladesh at that time.

We did have a very powerful board, and that was helpful. We trained the women, not just for secretarial careers but in handcrafts, embroidery, making dolls, anything women could do and for which they had aptitude. And of course anything which could provide some sort of livelihood.

While she admired Aengus and the way he, Jack and many others brought the organisation forward, she remains very loyal to the originators:

We mustn't wipe out the fact that the Kennedys were there at the beginning. Their drive was the beginning of it all, and Aengus always acknowledged them. We began as non-denominational with other founders, but a lot of credit has to go to the Kennedys, John O'Loughlin Kennedy and his wife, Kay. Kay was great stuff. They were both good, she was excellent. A very sensible person.

When I was head of the Volunteer Department in Dublin, I used to bring Raymond in to talk to the new recruits. His difficulty as head of the organisation was that he wouldn't always kowtow to government, and really you have to sometimes.

Aengus had vision too, but he added diplomacy and charm to it.

American volunteer Irwin Shorr firmly believes that Aengus:

... lived by a model espoused by President Kennedy. Even during the Cuban missile crisis, Kennedy always tried to get a good night's sleep so he could make good decisions the following day.

(Irwin, the common complaint is that Aengus wouldn't go to bed?) He brushes this off:

The point is that Aengus was always calm and methodical in his thinking and his plans. His thinking was always so clear.

But sometimes, as has already been seen, in the interests of the work, that charm of his, mentioned by Mary Humphreys, could be shed. Even this most fervent of all Aengus's fans, who really cannot stomach any criticism of his hero, does admit this:

Yes he had the ability to tell you as it is. Tell you something to your face that is actually quite critical....

And Irwin turns this into a virtue:

... he had the unique ability to have you listen and accept because he wanted you to get on the same side of the line as him.

7

'It is you who have ruined my vineyard;
the plunder from the poor is in your houses.'

– Isaiah 3.14

In 1976 and the first part of 1977, Concern's hull had hit a financial reef. With income running at 30 per cent below what the actual budget was, drastic measures and cutbacks were being discussed. Some of these financial decisions, like ceasing the practice of loaning out experienced volunteer nurses, engineers, logisticians and administrators to colleague NGOs, were implemented.

The organisation faced serious competition for funds within Ireland. Trócaire had been launched by the Irish Catholic Church in 1973, and by tapping into its own natural hinterland – the diocesan hierarchy and congregations who had ready-made access to parish collection points in its churches – had steadily made inroads into the finite pot of money available in Ireland. By 1976 it was outgunning Concern. Gorta, founded in 1960, with its agronomists and agricultural specialists, was also competing hard, and had now entered the ground in Bangladesh. And there was yet another competitor on the pitch. Under the aegis of the Irish Department of Foreign Affairs, the Agency for Personal Service Overseas had presented itself as the go-to body for volunteers interested in giving service abroad.

Meanwhile, Concern's head office faced increasing demands and grumbling from the fields. As operations grew and matured, the experience and confidence of field directors increased in parallel. So did the volume of calls for resources to enable the servicing of new and expanding programmes, both for existing clients and for those additional populations they could now identify as having no assets or services at all, and who were in desperate need of help.

As a result of these ever-increasing demands, communications between the fields and Camden Street had become somewhat tetchy. Instincts and demands from the fields were based on *spend now because the need is great; we can't wait until people die*, whereas for head office the imperative was: *hasten slowly and be prudent; hold back some funds in reserve so as not to run out.*

By this time Bangladesh was by far the biggest field, with at any one time up to seventy-six volunteers serving all parts of the country, from Chittagong in the far south, through Dhaka and up into various points north of the capital such as Mymensingh and Saidpur. Volunteers were running health, sanitation and livelihoods programmes in remote and rural areas, anywhere Aengus Finucane and his trusties had found the need for them. There is a line in Tony Farmar's book, *Believing in Action,* which tells us that in Bangladesh Aengus was receiving the greatest preponderance of all funding available from head office in Dublin.

On the other hand, he had become so expert in identifying co-funding opportunities and donations, he was able to source almost two-thirds of what he spent from co-funders and donations from elsewhere. In other words, he was receiving twice as much from external sources as he was from Concern itself.

Nevertheless, throughout 1976 and into 1977 there was a steady flow of correspondence, rather impatient in tone, between Bangladesh and Camden Street, 'always with carbon copies,' says Kevin Farrell, Aengus's eventual deputy, who, with his wife, Geraldine, had served there since 1973.

By profession an economist, Farrell was one of the people who 'did whatever Aengus wanted me to do'. Geraldine, amongst other assignments, taught in the Mirpur vagrants' home.

Farrell was taken on, incidentally, in rather an unorthodox way, which shows how Aengus and Jack Finucane operated on instinct about people, although not, as we'll see, without a little checking into their background.

Having gone to Canada after graduation from Trinity, Farrell didn't like it, and decided to spend six months travelling. He ended up in Calcutta in 1973, where he 'met a guy. "I'm interested," says this guy, "in having a look at this new place, Bangladesh." ' And so off the two of them went, by bus and by train.

In Dhaka, with funds almost completely gone, serendipitously Kevin Farrell met someone from the ICRC (International Committee of the Red Cross), who said to him: 'Listen, I'm going to a meeting with an Irish NGO called Concern, why don't you come along?'

Farrell, who is from Northern Ireland, had 'only vaguely' heard of this group, but on hearing the word 'Irish' he went along in the hope that somehow he could be directed towards contacts in Dhaka who might be able to offer some kind of temporary employment, 'and I end up meeting Aengus and Jack,' the latter then *in situ* with his brother.

The brothers talked with him, and heard enough to ask him to come back to see them the following Monday, 'but Aengus was heading home to Ireland the following morning for some meeting, so it's Jack I spent time with.'

Somehow, he managed to eke out his resources until the Monday. He met again with Jack, who offered him a job in Saidpur on a project to eradicate scabies, for which, as an economist, he felt less than qualified. A job, though, is a job, and he took it with some alacrity. Jack apparently told him that what the job required was spraying sufferers 'with some sort of Gentian Violet,' and giving them 'a supply of clean clothes.' Then, satisfied with his new recruit, Jack handed Farrell a pack of traveller's cheques to the value of $22,000, instructions about the quickest way to get to Calcutta, and directions as to where to go in that city and whom to contact in order to buy and transport large quantities of lungis and saris.

It may not have been as randomly trusting as it appeared. Kevin Farrell discovered some time later that in the time between the two meetings, the Finucanes had done a background check and found, inter alia, that he had a brother in the Kiltegan Fathers.

He stayed with Concern in Bangladesh until 1977. By that time, Jack had departed to run other fields and countries and he himself had climbed to the position of deputy field director. From early on in that year, although he didn't get involved, he says, he sensed that there was an internal 'but civilised' power struggle going on between the Bangladesh Field and Father Raymond Kennedy, one of the original founders who now, as CEO, was still a passionate driver of the organisation. As always, between field and head office it was: 'What do they know back there in Dublin?

From Farrell's perspective, he could see there was a bit of plotting going on:

> Meetings of council and the executive committee in Dublin were being followed very closely in Bangladesh, with tactics and strategy being discussed, and communications being made to Dublin with people Aengus trusted. There was a mischievous side to Aengus: it was the politician in him, and I think he revelled in sending instructions to his Dublin followers: 'There's a meeting next week, here's how you count your heads, we know we have to concentrate on The Undecideds ...'.

Aengus's deputy conspicuously abstained from taking sides, but was 'always very supportive of Aengus,' and emphasises that at the time he was – and is again now – making his judgements simply as a close observer.

He and Geraldine left Bangladesh, as planned, in May of 1977, carrying with them joint and abiding lessons learned from Aengus during their period there. The main one, according to both, was that motivation for all action was 'the dignity of the poor.'

When Concern set up in Bangladesh, its jostling crowds amounted to a population of seventy-six million. Latest estimates put the population at close to 160 million.

So this small land mass, (less than one and a half times the size of Ireland, an island supporting five and a half million people) has to feed, clothe, house and regulate an average of over 2,600 people per square mile. To put that in perspective, Bere Island, one of our most populous offshore islands, at seven square miles and a population of just over 200, would have to support more than 18,000. The first impression gained on arriving in Bangladesh continues to be of crowds and ceaseless movement, and this is not limited to the cities. P. J. Howell, an engineer and future chair of Concern, who at the age of 21 spent his first stint of volunteering in that country, remarks on this:

> Even in the remotest rural areas, on tracks between villages, you could never walk for five minutes in any direction without dodging people on bicycles, motor- bikes, rickshaws, people walking, walking, walking. The only space that was really your own was the room in your own house.

While working for Aengus, after some new disaster had befallen the country, Howell remembers his boss going into the appropriate ministry, offering Concern's help, and saying: 'We will go into wherever it is the worst.'

Given all of this, it would be all too easy to see the poor of Bangladesh as an anonymous swarm. Aengus, say the Farrells, always retained intact 'his sense of the individual's worth.'

Speaking in their home in south Dublin city, they agree that Aengus lived his spirituality and religion, but did not talk about his work in those terms; that he never preached or explained his view of humanity in terms of: *I must do this because it's my Christian duty.*

As to whether the priest saw himself as somehow embodying Concern and in that context, fretted that the organisation as run from Dublin was not up to his standards, Kevin said: 'he probably did envisage himself in charge in Dublin.' And he did remember a casual reference, made during some ruminative chat or other, 'that the only job better than the stewardship of Concern in Bangladesh was "the big job in Camden Street." '

Both Farrells agree that Aengus was not in the least interested in money per se, and saw it only as a resource needed to fund his cause. As far as that went, though, the more zeros on the donation cheques, the better.

They do say, as does almost everybody else interviewed, that he was nevertheless financially and organisationally competitive for Concern and its mission, although never, in public at least, critical of any other Irish NGO. While knowing that the organisation could never be as big as Save the Children or Oxfam, say, he strove nonetheless, says Kevin Farrell, to create an Irish-based organisation that could make a valuable difference, that could be the best in the class, that could provide the best service possible to the biggest and widest set of his 'poorest of the poor.'

In any event, whatever machinations were afoot in Bangladesh, or in other fields, from the beginning of 1977 head office was rumbling along under CEO Raymond Kennedy and the council, now chaired by Michael Fingleton.

That May, however, not only did Kevin and Geraldine Farrell resign as planned; so, very suddenly and unexpectedly, did Father Raymond Kennedy, sending shock waves through the organisation. Even those who had been disillusioned with him were stunned. His resignation was with immediate effect, and so, without warning, the organisation was, if not rudderless, at least temporarily adrift.

It was also significant that, following this event, others too resigned unexpectedly: the Overseas Coordinator, the

Bookkeeper, the Education officer and even the receptionist. In addition, Monsignor Bruce Kent, the English priest famous for his anti-nuclear stance, resigned his seat on the council, taking his international stature with him.

How was Concern to respond to this exodus of its staff? The resultant scramble ended with the quick installation of Father Michael Doheny as Chief Executive. He was another Spiritan who, having hardly any experience of running a business, which Concern now was, did, however, to his credit, have major field experience. He had worked in the enormous Salt Lake Refugee Camp on the outskirts of Calcutta, a 'hellhole' as it has been called by some sources. Father Doheny had a name for knowing what went on in the field, and like most of the veteran Holy Ghost missionaries had a sterling reputation for trustworthiness. He also had a wide circle of contacts, which ensured some form of welcome from those donating to Concern.

In the meantime, his predecessor, Father Kennedy, moved off with considerable dignity. There are a number of ironies here, of a type probably familiar to students of organisational matters. Africa Concern flared into public consciousness in Ireland because of Biafra, but with that state having been absorbed back into Nigeria, there was no longer any perceived reason to fund aid for it. It was Raymond Kennedy who, with Michael Doheny and his own brother, John O'Loughlin Kennedy, had scoped out East Pakistan as their NGO's next arena of aid, with himself as director of the operation. Moreover, he had ceded that post to Aengus Finucane so he could take up his CEO position in Dublin.

Bangladesh was fertile ground for a non-governmental aid organisation. In addition to its post-war difficulties, particularly amongst the Biharis, it was not just coming out of war, but was still suffering the after-effects of a devastating cyclone in November 1970. There had been huge damage caused to property along its Eastern coast, and 500,000 people had died or were missing, presumed dead.

A young Aengus Finucane, Limerick, in 1932.

A 36-year-old Aengus at a Biafran feeding centre, 1968.

Jack and Aengus in Bangladesh, 1973.

Aengus and Jack Finucane in Makele, Ethiopia, 1977,
beside a DC3 plane.

Mick Doheny with Aengus Finucane in Bangladesh, 1977.

Sheik Mujid Rahman, President of Bangladesh, being presented
with shamrock by Aengus Finucane, Mick Doheny
and Eithne Caffrey, 1973.

Captain of the *Colmcille*.

Paddy Reidy, Peter Fleming, Aengus Finucane and Mick Reynolds
in Kilkee, 1959.

Aengus Finucane and Raymond Kennedy at the Concern-run womens secretarial school, Chittagong, 1972.

Jack and Aengus Finucane in Addis Ababa, Ethiopia, 1977.

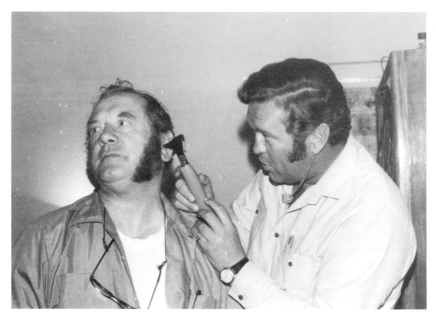

Aengus Finucane giving Mick Doheny a haircut in
Bangladesh, 1970s.

Geraldine (Walshe) Farrell and Raymond Kennedy CEO in
Saidpur, Bangladesh, 1975.

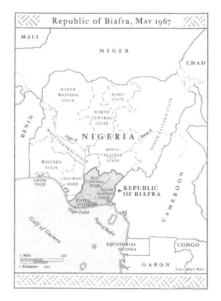

Republic of Biafra, May 1967.
Biafran-Controlled Territory, January 1970.

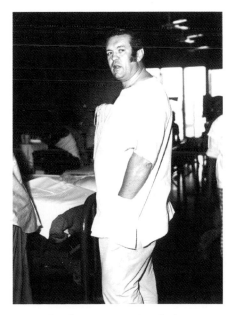

Aengus Finucane at feeding centre in Gabon, West Africa, 1969

Aengus Novitiate at Kilshane, Co. Tipperary, 1949.

Fintan Farley and Aengus Finucane with Irwin Shorr, Jack Finucane and Patricia Hickey, Dhaka, Bangladesh, May 1973.

In June 1971, during Raymond Kennedy's watch, Concern, having dropped the 'Africa' from its name, launched a fresh and very successful Irish appeal for aid. Following negotiations with the new state authorities in Dhaka, and in cooperation with local and international NGOs, Michael Doheny was instrumental in setting up the new Concern operation. The lawyer Abdur Rab Chowdhury, already mentioned in other contexts, proved to be particularly helpful in this. When he took the CEO's seat in Camden Street, Father Doheny was far from being a greenhorn, but always knew that his appointment was transitional while someone permanent was more conventionally recruited.

It should be mentioned here that there were already some small eddies of unrest to be detected about the seeming predominance of priestly figures in Concern.

To be fair, however, the original charter of Africa Concern did arise via the commitment of the Holy Ghost Fathers. Yet although the word 'secular' was never mentioned, from the very beginning, the organisation was firmly promulgated as non-denominational and along with Holy Ghosts, its board included a Methodist minister and lay people who were not Roman Catholics.

In any event, when the new CEO, Alex Tarbett, took over from the interim Father Doheny, there was a lot to do, although in his short time, just four months or so, Doheny had managed to steady the ship's course a little, and most importantly had smoothed over some internal differences.

Tarbett, who had studied for the priesthood in Maynooth without actually going forward for ordination, was by most accounts highly thought of, generous, and was, by reputation, familiar with every priest in the country. His arrival was welcomed in many quarters, and he proved to be an entirely different entity to what had gone before.

Books were his thing. He had never had anything to do with NGOs, the Third World, or indeed had any hands-on experience of Concern's work. Imposing, charming, articulate and courteous, he had been managing director of the book-publishing arm of Smurfit, and in addition had gone into publishing himself, specialising in catechetical and liturgical books. Many people may remember the bookshop he ran, Cathedral Books, beside the Pro-Cathedral, where he was much admired for his smiling demeanour, politeness, and willingness to go to the ends of the earth to find some volume not easily available.

On taking office he went immediately on a number of field trips 'to see for himself' what the operations were like and to get a feel of what he had got himself into. Over the next few years, on his watch the situation in Concern, including the grumpiness of the field directors, settled down as they accepted the true state of the organisation's finances. While insisting on their right to demand more, they accepted what they could get.

In Bangladesh in particular, the volunteers looked forward to his visits. 'Everyone loved him,' according to Ursula Sharpe. He would arrive fresh and energetic after his journey with British Airways, and while he would not stay in the Concern house, but in the Sheraton Hotel in Dhaka, he would invite squads of the volunteers to join him for a slap-up meal there, and always had gifts for them.

'He convinced you that British Airways was bumping him up to first class because he was going to interview Jesus,' according to Ursula Sharpe, who was working with Moira Conroy in a programme 'up-country'. Both had started with Concern as volunteers, but were now staff.

She also remembers him saying to her that her salary of £100 a month was not adequate. 'Oh, you'd need a lot more than that, Ursula!'

One of his first moves, apparently, had been to refuse to take an annual salary of more than £4,000.

Moira Conroy, a woman not easily impressed, was also taken with her new boss:

He had an amazing background. We were in deficit when Alex took over, and he took it all on and began to look at the bigger picture, places like Ethiopia, Yemen and all the other projects. He came to Bangladesh, I remember, and he was going on to Bangkok. He invited all the volunteers to a meal in the hotel. We knew he had travelled first class on the plane; he had an arrangement where he would write a report on the standards on board, and in return they'd give him a first-class seat.

8

*'"When it looks like everything is hopeless with no sustainable
solution – and some people think we should do nothing unless it's
sustainable – look, shut up! We're in a war zone here and some day
there'll be peace." I think that's a brilliant mantra.
We've become so theoretical, with so many academics and bullshitters.
Aengus had walked the walk as far as I'm concerned.'*

– Mike McDonagh (formerly Concern)

'Hokay ...', as Jack would say, exhaling, when transiting
away from a subject or segment of a subject that as far he
is concerned is closed.

Let's talk now about Mark Malloch Brown, Dominic
MacSorley, Mike McDonagh, Fred Cooney and Ciunas Bunworth,
and Aengus of course – some lives that collided in Khao-I-Dang
refugee camp on the Thai/Cambodian border in 1982.

Having left his job as a journalist with *The Economist*
magazine, Mark Malloch Brown was a UNHCR officer at
Khao-I-Dang. This man, later to be a Peer of the Realm,
in no particular order became Deputy Secretary General
and Chief of Staff of the United Nations under Kofi Annan,
vice president at the World Bank, vice chairman of George
Soros's Fund and Foundation, British Labour Minister in
2007 and vice chairman of the World Economic Forum. So,

demonstrably, he has dealt with people of influence from all over the world. Even so, he still remembers vividly the day he first met Aengus Finucane.

All services had broken down in the region because of the influx of refugee populations fleeing the Pol Pot regime, and at Khao-I-Dang a number of agencies were trying to house, feed and supply basic needs to 125,000 people. Malloch Brown's job at the time was 'to look after very highly skilled people such as surgeons, who had come to the camp on short-term contracts.' All were highly aware, he says, that they were 'doing good', and looked to him for answers: 'Where is our accommodation? Where is our transport?

'And here was this no-nonsense Irish charity that was just interested in getting the job done; doing it just for its own sake; largely women.'

One day he had been sitting quietly in his little UN-supplied 'bamboo hut' office when this big, indignant man rolled up to complain about some travesty in the camp:

> I forget now what it was about, but I seem to recall Aengus haranguing me about some shortcoming in camp services or management or some wrong that had been done to his team of young Concern volunteers. There may be elements of myth formed in my mind, but my first encounter with him was intimidating.
>
> Here he was, this instantly larger-than-life character, a veteran of Bangladesh, quite fierce, with this enormous no-nonsense efficiency and facility with soup kitchens and feeding stations established unbelievably quickly with his Court of Women. He'd been through Biafra and I sure as hell hadn't. And here I was, 27 or something, a callow ex-journalist in my first real job. Fortunately, I was in learning mode. He saw that and he adopted me.
>
> At that time the entire Cambodian border was populated with big characters. There was an adventurous side to it.

Fred Cooney, for instance, a consultant engineer with USAid, The United States Agency for International Development, was the man who designed and supervised the building of the A-frame houses in that camp and elsewhere. From Texas, with a heart as large as that state, he too was 'a big man', and according to Jack Finucane became a very good friend of Aengus's. Never without his Texan cowboy boots, after Khao-I-Dang he stayed in the aid and development world, but went missing while working in Chechnya later on, and there has been no word of his whereabouts for more than twenty years now. 'He and Aengus were far-seeing figures,' says Malloch Brown, 'veterans with very simple ways. They liked big theatres of operation.'

But Malloch Brown made a further interesting observation about his new friend when he got to know him better:

> It was my impression that Aengus might have been slightly unsteady in his stride in Khao-I-Dang, slightly unnerved that he wasn't the only big figure on the stage, because this was a field of great characters. These were all hugely exotic individuals with enormous back stories. Being in Khao-I-Dang was like being in one of those movies where there were lots of stars, an ensemble piece, and to a discriminating critic like myself, up to then Aengus had always been the first amongst equals. This wasn't quite the case here.

Three more significant Concern people worked at the Khao-I-Dang camp: Dominic MacSorley, Mike McDonagh and Brian Stockwell, the latter pair having taken their places in the annals of Concern's most prominent mavericks.

For both of these men, the physical world presents no boundaries. After Thailand, Brian went on with Aengus to Karamoja in north-eastern Uganda, where we will meet him again.

McDonagh, whose home at the time of his interview was in Addis Ababa, where he is now based for UNOCHA (the United Nations Office for the Coordination of Human Affairs), was in Dublin for a few days. The interview itself was so rapid-fire and wide-ranging that it was not easy to keep track of his odyssey through many of the most difficult and hostile places on the planet.

> I know where I've been every day for the last thirty years: the first four, Ethiopia, Mozambique, Bangladesh, Sudan, back to Mozambique, then back and forth for a bit, then another period in Sudan, the Jordan/Iraq border before the first Gulf War, Ethiopia again in '91, with a transfer to Cambodia with Dominic, Laos, Somalia, and all the time Liberia and Sierra Leone were going on. And when Kosovo happened and refugees started coming out to Albania, I got called to that.

He was the go-to guy who got called out to a lot of what he calls 'shortnesses', in-out rescues, necessary as a result of sudden catastrophic events: 'Or when I get called to do something absolutely specific.'

Given what they do, what they see and where they do and see it, the attitude of professional aid workers can sometimes stop you in your tracks.

> (Did he become addicted to danger, like the war correspondent who, by popular (mis)conception becomes a conflict and adrenalin junkie?)
>
> It's just that I found I wasn't like some others who would stay ten years in the same country; I would have been bored.
>
> (Inured to suffering of individuals?)
>
> I don't think I got inured, because I'm still not inured when the horrors strike. It's just that I feel I need to be challenged all the time, and there were a lot of challenges there to be had.

At one point he left Somalia, persuaded by Aengus that he would be the ideal person to head up the new office in New York, a prospect that did not exactly fill him with enthusiasm. But his master had called, and since Somalia, in McDonagh's opinion, was at the time 'quiet', he could not refuse, accepting that his high profile in the US, largely the result of his on-air, live TV reports from Somalia would be of benefit to the organisation. What is more, he brought with him another useful asset – he was known to some of the most high-profile journalists in US media; he had been the go-to guy for those who had flown into his theatres of operation in search of instant, compelling stories, analysis and sound bites about very complex situations – so his contacts book was priceless.

Understandably though, New York, when he got there, was a very big culture shock. There are, he says (or there were at the time – probably more now given the times we live in), 30,000 charities in that city:

> Everyone was nickel-and-dimed. You'd have two lunches back to back, everyone building a database, everyone selling a database. On the one hand it was fascinating. On the other hand you had actuaries there telling you exactly when you'd break even. Fundraising is a science. There's no pressure if you have four years to do it.

Then, the unforgettable:

> ... but, thank God, Angola broke and I could go back. I escaped. When Aengus asked me to go there for six weeks I went to the Angolan mission in New York [for visa documentation] like a bat out of hell.

It was a Tuesday when Aengus made his request, and what follows is a terrific illustration of how a Concern rapid-response unit actually works.

I got the visa on a Wednesday. I flew Aer France on a Thursday. I went into an office in the airport in Paris; Ciunas had faxed me out the names of all the priests in Angola. There were lots of Holy Ghost Fathers down there; some of them were even Irish.

I arrived on the Friday morning, I was in my first besieged city by the afternoon, and having read the fax from Ciunas I'd met a wonderful Portuguese priest and a wonderful Portuguese nun, Sister Marie Jose. They brought me to see the governor, a complete bastard, but we got on wonderfully.

Aengus was already sending people, amazing people. I was able to grab people who had already been in Somalia or South Sudan. The head of Save the Children today was a junior part of that team. And Brian Stockwell. And Sean Lee, who was Mary Robinson's bodyguard when she came to Somalia. And a whole plethora of nurses.

We had the operation up and running by that Tuesday.

He smiles, shifting on his bar stool. We are meeting in a noisy Dublin pub near where he was staying with his brother. The lights were dim enough, but that smile was fond.

Irish nurses! That's one of the big things about Concern, those nurses, people like Anne O'Mahony. They trained under brutal matrons. All these places, and they were there, hardy and fearless and tough as nails, but not so tough as to shut out what was going on. Just amazing people. I remember an American colonel saying to me in Somalia back in '93: 'Your nurses have more balls than my marines!'

Anyhow, we went front line into three besieged cities, landed under fire, spiralled down with South African pilots when the government side was being shelled by Unita. And then we went to a city where Unita was in charge and being shelled by the government.

So that's how I got to Angola and never got back to New York.

I think back on Africa of the 1990s and I don't know how I survived it – the madness in Sierra Leone was the worst of the worst. And if you read one of these books you wonder how some of these journalists survived too....

(Any plans for retirement?)

I'll do another year and a half in Ethiopia. There is one small caveat, though: I will let it be known that if there's something available for two months somewhere, then I will leave Costa Rica or wherever we are. I'll do it: John Ging I am here! Dominic MacSorley I am here! I'd like to do two months a year. [He looks into the distance] Or maybe three. [Laois-born, ex-Irish military man, John Ging, having become world-famous as head of the United Nations humanitarian effort in the Gaza Strip, now heads up UNOCHA].

Dominic MacSorley's first experience of a Concern field was in Bangkok, and then in the huge Khao-I-Dang refugee camp. It was 1982 and he was a 26-year old, fully qualified Belfast solicitor when in the *Irish News* he saw a Concern advertisement seeking nurses and engineers.

He wrote immediately: 'I'm interested in this kind of work, but I guess you don't hire lawyers?' His perception at that stage was that Concern was a 'South of Ireland only' organisation (there was as yet no office in Belfast), which hired only nurses and engineers.

He was impressed, however, to receive a very quick response to his enquiry, posted to Belfast on the morning his own letter had arrived in Dublin. What's more, he discovered on reading it that the organisation was already highly professional, staffed with accountants, administrators and systems people who supported said nurses and engineers. The letter was signed by Mary Humphreys, the Head of the Overseas Volunteer Department:

> We have an administrative structure in all our overseas fields, Bangladesh, Thailand, Tanzania and Uganda. In each of the fields there is a Field Director and administrative staff. We also have field officers in health, education and sometimes in engineering and women work programmes. We find that solicitors can be very effective in administration work overseas so we would be very pleased if you could fill in the enclosed application form....

She outlined the terms:

> All contracts with Concern are for two years. Return airfare, living and accommodation expenses are covered by Concern, and in addition each volunteer is given a small amount of pocket money and a holiday allowance.

Ten days or so later, MacSorley found himself, having been invited down for an interview, standing outside Concern's office in Dublin, and thinking that this had all happened too quickly, and also noticing, with a degree of alarm:

> ... the large religious statue of the Scared Heart, all in white, over the entrance door, and when I saw this I remember thinking, is this a very religious organisation?

Tangentially, this statue had been *in situ* when Concern took over its original Camden Street building from nuns, and according to various interviewees its presence or removal had been the subject, serially, of the most heated and prolonged debate ever held internally. It was Aengus who, despite his personal devotion, eventually had it removed.

MacSorley met Aengus 'very quickly', and like almost everyone else reports that his first impressions were of 'his size. And his warmth. He'd almost bear hug you even though he didn't know you. There was something very charismatic about the man.'

But ultimately, he says, what convinced him to join Concern was Aengus's:

> ... singular passion about the work, about what Concern did and does – he had that 'fire in the belly.'
> I went in thinking they'd be lucky to have me; I walked out knowing that if I get to work with this organisation it would be a privilege.

He was sent as a volunteer to Concern's administration office in Bangkok, where he thought: *okay, I'm a solicitor, that's fine, I can do this*. 'I worked there for a couple of weeks with Ciunas Bunworth as my first boss – they had big, big programmes on the Thai/Cambodian border, and had forty-five staff.'

One day during this period, Aengus comes up to the office from the camps. MacSorley has already gleaned that when Aengus is about to pay a personal visit some things are about to change, so when he is summoned he has no idea what to expect, and is curious. Some kind of administrative change, maybe....

For the first time, although he is too new to have heard them expressed, Dominic came up against two of Aengus's most often quoted mantras: *This is not a democracy* and *Give me the Makings*.... No questioning, he was about to move to Khao-I-Dang to run a youth training programme.

And within twenty-four hours, light has dawned. This is where the work is. This is why he, Dominic MacSorley, solicitor, has joined Concern.

Once again, Aengus Finucane's unerring instinct for spotting potential has borne fruit.

At the time, he says, the concept of caring for refugees in camps was the provision of shelter, sanitation and some food, and that was about it. But Aengus's ideas, many of them instituted during his time in Bangladesh, included micro industries, women's programmes and handcrafts, concepts he had brought into the Cambodian camps. There were schools for the small children, a women's training centre and a men's training centre. Men who had lost limbs, for instance, learned carpentry. And then there was this youth training centre – no other agency was running programmes like this at the time: they were new, bold and innovative.

Ciunas Bunworth, who is speaking in Concern headquarters in Camden Street, takes up the story:

> The people were coming in from a regime where all learning had ceased; the Khmer Rouge had destroyed all schools, all libraries, everything. Here you had a gen-eration whose expectations had been stymied.
>
> Aengus decided we had to do something about this, and started the new youth programme. There was a certain amount of book learning for these kids, but also other skills: football teams with a league, a table tennis league, there were guitars.
>
> A lot of the people who came across from the Pol Pot era were very disturbed, and at the beginning were hospitalised, sleeping all day, treated by a lot of the western doctors with western-type psychiatric medications. This was what kept them quiet.

The new approach to this disenfranchised group of angry young men running around in the camp or just hanging around corners was to establish fun programmes. 'They were active,' says Ciunas, 'and noisy and singing, and learning again.'

She also observed that, in rolling out these programmes, Dominic himself was in learning mode. While ostensibly having fun, he was discovering how to be an effective and innovative

Concern aid worker like his boss. 'Dominic,' she says, 'was another one who had clearly fallen under Aengus's spell.'

In many cases, host countries are very protective of their education systems. How did the Thai authorities react to this learning-as-fun project?

> At that stage there weren't as many restrictions as there might be now. You always have restrictions on formal education, and we're now [2013/14] working with a number of ministries of education in different countries where we're hoping to improve their methods and standards. But at that stage in the camps, what they were seeing was that the kids were happy. It was another inspirational Aengus initiative.

Mark Malloch Brown, who is not a Roman Catholic (although his wife is), is not all that keen on churches full of bishops and cardinals. He is keen, however, on 'a guy like Pope Francis, who puts the fight against poverty right in the front there, doesn't separate it from religion.' He loved drinking with this larger-than-life Holy Ghost priest:

> ... shooting the breeze. There was always this 'don't suffer fools' quality about him, a brusqueness at times, but what I loved about Aengus is the idea of the working priest, a doer, a practical man with a Catholic Church sense of alms.

He then added, surprisingly: 'Actually, I never quite knew whether Aengus believed in God ...'.

They kept in touch over the years, but in the latter years of Aengus's life did not see all that much of each other because their paths, not least their travelling routes, had diverged so much. Malloch Brown did keep abreast of aid matters, and would meet Concern people 'around the fringes of Davos. That kind of thing. So that way I would know about him.'

They met much later during many of the fundraising initiatives in the US after Aengus had retired from Concern in Dublin. 'A very dear friend of mine, John Scanlon, was very much one of the movers and shakers with Tom Moran in getting Concern US going. I got to know Tom very well, and also became very good friends with Siobhan Walsh (the executive director in New York).

> I helped with some of the early dinners. The way these American dinners work is that they choose a guest of honour that can actually help them sell tables rather than for their next-to-God credentials. So I got the Concern Man of the Year award or something with a magnificent 4,000-year-old piece of Irish bog oak.

As a non-Concern person, Malloch Brown's summation of Aengus's stature is interesting, to say the least:

> In his country of priests and storytellers and larger-than-life personalities, Aengus stood out. And it was a strange life he led with an itinerant quality; a Jesus-like life with disciples around. All these colleens? There were plenty of other figures to whom they could have flocked.
>
> I said earlier I wasn't sure whether he believed or not, that he wore his religion lightly; I hold to that, but another explanation for it is that for most of his life he lived in a world where there were a lot of other religions. And unlike other men of the cloth, he moved very easily in these worlds.
>
> Whatever the connection to the Church and the pleasures of the stage – the theatricality of the status it gave him – he was a man of relief missions, and that was his role in society. I'm sure he was never happier than when he was bundling into the back of a plane and going off to see his girls in Ethiopia or wherever. That was his milieu; he lived for this and this alone. And what

was nice about his later role in New York is that it was around that. If you'd left him in his flat in Dublin, he'd probably have died years earlier....

There are many, his family included, who would probably disagree with Malloch Brown's next insight, particularly with his use of the word 'alone'. There are others, however, for whom, belatedly or partially, his words might ring a bell. We will never know, because Aengus's inner, non-Concern thoughts or personal doubts are not on record.

Sitting in the London West End boardroom of the US-based FTI consultancy firm, where after his own honour-laden and peripatetic life he is now chairman of Global Affairs, Mark Malloch Brown said that 'It tore one apart' to contrast Aengus's years on earth with those of 'the rest of us who had stability with families and so on.'

Aengus, with his huge humanity, spent so much of his life in the midst of disasters and out of a suitcase. And then, towards the end, alone in a flat in Dublin for great periods. And then, at the end, back in the seminaries.

9

'He asks you to do something, and he assumes that you will be as honoured to do it as he will be honoured to receive it.'

– Ciunas Bunworth

There is no doubt that Aengus was ambitious, for his people, for his organisation, but most of all for the 'poorest of the poor'. Expansion was always on his mind – not with the target of world domination, but to garner ever more opportunities to serve them. Towards the end of the 1980s, for instance, he decided that the UK could usefully be colonised.

Paddy McGuinness, a former deputy CEO of the organisation, had been doing some fundraising from Newry and had identified a Belfast premises, formerly used by Quakers, in Frederick Street. The small team there included Patrick McManus, a Derry engineer who had worked for Concern in Bangladesh, firstly in Myensingh, where for the first time he encountered Aengus.

First impressions?

'Everything about him was larger than life.'

Aengus and Jack, who was country director, had plans for Patrick, and he found himself in the Haor District, one of the remotest and most poverty-stricken areas in the country.

On a crackly line from Lusaka, where he is now attached to Ireland's Zambian embassy as a development aid specialist, he explains that for six months every year in Haor, four million people were totally isolated by inundation from the sea and from a network of rivers. Concern was involved in building bridges, roads and culverts in an effort to give year-round access.

(To put this push into Northern Ireland in the context of the time, Belfast was still mired in 'the Troubles'. Behind the scenes, the British and Irish governments, along with people like John Hume and Father Alec Reid, were working towards securing an IRA ceasefire, but it was still the case that it was risky to drive your southern-registered car down the Shankill Road.)

The new Concern out-office was run by a small team of five people. Patrick was the development officer, a catch-all title that included responsibility for the development of education initiatives, PR, and the most important task of fundraising.

Then, moving on to 1991, when the Belfast office was on its feet, Aengus had another bright idea: *what about England now?*

'He asked me to set up a "presence" in England,' says Patrick: ' "Just start up and see what happens." '

Again, it was Paddy McGuinness who found premises, 'which for the first nine months was both my home [a sofa bed] and my office.' Aengus sent over two colleagues: Mick Goodman, and a former PA of his own, Ann Sheehan.

The trio rendezvoused for breakfast at 9.00 a.m. on their first day of business, and the way McManus tells it, virtually as they sat down and looked at each other – *Now what'll we do?* – the phone rang.

It was Aengus, phoning to wish them luck.

'No,' says McManus, 'to see if we're there!'

They started small, putting little, self-designed ads into newspapers such as the *Daily Telegraph* and the *Guardian*. Naturally, although there was some response, it was small.

But then, in April, Cyclone O2B, with winds up to 155 miles per hour, one of the deadliest on record, smashed into the Chittagong region of Bangladesh, causing 139,000 deaths and immeasurable economic and social destruction. There was massive global media coverage.

Those little ads in those English broadsheets now resulted in an influx of funds to this virtually unknown Irish aid agency – but one that had experience in Bangladesh. Concern was up and running in England, with a good and expanding database, and now a profile.

'The English are very generous in emergencies,' says McManus, 'very trusting. They were just looking for some way to help and somewhere to send their money.'

Inasmuch as there had been any advance planning, it had been negative: *not* to target the Irish. They changed their minds, and began communicating with the Irish communities, roping Aengus in to make speeches not just in London but in places like Birmingham and Liverpool. He would talk movingly and graphically about the Irish famine, 'and that went down very well.'

So well, in fact, that the Glasgow office of Concern opened a year later, and now the UK operation has a staff of forty-five.

Run by Rose Caldwell from London, it is an important advocacy, fundraising, lobbying and influencing source for Concern as a whole. It supplies technical experts to the field, for instance, and punches above its weight within the aid community, this time in the UK: 'London is a major melting pot for aid agencies,' she explains; 'all the big ones are here.'

As one of the thirteen-member Disasters Emergency Committee (motto: *Together We're Stronger*), the organisation's voice is heard on an equal footing with those of giants such as British Red Cross, Oxfam, World Vision and Care. When there is a major catastrophe, these thirteen agencies campaign as one for support.

'Concern commands huge respect in the humanitarian field,' Rose says (and here comes Aengus's influence again):

We get huge respect within these other humanitarian organisations because many of their humanitarian directors [she instances Cafod, the Catholic Agency for Service Overseas and Save the Children among others] started their aid careers as volunteers there.

As ever, that calling card opens doors.

Patrick McManus stayed with the UK operation until 1995, when he felt his Derry accent should yield to those indigenous to England. He moved to Haiti – where, after 1997, Aengus having transferred part-time to New York, the Haitian director had the pleasure of great nights and great chats during the honorary president's visits.

Great *late* nights....

As already mentioned, when the family, friends, even acquaintances of Aengus Finucane were asked if this priest, in many ways lauded as a paragon of all virtue, had any flaws, they would invariably mention the late nights he kept: ('He would never go to bed!')

From his sister, Patsy, however, the immediate response was the kinder: 'Days were longer for him than for the rest of us.'

During those late nights, however, it was not all sweetness and light. Passionate as he was about work, about his charges, about almost everything that interested him, when off duty, it was his fierce competitiveness over the Scrabble board that defined his leisure time.

According to Patsy:

> He *hated* to lose. When there was a family game at home in Limerick, it went on until three or four in the morning, and this was a man who'd be driving back in the morning to Dublin! 'We'll have Mass in the morning at eight,' he would pronounce while laying out the tiles for the next game, but when he saw all the rest of us getting up to leave the table, would ask, genuinely surprised: 'Why are you leaving?' He literally did not comprehend that people got tired.

Was it lonely at the top? Was that why he needed people around him during all those late nights in the field and in his apartment? Did he confide in anyone in particular?

'He was certainly a confidant for me.'

'And,' she adds, 'no matter what his faults or flaws, I am convinced he was superior to most mortals.'

As for his seeming need for social engagement and having people around all the time:

> He did love company whether it was night or morn-ing, with young or old, black or white. I think that was maybe the way he coped with the moments of isolation he had. He was making huge decisions involving thou-sands, even millions of people, and that's a lonely place, so it was probably an antidote.
>
> His nieces and their friends treated his apartment as a crash pad, and he loved that. Aengus would get up in the morning and there'd be one in the spare bedroom and another three on the floor of the sitting room. So many people had keys – and they came in at any hour of the day or night and he'd get up in the morning and he'd be delighted to see them. I could never fathom how he coped – no matter how many arrived or how long they stayed.
>
> (What else did he love?)
>
> He *loved* shopping. Loved going to Tesco, pushing that trolley.

Towards the end, when his health was deteriorating, she tried to persuade Aengus to do his grocery shopping online. He would not hear of it. ' "What would I do that for? I'd meet nobody!" He loved Cookery programmes on TV. He loved to cook.' One of Patsy's happiest memories is of him banging around in his kitchen creating cabbage soup for his latest diet.

What did he hate?

'The government not giving enough money; not just to Concern, but in general. People breaking up a party.'

Her reaction to the suggestion by some that her brother could be a bit, well, 'managerially autocratic', gives the lie to that of his faithful fans who would rebut such a charge: 'But it's true,' she says. 'He couldn't have done the work he did if he wasn't. Aengus had a vision. He had to get it across. He was a tough negotiator.'

She balances this, however, with the statement that nothing in life can be seen in black and white:

> He was quite sensitive, and was so capable of enter-
> ing into the lives of other people; a great comforter
> and a great listener, so compassionate. The more I think
> about him the more extraordinary he becomes.

And the opinions of those who have mentioned that Aengus could be imperious might be softened a little on reading a personal letter he wrote in connection with a volunteer he had had to ask to leave a particular field. 'In many ways it was a fairly painful experience,' he said to his correspondent. 'I made it as painless as possible, and stressed the unusual and extraordinary work circumstances pertaining ...'.

During the volunteer's exit interview, he told his correspondent, he had suggested training and mentioned specific options so that the person: 'could get a proper feel of things before again working in an emergency situation, and certainly not in a war zone with all kinds of additional problems.' And so it appears that whilst he could be autocratic when it came to defending his own standards and vision for Concern, on this reading, this trait was tempered by consideration for the feelings of the individual. One case that came to light during the interviews for this book was reported by Brian Stockwell.

In his sixties now ('I *think* I'm retired'), probably the best way to describe Stockwell is that while by profession he organises people, goods and jobs, he is by personality an itinerant adventurer. There is no doubt that he is unique, and for this project very interesting, because he is just one example – admittedly at one of the more extreme ends – of the extraordinary range and variety of personalities who flowed through Concern. He has spent by far the largest portion of his working life cutting a swathe through different zones of war, conflict and deprivation all over the world, not just for Concern but for many other NGOs and agencies, including huge international bodies like the UN and its subsidiaries.

He had no formal training or apprenticeships in logistics ('Ireland in the 1980s, it wasn't really an option then'), and says that his early schooling in the discipline began at home. 'My job in the house was to clear the table and wash the dishes – so I was moving stuff from A to B and working as efficiently as possible to get the dishes clean and dry.'

He lives in Castlegregory in County Kerry in two houses melded into one, and the interview was conducted in his living room/art gallery, the walls of which are hung with paintings from Vietnam that he offers for sale. He was one of only three people interviewed who came prepared with notes. His list was organised, flowed logically, and he ticked it off right to its very end.

He makes one rather startling announcement at the outset: 'People are numbers to me.' It's '50,000 here, and they need this for three months. It's cold, I know. It's *get the job done.*'

He first sought work from Concern after he returned from working with the government of Nigeria for two and a half years in the late 1970s.

I was teaching African literature, which was great because I was learning all the time, and then I came back to Ireland and there were no jobs. I wanted to get back to Africa, but there were no options unless you joined the missionaries, otherwise it was so difficult to get out of Ireland.

Like many another who joined overseas agencies with mixed motives – to help the poor and disaster-stricken, certainly, but also to escape from what was in those days a dreary and repressed Ireland – Stockwell was desperate to travel. With Aengus now working as Uganda country director, Concern was willing to give him a try. In 1980 he was dispatched to Karamoja, a state in the north-east of that country where, in terms of mortality rates, the famine raging was one of the worst in its history up to that time. 21 per cent of the population had already died, 60 per cent of them infants.

The first job Aengus gave his new recruit was to build bush schools. These were what it said on the tin: schools built in the bush to educate children whose families could not afford to send them to state-system institutions. The families of these potential pupils could not afford uniforms, so when these bush schools came on stream they went to school as they lived in their villages and compounds: naked.

Having arrived in Karamoja, Stockwell got stuck in, but the work involved:

> ... merely cutting down trees and cutting them up and throwing the wood into the backs of trucks. The locals did the building.
>
> I had to do that for about a month, and then I got into the logistics. Because someone was leaving, I jumped in, and was up and running.
>
> I love making decisions. I was there to make decisions.
>
> (No soul-searching?)
>
> Never. I don't think that on major issues I've ever made a wrong decision. I wouldn't make one if I wasn't confident. I can't ever remember asking for advice either. I'd say Aengus was the same. He knew his business.

Having taken anthropology night classes at UCD before he left Ireland, Brian knew a lot about Karamoja and the Karamojong, who, he had learned, 'are the second most primitive people in Africa after the Bushmen of the Kalahari – cattle herders like the Maasai or the Turkana.' By tradition, he adds, one of the local tribes, the Matheniko, believe that all cattle belong to them, and were known widely as cattle raiders, even operating beyond the borders of Uganda, and particularly into Kenya. Moroto, he says, the region's capital, is where Idi Amin kept his armaments in preference to risking them in Kampala, where they could easily be taken by some challenger.

What had led to the famine was that during the 1978-1979 war between Uganda and Tanzania, this Matheniko tribe had successfully raided Amin's arsenal in Moroto. Thus armed, they were then able to steal cattle from everyone else. As a result, thousands of Karamojong began to starve.

There was aid coming into the region, but one of the big problems about getting trucks into the famine-affected areas was that there are three sandy-bedded rivers in Karamoja (between it and Uganda 'proper'), and the heavy vehicles couldn't cross.

When Aengus, working from a base in Mbale, north of Kampala, came up to visit the Karamoja operation, Stockwell took immediately to 'this giant of a man, this genuine, fun-loving person,' and felt 'straight off that this was someone I could get to like, certainly to admire.'

And of course the big man's reputation for gregariousness had once again preceded him. 'He was infamous for his practice of arriving into field headquarters at about six o'clock, having traipsed around to see what had been going on,' and then saying Mass.

> Now I didn't go to Mass, and I'd say to him, 'I'll sit outside,' but it didn't matter to him, and he never made me feel uncomfortable about it.

While acknowledging Aengus's love of good company and late nights, here is an opportunity to point out that, frequently, there was more to this midnight socialising than sheer fun and chat. Aengus was a very social animal – a real people person, says Dominic MacSorley. He enjoyed people's company, but also used social occasions for his own agenda. Having a few drinks with Concern staff, donors and policy makers was deliberate, and gave him an opportunity to tell the Concern story – a story that wasn't written down, and that predated email and mass communications:

> When visiting Concern fields he insisted on meeting all Concern staff. It didn't matter if you had been one day or one decade with the organisation, he wanted to hear what you had to say.
>
> But more importantly, he wanted you to listen to him. He used these dinners and social occasions for enjoyment, yes – but also [for] propaganda campaigns. When you left his company you might be tired but you had learned a lot more and were motivated to do more.

In Karamoja, Brian Stockwell particularly admired two traits in his new friend. The first was independence of thought: 'He could go against received and trusted wisdom; he had innate understanding about what can be done.' The second was his discovery that, while Aengus did instruct, he could also listen.

To prove both points, he tells a story about how those aid trucks finally accomplished the fording of the three sandy-bottomed rivers.

Aengus, he says, tended to favour Food for Work programmes when he saw the necessity for them, while Stockwell did not. Now, however, faced with the problem of the stranded trucks and the need for labour to solve the problem, for once he compromised: 'I decided to build Irish bridges.' (Irish bridges, for the uninitiated, are structures built just a little below the surface of the water.)

He went to Aengus:

... and I said how important it was that these rivers could be crossed at all times, and that I'd agree to get the labour on an FFW basis:

> So I took Hugh Byrne [an engineer prominent in Concern, then and later] to see the river crossings I had in mind, but it was 'no, no, no,' negative to the three.

> The next time Aengus arrived on a visit, I told him: 'Hugh doesn't think it can be done, but I disagree.'

Aengus brought over another engineer, Sean Hogan from Roscrea, who concurred with Stockwell's vision, and with him drew up the plans and a long inventory of the materials and equipment required:

> The problem now was where to get these supplies. You could get nothing in Uganda, and Kenya was some five hours' drive away.

As usual, the port of call was Aengus, and it is here that a subplot emerges, again illustrating the intricate webs of missionary-based contacts pertaining at the time, covering all of Africa and most of the world.

Aengus gave Stockwell an introduction to another missionary priest, Father James Good, living and working across the border in Turkana. This was the same James Good who famously clashed publicly in Ireland with the Bishop of Cork, Bishop Lucey, about the issue of contraception and other controversies within the Catholic Church at the time. After he retired, Bishop Lucey went to Turkana to work as an ordinary curate with his former adversary.

Father Good was indeed able to source the necessary materials, and Stockwell (having met and greeted Cornelius Lucey with the phrase 'The Bishop of Cork, I presume?') returned to Karamoja knowing that his Irish bridges would be built.

All three of those Irish bridges were completed, enabling the trucks safely to splash through. They were, Stockwell believes, still in use 'up to a few years ago, anyway.'

> I thought it was amazing that Aengus went for my idea rather than Hugh Byrne's. I've since built bridges in Asia that military engineers said couldn't be done. Myself and Aengus [he adds with pride] ... because we're not engineers, we could see things differently.

There remains a sting in this story under the law of unforeseen circumstances. Just a year after the bridges were built and put to use by the aid trucks, the Ugandan Army used them to go in to Karamoja and to stay there.

With regard to Aengus's management style, at one stage Stockwell heard that one of the volunteers who was looking after a Concern programme in a very insecure [read 'dangerous'] area:

> ... wasn't handling it very well. She and I didn't get on, but I did feel I had to see her. So I took the car – and in retrospect I took the greatest risk that I ever took in my life, because I went across a river in a flash flood, letting it carry me down so I could get off at a certain point. Anyhow, I got up to see her. She was very tense, but holding up well, and was evacuated the next day.

At the next meeting, when this was discussed, Aengus would brook no defence. 'She was left up there for far longer than she should have been. I can assure you this won't happen again. I'll sit down with you all and we'll work out a system where everyone gets seen every ten days.'

> That's the first time I saw Aengus as a boss in action. So yeah, he could jump on you for the right reasons. It

114

didn't matter who you were, he was fair. There was no pussyfooting, no endless talking. Action.

At one point, Aengus sent Brian to head up an operation in Cambodia.

> This was a huge, major operation. The US was throwing money at it. Aengus was the CEO, and in the fifteen months I was there, I had one communication from him, a letter. He asked for a reply, giving him the reasons why Concern should stay on the Cambodian border. So I wrote back with the reasons.
>
> I wanted to say this because it shows what he was like. Once you were there you were allowed to get on with it and he trusted you.

The conscious hiring of such individualists by Aengus and Concern illustrates very well that the organisation was and is a broad church, not only subscribing corporately to Aengus's mantra of 'give me the makings', it also shows how he fitted the qualities of toughness and resilience to the exigencies of the work. Much of that work is in war zones, and certainly not for the faint-hearted.

Aengus and Brian subsequently became very close friends. They were never anything but enemies, however, over the Scrabble board. Brian would drive up from Castlegregory to Sandymount, where their two-person tournaments were played with ferocious concentration and competitiveness in Aengus's apartment late, very late, into many, many nights.

'Aengus *hated* to lose at Scrabble,' said Patsy. Said Jack, said Jim, said Joe, said nieces Sarah and Susan, all of whom know only too well and too sadly that Scrabble nights will not now come again.

10

'... a philanthropic Sir Bountiful,
who had locked himself in a world of make-believe.'

– Mr Justice Gleeson (the sentencing judge)

Having travelled through Concern's fields, with the aid of British Airways, Alex Tarbett settled in to Camden Street, where his first and most important task was to balance the books. Over the next couple of years he applied himself vigorously to the task, and by and large the council and managers went along with his decisions. These decisions included, initially, the need to cut back the overall budget by 25 per cent and to trim excess fat, as he saw it, from expenditure in the fields, including the new ones that had opened up in 1978: Yemen and Tanzania.

It was also in 1978 that Aengus Finucane left his beloved Bangladesh and went to lead Concern's team in that huge Khao-I-Dang refugee camp in Thailand, crammed with Cambodians who had fled the regime of Pol Pot. He followed that posting by moving to the region of Karamoja in north-eastern Uganda to set up operations there, and was apparently taken aback by the response of the Ugandan authorities to the very real threat of famine: 'The Karamojong have always been skinny!' (Karamoja, you will recall, is where we met Brian Stockwell with his three Irish bridges.)

Despite budgetary constraints, the organisation was, if no longer expanding at the same rate, beginning again to hold its own. Tarbett was continuing to urge caution, prudence and loyalty, in one memo admonishing: 'I intend to run the Concern office with a rigorous business discipline.' The CEO even initiated discussions, never fulfilled, about the sale of some or all of the Concern premises.

By 1980, these strategies seemed to be bearing fruit. Donations had started to pick up again, helped not a little by a hefty gift of $82,000 from a builder, Ted Foley, who, based in the US, was a contact of the former CEO Raymond Kennedy, and who had channelled his gift through the good offices of the Bishop of Orange County, William Johnson. Everyone was delighted with this particular gift, hoping that it was a harbinger of good things to come, and that at last this ship was again on an even keel.

There was good news all round, then, and so when Mr Tarbett announced in mid-1981 that he had decided to retire in order to pursue other business interests, the official response was to congratulate him on a job well done and to thank him effusively. A presentation was made to him by The O Morchoe, the organisation's Administrative Officer, and the search began for a new CEO.

The choice was obvious to some, if not to all, and in any event Aengus was called home to serve. He took office on 1 September 1981, and was to spend the next sixteen years, metaphorically, and a lot of the time literally, in his big chair behind his big desk in Camden Street. He still travelled to the field on visits, although towards the end of his period in office was struggling with his health. But for those first two months of September and October 1981, when he went on tour to get a feel for the entirety of the theatre of operations overseas, the whole situation was under control and the future looked good.

'Nobody was surprised it was Aengus,' says The O Morchoe, adding, elfishly, 'Aengus was not surprised either!'

Major General David Nial Creagh O Morchoe, CB, CBE, KLJ, Commander of the Most Excellent Order of the British Empire, Knight of the Military and Hospitaller Order of St

Lazarus of Jerusalem. The KLJ title is by invitation only, granted only to those of 'noble families' in Europe. With it, The O Morchoe is entitled to be called 'Chevalier'.

He is also the hereditary Chief and Prince of the ancient Irish dynasty, The *Uí Cheinnselaig*, Kings of Leinster. Just another of those people who were attracted to and stayed with Concern for years and years, adding their unique colours to the Concern tapestry. Now in his late eighties he lives quietly in County Wexford, but has featured largely throughout Ireland's commemorations of the start of the 1914–18 World War because of his presidency of both the Leinster Regiment Association and the Royal British Legion, Republic of Ireland.

Although 'Concern people' know all of this, and suggested that he be contacted for interview, he said nothing of this heritage while being taped, modestly electing instead to adhere to the agenda of talking about his long friendship with 'Father Aengus' and his own long association with Concern, firstly on the Dublin staff and then as a council member for a further twenty-six years.

His father had been in the Leinster Regiment of the British Army in India, serving also in Macedonia and Palestine and he himself, also an army man, is quiet and soft-spoken. 'They must have regarded me with some great suspicion in Concern, because here I was, a retired British Army Major General. I never used the title, quite deliberately.'

> I was born in Dublin, but I had my first birthday in Quetta. We managed to survive the Quetta earthquake in 1935, although our house was destroyed and we had nowhere to live. So our mother brought us home to Ireland. She went back to my father in India then, leaving us with her mother and a nanny on Raglan Road. This was the way it was then.

O Morchoe finished his own military career in 1979, 'commanding the Omani Army for the Sultan of Oman.'

Having returned to Ireland, he was 'looking around for something to do' when he saw the Concern ad for an administrative officer.

> I like to think that I knew a little about the work having spent some seven years in India, much of that time in similar work. I served during the Suez Canal crisis in Egypt, served in Kenya. So while I had no experience looking after the Third World, I had experience *of* it, and didn't feel that I would be lost. I knew what the Third World was about.

He got the job, settled in quietly, and after the 'black and white' of the army, thoroughly enjoyed observing the colours of Concern office life, with field directors coming and going amid flurries, even explosions, of frantic activity when some new disaster threatened in some far-flung part of the world. 'I didn't get involved in that, though. That wasn't my job for Concern; my job was to administer the organisation.'

In the course of this work he was required to balance the organisation's bank statements, and at one point in 1981, 'I thought there were certain cheques that should have gone in that didn't go in,' so he reported this to the chairman, Michael Fingleton.

That November, Concern's auditors came to a similar conclusion, reporting that cheques that had been sent from the Cork branch could not be traced. Almost simultaneously, the Bishop of Orange County in California complained that he had not received a receipt for that donation of $82,000 so kindly given by the builder, Ted Foley. The bishop made it abundantly clear that he wanted one.

Alerted by firstly, O Morchoe and then the auditors, Michael Fingleton went to work. He crossed the road, entered the AIB branch involved and insisted on seeing the stores of cancelled cheques that had gone through the two Concern accounts. In fairness, AIB cooperated.

Patiently then, over many, many long nights back in Concern headquarters, Fingleton, using the cancelled cheques as a base, trawled forensically through all the files pertinent to Tarbett's tenure, cross-checking and matching them up, searching in particular for that cheque from Orange County. AIB searched too and jointly the bank and Fingleton found it – in one of two accounts in the name of Alex Tarbett.

It turns out that there were four accounts: two for Alex Tarbett, two for Concern. Tarbett had deliberately confused AIB tellers and officials with four separate bundles of cheques: 'Put this lot into that account, please, but this one in here, that in that one', and so on. The staff and tellers of AIB, who knew him so well from coming in and out and doing so much good for the world, never suspected a thing. They all knew that Mr Tarbett, with his pleasant, courteous and well-spoken manner, was very 'well got', and even had lots of Irish bishops and other Irish notables in his contacts book. So impressed with him were the tellers that they accepted Concern cheques with only one signature when in fact two were required, and crucially let cheques be deposited into accounts other than those of payees.

When Fingleton was sure he had all the evidence, he confronted the former CEO, whose response was feeble, in that he apparently would not admit what he had done.

The next step was the law. It was a very difficult prospect, but this is where Aengus and his organisation proved the depth and strength of their convictions. Knowing how it would look publicly – and the damage it might inflict – Aengus called on his reserves of physical and emotional steel, and, with Fingleton and colleagues, called in the Gardai.

As Ursula Sharp, who was one of the confidantes with whom he discussed the affair at the time, recalls it, one of Aengus's fears at the time was that, out of loyalty to Tarbett, the hierarchy, many of whom the former CEO of Concern would have known from his time at Maynooth, might remain loyal to him in his difficulties and as a result could attempt to 'take down' the new CEO in his efforts at redress, causing even further damage to the organisation.

So, she says, he tried to arrange meetings with individual bishops, including Bishop Comiskey of Ferns, who belonged to an order and was therefore not subject to hierarchical control.

It was all to no avail. Some of the bishops, she says, did come back to him, but only to ask him not to proceed with the court case. Again, showing the independence of thought that had seen him through so many vicissitudes and situations of life and death overseas, the new CEO of Concern decided to do what he did best. He brushed down his best black suit, put on the clerical collar and went on the road.

According to Ciunas Bunworth, he visited every parish in Ireland:

> He stood in front of the people of Ireland and with honesty and directness, did not shirk the facts but asked people to have faith in him personally.... In every town, big and small, every parish hall and meeting house, literally standing tall, he told anyone who would listen that his word was his bond, that they could trust him with their donations, and if they did, their money was going to be spent overseas.

And according to Tom Arnold, future chairman:

> ... yes, he had inherited a meltdown, but through dint of personality, determination and warmth, he was saying to people: 'Concern is not gone. Trust me.' His capacity to inspire people was remarkable.

By dint of this tour, almost theatrical in its presentation and scope, with parishes in the smallest, postage-stamp-sized hamlets being challenged to set up a 'Concern home volunteer' fundraising and support group – another new initiative of his – he has been credited with saving the organisation during what was a very difficult time.

121

Despite the obvious difficulties, and with significant levels of scepticism and anger to overcome, large numbers of people did listen to his message, did react positively to his persona, and did believe in him and give him their trust.

So many, in fact, that he was able to organise multiples of individual cells of Concern supporters and fundraisers all over the country, who would by their own influence in their communities begin to rebuild and repair the damage.

On 22 July 1983 the case went to trial. Alex Tarbett, representing himself, attempted a defence and handed in numerous character references including those offered by Cardinal Tomas O Fiaich, Father Austin Flannery O.P. and the broadcaster Seán Mac Réamoinn. But a jury convicted him of all ten charges of larceny and embezzlement, the judge sentencing him to three years in gaol. In doing so, he remarked that Tarbett had seen himself as 'a philanthropic Sir Bountiful, who had locked himself in a world of make-believe.'

Seated in the Medical Missionaries of Mary's residence beside the Lourdes Hospital in Drogheda, Sister Ursula Sharpe still cannot believe that they were all so easily fooled, and harks back to Alex Tarbett's visits to Bangladesh: 'Chocolates and drinks and all the things we couldn't get! We looked forward so much to his visits!'

She remembers, however, something Aengus said at the time: 'He said to me once that Alex was "dangerously plausible." '

And she recalls Michael Fingleton's role in keeping Concern's reputation afloat:

> One of the sad things for me is the whole story around what's being said about Michael Fingleton these days. Aengus used to say of him at the time that he 'slept in his suit,' that he never seemed to go home.

Eventually, and not without a degree of moral pressure having been exerted by Aengus and corporate Concern, AIB acted honourably, accepted its part in the debacle, and all the money fraudulently placed into Tarbett's accounts was repaid. 'I think we were all shocked, but we just wanted to get on and make sure the place was operating correctly,' says The O Morchoe.

But the last word on the affair goes to Mary Humphreys, who credits Aengus with 'taking the phoenix out of the ashes':

> He handled it very well. He was open about it at a time when it was the culture not to disclose. He showed great leadership there, and, to his credit, so did Michael Fingleton. We had had a good name up to then, and I think it was that openness that reflected well on us. Because it had been so well handled, I never thought the end of the world had come.

By all accounts, while others were extolling Aengus from the rooftops about his role in the affair, Aengus himself never presented it as a sort of solo rally, and in fact probably learned a great deal from the experience.

It had been a harrowing and disruptive episode, but as the cliché goes, what doesn't kill you makes you stronger, and the organisation did overcome being targeted.

By common consent, by laying his own reputation on the line as he did, no one but Aengus could have so quickly regained Concern's reputation.

Bottom line? Aengus triumphed. Concern won.

11

*'I suppose being young and male I initially saw this as a bit of
an adventure. But when you got into the reality of it, that's when
everything changed, and whatever romantic notion you had about this
great foreign assignment dissolved.'*

– Donal Byrne (journalist)

On 23 October 1984, a BBC TV news report fronted by
Michael Buerk, one of the corporation's correspondents,
was broadcast from a desolate plain in the north of Ethiopia
near the town of Korem. It was bounced around the world, and
those millions who up to then had been enjoying the luxury
of watching TV from the comfort of their couches reeled in
shock. Famine, harsh and undiscriminating, was stalking the
rural landscape of Ethiopia consuming everything in its path,
and on that night TV had given us pictures of those who had so
far not yet succumbed: the living dead. Huge numbers of them,
maybe 100,000, crouched together on open ground waiting for
help. Any help. From anybody.

Buerk's interview with the aid worker from *Médecins Sans
Frontières* showed that he was clearly overwhelmed, and the subtext,
too, was clear. There were more, far more, in the same position
and condition, in areas the cameras had not yet penetrated. The
journalist himself had been weighed down by 'this cacophony of

misery', as he called it when giving an interview later, in which he confessed that he had come very close to the limits of being able to function professionally. A job-hardened journalist can usually take psychological refuge in the mechanics of the work he or she is required to do, but in this instance, particularly watching aid workers' struggles with little or no resources in the midst of this 'biblical famine', he was overwhelmed with a sense of inadequacy and uselessness.

Buerk's report had not been the first about this famine; that honour, if the word is appropriate, is given to another BBC man, Mike Wooldridge. For some reason, however, the world had not noticed his transmission to the same extent.

Wooldridge's piece was noticed, however, in Camden Street. There, Concern people had not needed pictures because they already had workers on the ground, with Jack Finucane sending a stream of urgent messages to his brother Aengus to send more resources. Long before the world reacted to the Wooldridge and Buerk reports, both men and their staff had known only too vividly about the escalating crisis, but prior to the second BBC broadcast of what are now universally named 'the Buerk Pictures', the organisation had not managed to influence Ireland, and much less the wider world, into listening or responding with an adequate sense of either the urgency of the situation or the scale of the aid effort required.

Jack had been Concern's country director previously in Ethiopia during the famine of 1974 and had recognised the portents of this one from an early stage. He also had proof. A few months earlier. '[Father] Mick Doheny had been in Wollaita in the south, and had picked up a famine situation there. He made a film of it, but it wasn't professional enough to garner wide attention.' Consequently, however, Jack went to the Ethiopian authorities to request permission to go and see for himself:

> But because the Dergue was holding a celebration of the
> founding of the Communist Party in Ethiopia, and had

decreed that no one could enter or leave Addis [Ababa] within a month or two prior to that, we weren't given passes to travel.

So for the duration of the travel ban, he and his colleagues had to cool their heels in Addis, while knowing instinctively – and via the ever-reliable jungle drums – that the situation in various parts of the countryside was worsening, literally by the minute.

At that point in its history, 85 per cent of Ethiopia's population was rural. While official estimates record the death toll as a result of the famine at a million people, the true figure will never be known. What is known is that many millions of survivors were rendered destitute.

Jack Finucane:

Immediately after that 17 September bash, I went to Dawit [Major Dawit Wolde Giorgis, educated in the west, chief of the Ethiopia's Relief and Rehabilitation Commission], and he gave us permission to travel up north. I went up with Aengus and Moira Conroy to Wollo and Tigre, and as we went up we saw people on the move in huge numbers. We were shaken by its extent.

After we got back, I went into Dawit again and said: 'Do you know what's going on?'

'Look,' he said, 'bring in as many people as you like, bring in anything, cars, nurses, doctors …'.

So, for us that was the beginning of it, but in situations like this something unexpected usually happens; it will run and become a huge story overnight.

In this case, the 'something unexpected' was the Buerk Pictures.

Very soon afterwards, on 31 October, a small group of nervous Irish journalists gathered with the chairman of the RTÉ Authority and an RTÉ TV crew in the departures area of Dublin Airport. For everyone it was an unexpected dive into the deep end of horror; none had personal experience of what Michael Buerk had illustrated to the world but what the Finucanes knew so well.

All of us had been hurriedly vaccinated against typhoid, cholera etc., but had been cheerily advised that many of these prophylactics would not really be effective for many days yet. (Someone in the party advised that morning that the best thing to do was to drink loads of gin and tonic: gin to kill parasites in the gut, tonic for its quinine, reputed to prevent malaria.)

The aid flight had been instigated by RTÉ Chairman Fred O'Donovan, whose big, buttery heart had almost seized with empathy when, like so many, he had seen the Buerk broadcast. He immediately began to tap into his many business contacts for donations, donations-in-kind, and also, crucially, for an aircraft to fly them to Addis Ababa.

Tony Ryan and his aircraft-leasing company GPA stepped up to the plate, and were represented that morning by Jim King, Ryan's right-hand man. In the livery of Air Nigeria and with Aer Lingus pilots, the plane was on the tarmac, already loaded from floor to roof with blankets, foodstuffs, clothing, medicines and medical supplies courtesy of the Irish public and other more official sources where Concern's urgent signalling had been recognised. There were even a couple of securely bound pallets of Foxford rugs amongst these offerings, donated by the nuns who ran the mill in the Co Mayo town. This was no whimsy: much of the country is part of the East African Rift Plateau, with a general altitude above sea level of between 1500 to 3000 meters. So at night it is very cold.

This author, then a journalist with the *Sunday Tribune*, had been briefed by her editor, Vincent Browne. He had taken her aside to give her a long verbal history of Ethiopia, outlining details of Emperor Haile Selassie's regime and overthrow by the current Communist, Russian-oriented authorities, the Dergue, now headed by former army colonel Mengistu Haile Mariam. He also explained that members of the former royal family were at that time still in prison, in addition to other historical and political facts she had never previously had reason to know.

He then gave her the best advice anyone can give to any journalist:'Now forget all that. Just keep your eyes and ears open.'

Also there that Hallowe'en morning to see the group safely on its way were Father Aengus Finucane and the flame-haired Jacqueline Duffy, respectively the CEO and press officer of Concern. Jack Finucane would pick us up on the other side.

The Concern people had good reason to be grateful to Michael Buerk. As Jacqueline confirmed:

Before Ethiopia became a big story, it was an uphill strug-gle trying to get people interested. Aengus used to say:'We might get two lines inside *The Irish Times* about hundreds of thousands of people homeless or dead in the floods in Bangladesh or famine in Ethiopia – and there are front-page headlines all over the place about the Tolka [River] floods here. Of course that was awful, *but ...*'.

He did have a 'thing' about media, but was much more clued-in about it than he got credit for. We had a very close working relationship. We were a team, spent a lot of hours working together, and I never once heard him say a bad word about anyone.

He did pull me up once when I made a comment about someone prominent who had dirtied his copybook here in Ireland.'You don't know the full story, Jacqueline; that man has done so much good work. And the number of people he influenced and helped!'

We were called to depart, and Jacqueline's was the last smiling, encouraging face and waving hand to be seen as the boarding party moved out of the departures area and into the plane, in which space was extremely limited. Above a full cargo bay, every seat, bar the nine occupied by the passengers, was stacked high. The smell was of canvas sacking combined with disinfectant.

The flight plan filed for Addis was via a refuelling stop in Rome and another in Cairo. The travelling party disembarked in Rome, but none of us was allowed anywhere near a terminal in Cairo, where, on the apron, the plane was ringed by soldiers, ghostly forms in the foggy halos of floodlighting, the bristle of guns clearly visible on arms and uniforms. This did not help with the nerves. What did, however, was the realisation of how inconsequential these flutterings were in light of what we would have to see.

In his interview, Tom McSwiney, who was reporting for TV, conveyed a vivid image of the plane's arrival at Addis Ababa in the early hours of the next morning. He was behind the pilots as they made their approach to the darkened airport, and suddenly thought to himself: *this is serious. This is real.*

> Apart from everything else, none of us had visas and this was an embattled country. I heard the pilot talking to air traffic control in Addis. He was told the airport was shut. Then this pilot said, in a really firm, slow voice: 'We are coming in. We are an Irish government aid flight.' A heated argument ensued, with the pilot continuing to insist that, since this was an official Irish government flight, it could not be interfered with. Of course I could hear only the pilot's side of it. And then he said: 'We are running short of fuel. We are coming in. Please switch on the landing lights.' Apparently there is a universal convention, or law, that if an aircraft is running out of fuel ... Anyhow, the lights came on and we landed.

For Tom, then, the next thing was the question of what would happen after disembarkation. Troops again, but also compliance, because as the group straggled off with luggage and equipment, the plane was already being unloaded and refuelled.

> We were standing there in the middle of boxes and all this stuff, and then the pilot stuck his head out through

129

the side window of the cockpit and said: 'Good luck, lads, I'm heading!' And I remember standing there with all these soldiers and all this stuff on the tarmac, and looking up and seeing the red lights of the aircraft vanishing into the night of African stars. It was the loneliest feeling in the world.

Then, out onto the tarmac came this man I didn't know. He struck me as this really tall guy with a commanding presence. And he said something completely irrelevant: 'Good morning!' Then this tall, commanding figure said: 'Grab your cameras and your own stuff and follow me. And if anyone shouts at you, shout back in Irish.'

Like sheep we all marched in behind him, shouting: '*Beannacht Dé leat*' and '*Dia dhuit*', straight through and into the Concern jeeps outside.

That man was, of course, Jack Finucane.

Michael Lee, young and just married, had been in the RTÉ newsroom for only a few days, and at the time was an assistant cameraman rather than a full one. Like everyone in the group, he had had less than twenty-four hours' notice. 'My wife was in a total panic. Neither of us knew where Ethiopia was; just somewhere in Africa.' They took down an atlas....

When we all met the next morning, I realised that all these 'experienced people' were doing this for the first time too. None of us really knew what was going to happen, just that we were going to the land of horror, Joseph Conrad's *Heart of Darkness*. Your mind plays tricks, especially when you don't know where you're going.

It was Fred [O'Donovan] who put my mind at ease. I felt if this older man, well respected in Ireland, could manage to do this and get a plane together with supplies, it was up to me to get myself together.

From Donal Byrne, then of *The Irish Times*:

> Like the rest of us, I had no idea what this was going to be about. I had a vague notion, I suppose, having seen the coverage of previous conflicts, Biafra and so on. That era did bring reality home to you on screen.
>
> Michael Buerk's pictures were the 1980s' equivalent of today's high definition. You saw the reality of famine in Africa.
>
> Both those Finucanes were the architects of bringing this to the public imagination.
>
> Their response was: 'We can do this ...'.
>
> I don't think they were deflected in any way by the fact that they belonged to a relatively small organisation in a small country like Ireland. They had a much larger vision, what is now called a Mission Statement. Nowadays people pay consultants to think this out, but these guys had it intuitively and instinctively; most of all, it was rooted in their own Christian response to a tragedy.
>
> It was immediately evident when we got to Ethiopia that these guys knew what they were doing, and that they were a team with skills quite different from each other. Aengus was the type with Buddha-like silences when they were required. Jack was the Stewart Granger rangy guy, happiest out there when he was doing it. And boy did he do it, from morning to night. You could see that. I had been used to dealing with priests. I never dealt with priests like these guys, they were a different breed.

Then, after all the nerves and anticipation, nothing! Each one of the group was as frustrated as every other at the ensuing delay in getting to the story, which was taking place outside the city limits. After the blanket permission to 'bring in as many people as you like, bring in anything,' Jack was having difficulty with suspicious officialdom in securing travel visas for a bunch of hacks. In fairness, here were nine people descended from the sky without official permission, and only Irish passports as proof of who they were and why they were in Ethiopia.

The only distraction during those two lost days in the Ethiopia Hotel in Addis Ababa was the momentous – in his own eyes – arrival of the twenty-two-stone Robert Maxwell, who then held lengthy court in the lobby for some of the tabloid journos he had in tow, proclaiming loudly about the *Daily Mirror*'s saving of Ethiopia with its *Daily Mirror* Mercy Flight: 'The first mercy flight to get here.' No one from the Irish group disabused them, or indeed him. And yes, his flight did bring much-needed aid supplies. This was the bottom line, and would have been, everyone felt, the response taken by Jack and Aengus.

During those stifled two days, when all of the energies of Jack and his three office staff were directed towards shuttling between various ministries to secure permits for the group, there was a limited opportunity to explore Addis. Some of the main business streets were paved, but just off them were the corrugated lean-tos, shacks and open sewers of the poor. In one kebele, the Amharic word for the equivalent of a ward in an Irish city, there was only a single shop for a population of 4,500. A man with a rifle guarded its stock, which consisted in total of three sacks, one each of maize, chickpeas and tef, a grain staple, a few rows of white canvas runners, a small stack of copybooks and three light bulbs.

Spread out on one sidewalk was a selection of tattered books for sale, including *English for the Young Ethiopian*. A 'restaurant' was accessed through a hole in a hedge; inside, however, although the floor was of packed mud and the seating consisted of tree stumps, it proved to be spotless. The menu was fairly limited: ingera – a sort of large pancake, pockmarked and as grey as the surface of the moon, flavoured with wat, a sauce so highly seasoned with chillis that it was in danger of corroding an unsuspecting Irish throat.

Back at the hotel, a pair of nuns buying takeaway bread said that they had heard that children up-country were throwing themselves in front of aid jeeps.

The visas eventually came through by dint of Jack's ingenuity. Of *course* we were all aid volunteers for Concern, weren't we? We had come to help Ethiopian people through their difficulties.

Here is part of this author's contemporaneous account of some of that first journey into the famine fields of Ethiopia in two Concern jeeps, each containing an official government minder.

We get going, and after a while the landscape deteriorates and we begin to see bare, stunted trees, withered stalks just a few inches high, and streams and streams of people using the same road. Apart from the jeeps' engines, the only sound is the continuous slap-slap-slapping of hundreds and thousands of feet on the ground beside us, doubly audible through the windows of the vehicle every time it stops, which is frequent.

During this phase of the journey, still relatively near Addis, the people are thin, but they can walk. No birds are in evidence though, no wildlife, no green vegetation of any kind, just stubble, stalks and straw. Anything edible is already gone.

Every so often there is a pathetically thin donkey, staggering along under an overload of entire families and all their remaining belongings.

A note written about this journey remarks on:

... women as beasts of burden. If a man has no donkey, his wife will substitute. Or his daughter. Or his niece. Or any female. Even if he does have a donkey, she may carry the loads anyway, as he may decide to ride.

But with few four-legged beasts of burden evident, the division of labour by gender is also evident.

Men loop hands and forearms over the protruding ends of the long sticks they carry across the backs of their shoulders. The

133

women, dead-eyed, pace behind them carrying whatever goods and chattels they have left: a pot, a bowl, an enormous bundle of firewood or dry sorghum.

After this first phase of the journey, we pull in to the town of Dessie. A man, who must weigh no more than five stones, lies beside a lamppost. His rags are too few to cover him, and he is almost naked. Another, older man tries to move him on, kicking him and prodding him with a stick. The man just lifts his head and puts it down again. Pat Langan, the *Irish Times* photographer who has arrived during the lacuna in Addis, could not eat his spaghetti during a lunch stop while being watched by a gallery of hungry faces peering in at him through an open door. He hands it out, which leads to another mad scramble.

We walk past a little girl. Her chronological age is easy to judge because her mouth is open and she is missing her two front teeth, twinning her with many a 7-year-old Irish First Communicant, already anticipating her silk and satin dress, her patent shoes. This little girl is lying in sewage.

Across the street, there is a bundle of rags on the footpath. A small child of about 2 years old enquiringly lifts the top of the bundle. Underneath is a woman. The child replaces the rags and settles down, yoga-style, her little legs crossed, beside them.

Progress is slow after we resume our journey. We pass groups of people holding out the most intricately beautiful jewellery fashioned in heavy silver, a ceremonial sword, even clothing. The very last of their family heirlooms. That treasure trove, we heard later, had recently begun to be sniffed out by dealers, bought for less than nothing, only to pitch up in the smart antique shops of Europe, where it was for sale at hundreds and thousands of pounds, dollars and francs.

We're told that these people have probably already sold the roofs of their houses for four Birr, the equivalent of four cents in today's Euro. God alone knows how little the Birr was worth thirty years ago.

Groups with nothing left to sell form human chains across the road as our jeep approaches, parting at the last minute only when the driver of the jeep, leaning on the horn, guns the engine and charges at them. We hear later that the jeep some distance ahead of ours, the second of the two, with Jack Finucane and the RTÉ crew on board, had frequently to stop because, as the bread-buying nuns had foretold, groups of children were throwing themselves prone on the road in front of them.

And we heard about Father Kevin O'Mahoney, a White Father here, who was approached by a woman at whose marriage he had officiated ten years earlier. She asked him for food. He had to refuse her because he had none to give. She asked if he had a revolver. He said that he did not. She asked if he could get one: 'If you shoot my two children first and then me, at least we will be dying with love. It is better than dying every day.'

In our jeep, Fred O'Donovan's emotion gets the better of him. He opens the window beside him and begins to throw banknotes and coins out into the dirt road. Dollars, cents, pounds. It is a dangerous thing to do – a riot ensues as people rush to get it. It's also futile. There is nothing to buy.

The rest of us are no better at resisting these impulses. This journalist remembers she still has some Hallowe'en nuts and raisins in the bottom of her bag, and at one stop where there are not too many people, distributes them slowly, one by one, which means, at the end, fifteen small nuts to each pair of outstretched hands under bowed heads. The subservient gesture has become familiar, but is still upsetting. The recipients do not talk to each other as they eat, but concentrate on each nut as it is transferred, slowly and carefully, from palm to mouth.

Tom McSwiney, against the advice of all the experienced hands, relinquishes his bottle of water....

It has to be emphasised here that all this was thirty years ago. Although its troubles are not yet over, and climate change and cyclical droughts remain as very real threats to food sustainability, Ethiopia is rising on its bootstraps. It has even become a trendy tourist destination amongst a certain cadre of travellers who are eager to be different and to experience its scenic glories (for instance a portion of the spectacular Rift Valley), its diversity of ethnicities and religions, its extraordinary archaeological wonders such as the rock-hewn churches of Lalibela. This country, many believe, was the original Garden of Eden.

But that sadder journey of November 1984 was to continue for many days, culminating in a place called Korem, where Michael Buerk, almost despairing, had stood and addressed us through his camera lens; a place that many who saw it still believe was the physical manifestation of Dante's hell, over the gates to which was metaphorically inscribed the poet's euphonious but terrible words: '*Lasciate ogni speranza, voi ch'entrate*', abandon all hope, you who enter here.

But there was hope. Thanks to the shocked reaction of international political and public opinion, and the Dergue's belated acceptance of the situation, a wide coalition of aid agencies, including Concern, was already rushing in.

12

'*It becomes all black-and-white,
because the viewfinder is black-and-white.
The odd time, though, I would peep with my left eye to see what was
actually going on.*'

— Michael Lee (cameraman)

'*It's hard to match a good nurse from Roscommon.*'

— Donal Byrne (journalist)

It is virtually certain that, for Jack Finucane, having to nursemaid a crowd of journalists would not be one of his favourite assignments, especially in this critical aid situation where his skills and commitments could be far more usefully employed. He makes the best of it nevertheless, and it is clear from his conversations that he loves Ethiopia, its stunning beauty, its wide, high spaces, its Rift Valley. Most of all, though, he loves its people.

In Harbo refugee camp, still in its infant stages of construction, a man approaches. He has a small child with him. He makes his sign for hunger, slowly patting his breast. There are vertical lines on his sunken stomach, so at one time he had been a prosperous citizen with a well-fed belly. Now in rags with not a single possession, he comes up to a foreign white journalist, begging for a biscuit.

The separate water queue is so long that those at the end will take five hours to get to the top. There are those who have nothing as a container but an empty sardine tin.

It's possible, probable even, that a large number of these people had been merchants, farmers, professionals. Now they must be herded like cattle. Controlled like cattle. At the sight of a food truck or a bale of blankets they surge forward. Like cattle, they stampede, so the men with sticks bang the ground and they jump backwards if they're able. If they are not fast enough in retreat, they receive a substantial clout.

When confronted with catastrophe of such immense proportions, seizing on details can sometimes be the only way to assuage the horror as our cosseted, middle-class sensibilities are offended at what seems like brutality against these patient, gentle people. So it has to be explained to us, just as patiently, that without these guards and their very effective, if seemingly cruel, crowd control, none but the healthier would get food, blankets or any kind of medical attention.

In a little area outside one of the PVC and wattle shelters already set up, Michael Lee and sound engineer John McGlinchey are recording a little group for RTÉ: a father, mother and three children. Marama is one of the daughters. She is 5 years old. She looks to be about 2. Yesterday, when the family came in, the Concern nurse Moira Conroy tried for hours to get her to take some food. Now the child lies under a piece of sacking, her eyes like milky opals and only half open, her father wiping bubbles of froth from her mouth. Her eyes close slowly until they are fully shut. That's all. She has died creating no bother.

Moira Conroy, who is setting up this camp, is from Limerick, like Aengus and Jack. Donal Byrne marvels at what she is able to accomplish:

> The scale of what Moira Conroy achieved in any one day … This is the great thing about Irish people. We

have highly developed and sophisticated organisations like *Médecins Sans Frontières* and so on, but it's hard to match a good nurse from Roscommon, down there getting her hands dirty and her feet dirty and her hair not washed. You watch what they do, day in day out, and you know this isn't a photo opportunity. Things were the same the day before you arrive and will be the same the day after you leave.

They're out there weighing babies dealing with malnutrition, doing the very essence: caring. The very essence of what nursing is all about: caring for and preserving life.

To see that applied practically, to see the little parts of the jigsaw that needed to be put together to set up one of these feeding stations: a little bit of food, a little bit of milk, weighing scales, the medicine that was needed, the attention and care… I don't like the word 'radiating', but that's what you saw. Most importantly of all, sometimes you saw, as a result of this caring, light coming back into the eyes, particularly of mothers. There was hope coming back.

Moira Conroy is petite, with the heart of a stallion. In the 1970s, having originally signed up with Concern to go to Nigeria, she found herself instead in Bangladesh with Aengus:

And when he shook my hand, honestly I thought it would fall off. It was quite a shock. I'd heard that he was from Limerick, so that was great and I suppose in my imagination I had visualised him as a Limerick priesteen. I went into my shell.

But there was another shock in store. Having passionately wanted to serve as a nurse midwife in the slums of Dhaka, she was instead sent up-country to work alongside the magisterial Ursula Sharpe in a makeshift clinic in one of the remotest of the rural teagarden areas. An advantage of this posting, however, was that these two proved to be kindred spirits:

> We hit it off instantly.
> Every day when we'd arrive out there'd be two long, long lines of people waiting for us. But there was no way you could see everyone; it was physically impossible. So we used to go up and down these lines identifying people we would have to treat now instead of waiting until the following week, those who we would have to send down to the doctor. When I think of it now, it's all so basic.
> We also realised right away that the conditions people were coming in with could have been prevented: scabies, diarrhoea, worms, chest infections, malaria, TB.

She got back to Aengus, telling him that from what she had seen: 'these people in the villages don't need people like us telling them what to do. They need their own people to be trained.'

> Aengus arrived up to see for himself. He saw the long lines of people, and said: 'I agree with you that you need trained health workers, but there is no way to train them right now in this country except to do it yourselves.'
> 'But we're just simple nurses ...'.
> 'Why not? Why can't you do it?'
> They put up all the objections, but Aengus said he didn't accept any of the criteria they were giving him.

> 'Of course it is possible. There's nobody out there to treat people. You are the people qualified to do it. It's up to you. The ball is in your court.'
> 'Well even for the most basic stuff it would take three months ...'.

'Very well. Three months. I don't see any problem with that. I'll pull the strings. Why don't you get down to it and write out what you need, and I'll take it with me and I'll go and get funding for it.'

Eventually, after I had got to know Aengus a lot better, I asked him why he had sent me up there instead of Dhaka. And he said that if I really wanted to know the truth: 'I didn't think you were going to survive. You were shy, you were quiet, you just needed somewhere that gave you a chance to come out on your own. If I had sent you to one of the camps you'd have been sick within a week, and before I knew where I was you'd probably have been going back home again. And now look at you.'

Indeed, now look at her. Barely a decade has passed, and on the morning of just the third day of this new camp at Harbo in Ethiopia she is dealing with 9,000 people who will all be fed. By the end of the day they will all have been organised into specific groups according to their home kebeles with an appointed chairman, and she is sure she will manage to have fed them all twice. The latrines are already dug, and many of the shelters already erected. She has isolated two separate cases of infectious diseases – one of measles, one of hepatitis – in two separate tents. She has no vaccines yet, and fears that if these diseases spread up to 50 per cent of the children here will die. Later, within a matter of weeks, her fears were realised.

Five exhausted orphans had arrived the previous evening. Their father died the day before that. Their mother died on the roadside just hours before their arrival. Leaving her where she lay, the 9-year-old picked up the baby and chivvied the three others towards the camp, where they were immediately admitted. After registration, however, he brought them into the group run by his own kebele instead of into the intensive feeding tent where they all belonged. All through that night and the following morning these five children sat uncomplainingly, without a morsel in their bellies. RTÉ wanted to film them, and they were found with the aid of a megaphone.

After filming, these five children, newly without a mother or father and their head of household now just 9 years old, are given their biscuits. They thank their new white friends, accepting the food with bowed heads and both hands outstretched, cupped, like those of Irish Catholics receiving the Body of Christ.

Even in situations like this, however, these Irish nurses manage to extract humour. There is the woman in the medical tent queue waiting to be assessed who collapses dramatically into the aisle every time a volunteer walks by. Beth Lane is one of those volunteers: 'Would you look at her, there she goes again ...'.

The woman gets the attention anyway.

Then there is the woman who gives back her magnificent, pure wool, hand-loomed Foxford rug that would have kept her warm for the rest of her life without shedding a thread. It was blue. She'd wanted a red one.

The Irish press pack leaves Harbo and drives farther north, passing through an increasingly desolate landscape – one you would expect, in imagination or in a movie, after a nuclear holocaust. An unrelieved, barren brown, the surface of the ground has crumbled to dust which is the consistency of finely milled flour. Dust devils, tornado-shaped plumes hundreds of feet high, chase each other and sometimes collide or meld all over this plain.

Next morning, Korem is dimly seen in the blue pre-dawn light ahead of the jeeps. The camp has been set up behind a vast set of hillocks, perhaps low sand dunes.

As we approach, through the open window of the vehicle can be heard an extraordinary, high-pitched but faint hum, almost a vibration, like that sometimes heard on a still day in Ireland when standing near a high-voltage ESB installation. (Or, during an Irish childhood in the 1950s, under a singing overhead telephone wire.) It fills up the ears, feels uncomfortable.

Both sunset and dawn happen quickly in these parts, and through some trick of the rapidly increasing light these hillocks, or sand dunes, seem to be undulating. Perhaps after all they are not hillocks but some form of lake, or swamp, ruffled by an early morning puff of wind. Could that sound be coming from a generator, or set of generators, for the camp?

The light increases further. We are still 200 yards away, but now we can see tiny puffs of smoke rising into the still air.

That sound increases. We are very close.

And those moving hillocks are the swarmed, living bodies of 100,000 human beings stirring to face another day of waiting for the possibility of gaining access to the camp. That sound is the sound of communication, mixed in with keening at the loss of a child or other family member who has died in the night.

Donal Byrne remembers that sound:

> ... it was that first, before I saw anything. I don't remember
> a word being said in that darkness, when daylight was just
> emerging. Just that wailing. It was all on such a large scale.

Inside and outside the camp compound, 'only' forty-two people – men, women, teenagers, children and babies – had died overnight. On the same day the previous week that number had been 120, so there had been 'quite a bit' of improvement in the figures. The aid workers had been working flat out to improve them further, but this morning, a sad row of shrouded bodies, some so tiny they would fit into a shoebox, lie on the ground to be borne away in the arms and on the shoulders of their loved ones.

Outside, the multitudes have been growing in number by the day. The crowd is now so vast that the naked eye, at least this naked eye, cannot see to its outer limits in order to distinguish between people and the horizon. These people are waiting outside the perimeter of the camp for their health and nutritional status to deteriorate to the point where they qualify to get inside for help, or to carry a newly dead body to where the formalities of death can be officially registered.

There is no point in shirking this: Korem camp, run by a cooperative group of NGOs including the Ethiopian

Red Cross, Concern and World Vision, was at that time an apparition of a world beyond the apocalypse. The grain silos and meat storage facilities of America and Europe were full. Obesity was becoming a recognised and growing problem in parts of the developed world.

Three years before the construction of Korem feeding camp, a huge Irish story generated a furore and was given miles of media print coverage, dozens of pictures and solemn, nightly readings by newscasters on radio and TV, not just in Ireland, although it dominated the news cycle here, but internationally.

Ten Irishmen − Bobby Sands, eight other hunger-strikers from the Provisional IRA and one from the INLA − died slowly, by choice, in the furtherance of their cause. Prime ministers of various countries, including Ireland, made statements of concern. Whole populations debated whether these men's lives should be forcibly saved by tube feeding. The contrast between their successive deaths and funerals − for the most part, dignified, sombre, laden with significance − and those of the skeletal men, women, children and babies who were borne away in the arms of their kin from Korem feeding camp could not have been more stark.

The media is not to blame for famine: that burden is shared between nature, politics and social indifference, and to be frank, if it were not for the BBC, the scale of the Ethiopian famine may have been exponentially worse.

Yet, to stand in that field of nurses, doctors, trenches, tents and winding sheets, witnessing the grief of fathers and mothers as they carried off their wrapped bundles, frequently no bigger than a forearm, was emotionally and psychically shocking.

There was no need crassly to write notes here. Memory would serve forever.

13

'There is no point in trying to suffer with the people who are suffering. If everyone went the same way, there would be no one to help anyone.'

– Aengus Finucane

In Korem camp, a few of the lucky ones who are inside wear donated cast-offs from alms-givers in foreign countries. Outside, those still waiting and hoping for some type of intervention from the Moira Conroys of this world search ceaselessly, grubbing through drifts of dust as fine as talcum powder for single grains that might have fallen through a tear in a sack being delivered. If they don't get admitted, their only hope is that death, when it comes, might be relatively painless and quiet. God alone knows how they feel as they watch their babies and adolescent boys starve to death with no way to alleviate either their hunger or their despair.

The commitment of the aid workers in this scenario is heroic. Minute by minute, they have to make choices between who might live and who might not, working with resources that at this time are stretched far beyond their limits and in many ways, within a milieu of casual indifference from many of the rest of us.

Michael Lee remembers that he was minding his precious camera gear while, like the rest of us in Korem, he was almost dazed by what he was seeing and feeling:

The mornings were very cold, and that was a surprise; to me Africa was hot. When we got to the camp there was this keening sound. And another thing I remember was the smell – and there was this beautiful haze in the mornings ... I was embarrassed even thinking that, a fat westerner with a lens instinctively looking for pretty pictures. I felt we were all voyeurs. *We shouldn't be here....*

But you had to get this out of your mind very fast, and nobody better to do that for you than Jack Finucane.

Jack was to me like Gandalf. He was the man you felt could manage anywhere. And he *told* you this was the way it was, that you're not here on a holiday or as an ambassador. You're here to show the Irish people what's going on.

In that context, Lee remembers specifically, probably while in Harbo:

Jack said: 'Come and have some lunch,' and he took us in behind some kind of canvas curtain where there was lovely soup. And I refused. 'There are all these thousands of people behind this curtain absolutely starving ...'.

Jack withered that protest with one look: 'You not eating will not save one of these people. But you may save many by filming. You have a job to do. You have to eat. You are no use to us if we have to fly you out of here. Come in and eat your dinner.'

That was a great lesson.

I was actually very proud that we were in Ethiopia with the first Irish Aid given by Irish people, but it took me quite a while to feel that I wasn't intruding. We had decided we were going to film everything that moved, but you'd go under a piece of sheeting – I won't call it even a tent – and you'd see people in the last throes of dying. It was very emotional.

It is not often that camera operators reveal their own survival mechanisms in such situations. Lee developed a small technique that subsequently stood him in good stead during many overseas trips to cover similar human catastrophes. It saved his sanity, for instance, when nearly ten years later he went to Rwanda, again with Concern, to cover the 100-day genocide there. Phrases he uses about that conflict will stick forever in memory: *There were corpses everywhere. They were using corpses as roadblocks.*

> By keeping my left eye closed, and burying my right eye in the viewfinder, it becomes all black-and-white, because the viewfinder is black-and-white. The odd time, though, I would peep with my left eye to see what was actually going on....

What is going on this day in Korem is that the forty-second casualty of the previous night is being borne away. One of his or her male relatives picks up the bundle so easily that he walks away with it as though the shroud dangling from his forearms is empty. A woman follows, holding something to her chest: it is a training shoe, in a size that would have fitted a 10- or an 11-year-old.

As the reporter with the TV crew that day, Tom McSwiney is following the filming.

> We're in this long, long, long shed-like structure. And Michael with the camera on his shoulder and John on sound, filming people, worrying about invading their privacy when they're at death's door. Worrying that we are just using them as objects to get the story out....

Later, Tom talks about being shocked, suffering from a feeling of uselessness. 'There wasn't anything practical I could do. Not like the Concern people. I kept having to rationalise that the reason we were there was a real one: to bring the story back.'

Like Michael, he too lectured himself with a lesson he had been given, this one by Aengus. 'He said there was no point in trying to suffer with the people who were suffering, or identifying with the discomfort of the Concern workers.' [Tom had plied Concern staff with the stash of foil-wrapped airline food he had whipped from the GPA aircraft. 'They dived on it. Treated it like Manna!']

> The logic was correct. If everyone went the same way, there would be no one to help anyone. But it was the size of the problem, the scale, the sheer size of this operation ... I felt really proud of the nurses and all the Concern people, and I kind of envied them. They were doing practical things, actually helping. I couldn't help thinking right then that it would have been great to have been a doctor or a nurse.

Right now, those doctors and nurses have no time for entertaining meandering scruples like those of their temporary visitors. Yesterday has gone. Today presents the usual long list of genuine dilemmas and life-or-death choices. A new daily death column is about to be started in the ledger where the first entry will probably be the name of the teenage boy twitching in the last throes of life on the floor nearby. His lips have already drawn back from his teeth like those of a cadaver discovered in an Irish bog.

Near him lies another boy, a little younger, barely adolescent, cheekbones sharp as knives under smooth, young skin. His eyes look up for a second and lock with this observer's, and then they glaze. He is dead in seconds.

In front of him a nurse is trying to force liquid in between the teeth of a beautiful young woman, succeeds in getting a little in, but the woman's shrunken stomach rejects it and she vomits all over the floor. In three minutes she too is dead, while a tiny baby, beyond hope but all life not yet extinguished, is stroked by its grieving mother.

So that's three for the ledger, soon to be four. And all of this represents only a glimpse of life and death as a result of (preventable) famine.

This is what Aengus Finucane was all about, what Jack is about, and Moira Conroy, and Ursula Sharpe with her Ugandan Aids victims, and Anne O'Mahony and the indefatigable cohort in damned places like Sierra Leone, Somalia and Southern Sudan. And what countless volunteers, staff and leaders of Concern have always been all about. Staff and volunteers working for other agencies too. *It's hard to match a good nurse from Roscommon.*

We see here what, as an organisation, Concern itself is about. Ministering to the lowest. People. Individuals. Teenage boys with clouded eyes who meet yours for a millisecond before they close forever. The tiny feet of a newborn baby protruding with its mother's from their joint shroud.

This is why, when Concern locks in its hooks, they stay locked. While for our party, Korem would forever leave its stain on our souls, for the organisation, the practice of which is to marry development with disaster relief, Korem was not the toughest assignment it has taken on over the years. The jury is out on that one. It was tough, but just a precursor to what was to follow.

In no particular order or chronology, there was, and still is in some cases, Sierra Leone, Karamoja, Rwanda, the Democratic Republic of the Congo, North Korea, Kampuchea, South Sudan, the Central African Republic, Liberia, Haiti, Somalia and Angola. Iraq, Afghanistan, Syria, and forever Bangladesh – although most of what is happening there is in the charge of local staff. At the time of writing, the total number of countries where Concern serves is twenty-eight, with some yet to emerge and some to be revisited.

In Korem, those not inured in human mind and soul, now shocked beyond all previous experience, can handle only so much at a time before looking for even a tiny shaft of relief. And in Korem that November of 1984, there was one heartening episode, illustrating what the Moira Conroys and Concerns of this world can actually achieve given commitment, experience, a strong will – and enough support, financial, political and individual. It is why they keep going.

Within an area of the camp, set a little away from the main action, was a corral full of children, hundreds perhaps. These were the under-sixes who had recovered their health quite quickly after intensive feeding. It was not clear what proportion of them were orphans.

Waiting for their next biscuits, they sat in a tightly packed, patient and bubbling rectangle, cheering and waving when anyone, particularly from our group, approached. One 2-year-old crawled out, eager to add her personal greeting, and was hauled back by a tot who could not be more than 3. You waved. They waved. You clapped. They clapped. You took their photograph, they all cheered. You thanked them with little 'thank you' bowing gestures and they all clapped again.

Thereafter, anyone who snapped them got a round of applause.

And there seemed to be a certain amount of cachet in shaking the hand of a *ferengi,* 'foreigner' in Amharic. As our group boarded a truck to leave, they crowded around, reaching for hands. In the midst of the excitement, this *ferengi* noticed two sets of tiny fingers clamped to the tailboard and, leaning over, found they belonged to a minuscule 2-year-old, little feet on highest tippy-toe, little face bearing an expression of fierce determination. He had no intention of being left out of this meet-and-greet. He wasn't, and, job done, toddled off, delighted with himself.

14

*'One of the things I learned from Aengus Finucane is that it helps
to be less serious about yourself. That humour and having a warm
personality is a very important part of influencing change. Aengus in
particular had that in a very big way.'*

– President Mary Robinson

The Somali conflict was catapulted into public consciousness
throughout Ireland and the world, not just because of its
multiples of horrors, but because television networks adopted
it for nightly and twenty-four-hour news. And there was
worldwide publicity given to the visit of Ireland's serving
president, Mary Robinson, which added to this engagement.

Along with other NGOs, Concern was in the thick of it.

By the time the situation had been deemed horrific
enough to dominate the news cycles, Aengus Finucane
might have been, one would think, accustomed to such
appalling situations. By this time, starting with Biafra, he
had spent almost twenty-five years in the 'aid business' as
it was now becoming. He had seen and experienced mass
starvation, death and cruelty in Karamoja, sequential floods
in Bangladesh and two major Ethiopian famines in 1974 and
1984. Even he, however, was deeply shocked by the carnage
and depth of suffering in Somalia.

He issued a press release in which he tried to individualise the general, the extent of which could not be encompassed in a thirty-second, or even one-minute segments on the *Nine O'Clock News*. In it, he told us about the little family, father, mother and child, who had made it to a place on the road just opposite the Concern feeding centre, but died there. 'An ordinary wheelbarrow carried off the mother with her child piled in beside her for burial in a shallow road. Then the wheelbarrow came back for the father.'

President Robinson was equally shocked. Voice shaking, eyes tearing after her visit inside the country, she could not prevent her emotions from showing during her 'wrap-up' press conference in Nairobi, Kenya, just hours after her visit to a Somali refugee camp at Mandera inside the border with Kenya.

Arriving at the venue in a 'drained and emotional' state, President Robinson nevertheless thought she had prepared well what she wanted to say. When the time to speak came, however, she was betrayed, as she saw it at the time, by emotion. Her response, caught in close-up by dozens of lenses, was raw, desperately honest, authentic, and probably because she had not planned it had more effect all over the world than a thousand speeches of sincere but rehearsed, pre-written outrage.

She was 'shamed' by what she had found: 'that the developed world had lost its humanity and watched as others suffered.'

On 3 October 1992, she and her party had flown in a small plane to Baidoa via a stop in Nairobi. They arrived on a dusty landing strip that was really a field, where in the sweltering heat they were met by a welcoming party consisting of various NGOs, local officials and a squad of 'Technicals' – 'sullen and cocky' young Somali men, according to one informant, sitting in trucks and jeeps bristling with machine guns and other armaments. They had been hired to provide security.

Had that 1992 trip kicked her sense of what was happening to entire populations in some developing countries into a higher gear?

Yes. I remembered setting out my stall during my inau-
guration speech as president – what I was promising the
people of Ireland and what I would live by. I had been
very tied to that, sometimes without having a sense
of humour about it. And I had worried about how it
would be possible somehow to fulfil it in the human
rights arena without breaching political boundaries.
Somalia for me was a huge opportunity to do that.

The invitation to make the Somali trip had been carefully
orchestrated by the formidable Bride Rosney, President
Robinson's Special Adviser, who was well versed in the political
sphere from her time in RTÉ as communications director.
Any trip abroad to be taken by the president had to be with
government approval, and as a first step Bride had organised the
issuing of invitations to the heads of all the Third World agencies
in Ireland to come to the Áras to brief the president on the
current situation. After such a briefing, President Robinson was
to make an anodyne remark along the lines of: 'Is there anything
I can do?'

Bride had also teed up Aengus Finucane to respond with a
suggestion that the president could make a personal visit there
to see for herself. Mary Robinson reports on this in her memoir,
Everybody Matters:

> ... at a particular point Father Aengus Finucane, the
> head of Concern, would ask me – in this very public
> setting in front of the press – if I would consider going
> myself to Somalia, and perhaps reporting to the UN
> afterwards.

That United Nations reference was crucial – and indeed after
her visit she did fulfil that part of the commitment.

The whole ruse, however, nearly fell apart. Reporter Charlie
Bird was there for RTÉ TV News. Not being privy to what had
gone in on the background, he saw this as a routine assignment,

and when he had what he felt was sufficient material to put together a reporting package, began quietly to leave the room. But coverage on the TV bulletin that evening was a critical part of the plan if the government and the public were to be influenced, and so Bride Rosney sprang into action to head him off. As the former President Robinson put it in *Everybody Matters*:

> Bride had to sit him back down again and suggest to him that he wait another minute or two. And so the question was asked and I replied: 'Well, this would be a matter for the government, but of course on a personal level I would be delighted to go.

There followed a little to-ing and fro-ing between the Áras and various departments, including that of the Taoiseach, but permission was very quickly forthcoming.

Once *in situ* in Baidoa, the president and her party travelled to various feeding stations, to see, as she wrote, 'the rows and rows of people, men and women and emaciated children.' It was 'an eye opener about the extent of hunger and famine and malnutrition of children. I hadn't been exposed to that before and now I was exposed to it in a very direct way ...'.

In one of these stations, Mary Robinson knelt down beside a woman and asked her for permission to hold the woman's tiny baby, 'ill-looking, with sores on his scalp, and flies crawling over his face and eyes.' But as she picked him up there occurred one of those unexpected but seminal moments that can turn a person's comprehension around by 180 degrees. When a press photographer shouted at her to turn and 'look this way' she automatically obeyed.

Instantly, even as she was turning her head, she recognised that on a human level this was the wrong thing to do. 'I got it wrong because I was playing to the camera. It was a moment of deep realisation about why I was there, and what I was trying to do.' She did not respond to such demands or instructions again.

How surreal was it to find herself trying to comfort a child covered with flies and with a swollen stomach, all the while surrounded not only by a cicada-like chorus of clicking cameras, but by officialdom, minders, security, and the rest of the presidential 'stuff'?

> Exactly. It was a very strange way to be exposed to it.
> When I was UN High Commissioner for Human Rights, that specific experience in Somalia in part played into the emphasis I kept placing on rights to safe water, food, health, education, economic and social rights, and that brought me to Realising Rights, which then brought me to Climate Justice. So in a way it was a continuum.

Both of these bodies, Realising Rights and The Mary Robinson Foundation – Climate Justice, were set up by Mary Robinson herself, with assistance from Bride, who had served with her not only during the presidency but during her UN stint, and others. The aims of both bodies are synchronous. Realising Rights aims to put human rights standards at the heart of global governance and policymaking and to ensure that the needs of the poorest and most vulnerable, including justice for those people vulnerable to the impacts of climate change and who are usually forgotten, are met.

From Baidoa, she arrived at that famous press conference in Nairobi at the end of the Somali trip, which that morning had included a visit to the Somali refugee camp in Mandera, very near where the borders of Kenya trisect with those of Somalia and Ethiopia. Again she was deeply affected by the conditions she saw there, without showing it overtly.

> I literally had no sense of being overwhelmed during the long days that we spent in camps. At one stage we went straight into an operating theatre [where surgeons were amputating limbs without the benefit of

155

anaesthetics because there were none available], and that wasn't funny. I had planned to tell the world coherently and professionally about the huge injustices I had seen.

When she got up to speak, public composure deserted her and in words that rang significantly in newsrooms all over the world and engendered huge public reaction, she said:

It has been a very difficult three days. Very, very difficult. I found that when I was there in Baidoa and in Afgoi and in Mogadishu, and this morning in Mandera, I had no real difficulty in remaining calm and in not letting my emotions show. And I find that I cannot be entirely calm speaking to you because I have such a sense of what the world must take responsibility for.... I have an inner sense of justice and it has been offended by what I have seen in the last three days – deeply offended.

Beside her, she has written, Minister for Foreign Affairs, David Andrews, was:

... banging the table with the flat of his hand to control his own emotions. That people would be treated this way literally overwhelmed me. It was a very strange experience. I saw before me a full press meeting in Nairobi, not only Irish but from all over the world. I wanted to try and tell the story in a compelling way. I had prepared what I was going to say. And instead of that, I was overwhelmed with emotion. I was furious with myself.

(You let the bridle slip?)

Yes, I went up to the bedroom in the hotel afterwards and Nick was trying to say: 'No, it wasn't too bad, Mary...'. No. I shouldn't have lost it. I've embarrassed myself.

She must have told this story a thousand times, and she has written about it too, but the memory still smarts. She looks, almost shyly, up from the polished surface of her desk in the beautiful old Dublin house inhabited by her foundation and recalls something else she has also officially chronicled: 'Believe it or not, Vincent Browne put a note under the door: "that was brilliant, Mary"', something like that...'. It was a small happening but: 'surprisingly touching.'

> No. I didn't like it [losing control] at all, I still don't like it, though I have noticed that it has happened again since then, so it wasn't the only time ... I can't always guarantee....

She has been convinced by others, however, that being authentic, i.e. being human, is an effective way to convey a message.

> One of the things I liked about both Aengus and Jack Finucane is that there was a spiritual dimension. They never laid it on, but it's one of the things I think about a lot: what is it that connects us as human beings? What prompts that sense of outrage when you see malnour-ished, stunted children who will never develop their full emotional or physical capacity?

She instances Article One of The Universal Declaration of Human Rights: *All human beings are born free and equal in dignity and rights. They are endowed with reason and conscience and should act towards one another in a spirit of brotherhood.*

> I often think about that when I see terrible destitution, sick people with not enough to eat, and desperately cold. That's the ultimate lack of dignity, and yet millions and millions of people have that as a daily reality. And they die alone.
> (And die invisibly?)
> Yes.
> (You feel a soul-to-soul thing?)

Exactly. I often think of the African concept of Imbuntu: I am because you are. My life has meaning because you're there, that kind of thing: *Ar scáth a chéile a mhaireann na daoine.*

Concern 'gets' this. It goes where no one else will go, and it stays.

She goes on to say that there were quite a number of times when she was High Commissioner for Human Rights, finding herself:

... in the back end of the far end of Goma, beyond Goma even, and I would hear laughter and I would hear an Irish accent ... I think that's the staying power, very visible, very appreciated.

One of the things I've learned from Aengus Finucane is that it helps to be less serious about yourself, that humour and having a warm personality is a very important part of influencing change. Aengus in particular had that in a very big way. Gregariousness. The fire in the belly. That's the kind of language that appeals to people.

In that context she has watched replays of a speech she made about the Diaspora on the second occasion she addressed the Oireachtas. Although she does not use the word, it's clear they make her cringe: 'There wasn't a joke in it; there wasn't a human moment in it. I delivered it in a preachy voice. It went down very badly in Leinster House and now I know why. I would never do that now.' She has now learned, she says, to be:

... a bit self-deprecating. Madiba, whom I admired more than anyone on the planet, had it, Tutu has it, Finucane had it.

(Would she place Aengus in the same league as the people just mentioned?)

Yes. In context. He became an elder in that context.

[She smiles in reminiscence. Mary Robinson has a great smile.]

These are lessons learned in later life. I can be awfully boring and I get teased by my family for name-dropping!

She brought all of this to her later job as High Commissioner for Human Rights. She never lost her support for Irish NGOs, and had a very high regard for Concern as an organisation, not least for Jack and Aengus.

I had a lovely relationship with both Aengus and Jack. There was a lovely humour in both of them. Aengus, a larger-than-life figure, very much a fixer of things, made things happen. Jack to me was not exactly in Aengus's shadow, more reserved but very knowledgeable.

Interestingly, when I was in Somalia, and subsequently Rwanda, neither wanted to be standing beside the president all the time, or travelling in the car with the president. They were very good that way, the ego thing wasn't there. It was: 'give the president the person who would be most useful to the president, the person with the most insights, they're the ones that know more than we do.'

Marian Finucane was one of those following the president during that trip, and she too noticed that discretion by the Concern people. In the course of the visit she got to know Aengus and Jack a little, and when seated with the former over dinner in Nairobi found him:

... very affable. We didn't go too deeply into philosophy, but I did get some feel as to what was going on in his life.

(And what was going on in his life?)

Fundamentally, I got the impression he was very deeply into his faith, but that he was a man who wore his Christianity very carefully and didn't foist it on others.

During that trip, the broadcaster also noticed the different ways people had of dealing with the horrors to which they were exposed. Gallows humour, false cheeriness, anything to cushion the mind against what their eyes and ears were telling them.

Marian's own method of coping was to stay in work mode, observing, occasionally interviewing. She has been to various parts of Africa, including Liberia and Sierra Leone ('the worst place I've ever seen'), but as a consequence, she and her husband, John Clarke, set up and still run an African charity of their own, Friends in Ireland, looking after Aids orphans in the Eastern Cape.

Meanwhile, the ever-changing map of the planet is now Mrs Robinson's focus. After Somalia she made subsequent trips abroad, where she bore witness to almost unimaginable ferocity and suffering. In Rwanda, for instance, she was shown 'a wooden stump, darkly stained,' where dozens of people had been beheaded. As she intimated earlier, she brought all of these experiences into her later job as High Commissioner for Refugees, and after that into both of the bodies she founded personally:

> I remember when I went back to Somalia in 2011. I realised Concern had been working solidly there since 1992, and in difficult areas, such as Mogadishu, where very few organisations were working. It's persistence of the right kind – work for as long as it takes – but also a realisation that if possible there needs to be a handover to those who live in the place, as has already happened in Bangladesh.

She seems to have kept up with Concern organisationally:

> I'm of the view that Concern has proved its worth as an organisation, and necessarily does evolve. Dominic will have different ideas than Tom Arnold before him, and that also is positive.

Also on that 1992 trip to Somalia, was the journalist/broadcaster Vincent Browne, who knew that since she was the first western head of state visibly to engage with the humanitarian crisis there, President Robinson's visit would create an international and Irish media scrum. He decided to go a few days early to try and find something different to write about for his paper, the *Sunday Tribune*. Like many, he found accommodation in the Concern house in Baidoa.

With Mrs Robinson's visit imminent, Vincent planned to get up early to go with the Red Crescent truck that every morning did the rounds picking up dead bodies. This he achieved, paying his respects alongside the RC workers who simply dug holes, said a prayer and put the bodies in.

He recalls a particular event that occurred while they were driving back to Baidoa:

> People started to gesticulate for us to go down a lane-
> way and a further laneway off it, and we came across a
> group of huts. The people there were indicating for us
> to go into one particular hut.

One of the guys got out, and when he came out of the hut again was holding a live child 'that looked aged 2 or 3.' Quickly, he went to pass this child to Vincent, but in the process they dropped the poor creature into the embers of a fire. Vincent managed to retrieve the little thing (it isn't clear whether the child was a boy or a girl), and they rushed with it to a nearby orphanage, where a nurse took it in. Later that day, 'the baby that I had brought in was thrust into Mrs Robinson's arms, and she was told that the name of the baby was Vincent.'

He met Aengus first in the mid-1990s, he thinks, struggling to remember the exact date:

> I think he asked to see me. Anyhow, he persuaded me I
> should go to Burundi, telling me that there was going
> to be a spillover from it – and the situation in Rwanda

161

– into the Congo, and the whole thing was going to be disastrous. A holocaust. And I remember thinking that this was way over the top, but I did go [and repaid his fare to the organisation afterwards]. I stayed with them in Kigali and moved into Burundi, which was an amazing experience and terribly depressing, a slow-burning genocide, with each side believing if it didn't annihilate the other, they would themselves be annihilated.

He says that he is 'hugely grateful' to Aengus for introducing him to Africa, and that it was 'almost transformative.' He travelled back to the Congo, and then back to Rwanda in 2004, and would love to go back again.

Vincent Browne is not the type of person, you would think, who would allow himself to be influenced by any other human being. As evidenced by his empathy with development issues (and indignance at what he sees as political indifference to them) in his subsequent broadcasts, it is clear, though, that at some level he was swayed by the passionate advocacy of this prescient priest.

15

'You get to know about terrible things. But maybe some of these things
would be worse if Concern weren't there. This is the trade-off.'

– Tom Arnold (former CEO of Concern)

The overall view of his predecessor's style by the man who succeeded Aengus in the latter's big chair, is that when it came to formal strategic planning 'Aengus's instinctive feeling was: why are we doing all this talking when there are so many obvious things staring us in the face?'

Arnold had taken up the chairmanship reins of the council in 1995. He had been elected to it as an ordinary member in 1985, so he knew the stage and its players pretty well. 'I wasn't terribly involved for the first few years, and then got in more and more.' His bridge to deeper engagement was membership of a subcommittee established in 1990 to prepare a policy review, the core focus of which was to identify and quantify what the balance between management and council should be. 'There had been a few bits of tension in the late 1980s about that.' When work began on the review, Aengus had been CEO for nine years or so.

Soft-spoken, with a focused gaze, he is speaking one afternoon in the lobby of the Herbert Park Hotel in Dublin, and clearly finds it painful to articulate some of what he feels he must say.

There has to be an honesty about this. I'm giving you the honest view from my perspective and as I remember it.

Aengus, shall we say, wasn't into management systems, especially when the words 'strategic planning' started being mentioned. He had strategic planning in his own head. He knew what he wanted from Concern, and he felt that people should fall in behind him. But at staff level, reflected to some extent in council, there were people beginning to approach things from a different angle. It was a legacy of Development Studies – there were people working there who had degrees in this – but he would have had a very strong level of impatience with some of it.

(How did this show?)

Impatience with those who were advocating for it. It would have crystallised a bit around the debate between the emergency and development people; we grew through it and out of it, but it was a real dichotomy. These are people with different mentalities. The development people take the long-term view; the emergency people have a tendency to come in and get things done.

His gaze softens, and he smiles, a little ruefully. It is diamond-clear that, whatever about his predecessor's holding of contrary views, he loved Aengus Finucane. In any case, his CEO, he adds, had:

... a much more subtle approach to these matters than many people gave him credit for. He would lay down the elements in an emergency situation: how recovery could start, what the long-term implications and prospects were, and would have a plan to work his way through it. But those two schools wouldn't have felt this.

As far back as 1977, when Aengus was four and a half years away from becoming the CEO and was still directing operations in Bangladesh, he wrote a lengthy 'Thoughts on Concern' document, analysing, from his perspective in the field, the shortcomings of the organisation, and particularly the regime in Dublin, including, predictably, the gulf that existed between Camden Street's understanding of the needs of outposts and what was actually necessary.

After some introductory praise for the work of the organisation, summarising it since Concern's inception, he gets down to the nitty-gritty. Acknowledging that the up-and-down income stream had survived in general (as a result of a series of emergencies and disasters, 'sad to say'), he articulates the need now to go onto a more professional footing:

> Management must be one of the matters of gravest con-
> cern for us; as soon as it can afford it, the organisation
> must put an increasing emphasis on professionalism and
> a stricter scrutinising of new job candidates under 'busi-
> ness' and 'commercial' heads.

Remember the words of Kevin Farrell, Aengus's deputy at the time? He who, although refusing directly to get involved, was that astute observer of the 'internal, but civilised, power struggle' going on between Bangladesh Field and Dublin headquarters? In 'Thoughts on Concern', Aengus also addressed the perception that there was now some grumbling about the clergy's continuing high profile in Concern: his own, Kennedy's, Jack's and that of the two Doheny brothers, Fathers Michael and Kevin, for instance. He defended this to some extent:

> We were long accustomed in Ireland to having priests
> and religious upholding our image and discharging our
> obligations as a nation to the poorer nations. It was
> very much in line with the thinking of Vatican Two that
> we realised that our concern for the poorer half of the

world could no longer be discharged on spiritual terms alone. Previous and continuing missionary efforts have always had a much greater genuine humanitarian content than they are fashionably given credit for.

He emphasised the increasing role of lay people and volunteers, many of whom went on to staff Concern, or at the very least joined the council.

What's more, he was pragmatic about the fact that the organisation's coffers benefited greatly from the labours and altruism of 'young Irish lay people in increasing numbers working for the underprivileged overseas,' who 'caught the public imagination,' which meant that 'Concern benefited from the very strong Irish readiness to back "one of our own." '

As for the issue of the participation of clergy at such a high level:

There is room and indeed need for us, but whether or not we should fill certain managerial posts should be on a basis of competence rather than considerations of service rendered or being ready to serve voluntarily or at markedly low rates.

Aside from these barely disguised spats, however, the general context, tone and thrust of that 1977 document was the tacit acceptance and understanding that Concern, having grown, now had to change and adapt.

Two years later, in 1979, and with his departure from Bangladesh imminent, Aengus took a reconnaissance trip through Kenya, Zambia, Tanzania, Egypt, Thailand, India and Nepal. On 16 June, his last day of service in Bangladesh, he sat down again to put pen to paper. *Pace* his desire for managerial professionalism, his views on the growing preponderance of 'development' had, if anything, become further embedded:

It is unfashionable today to use words like 'charity' or 'relief'. Voluntary agencies have been stampeded away

At an *Áras an Uachtaráin* reception, 1997.

Jack Finucane, Mary Robinson and Aengus Finucane on the 25th
anniversary of Concern Worldwide, 1993.

Aengus Finucane in Bangladesh, 1998.

Image from the 'He Ain't Heavy' TV advert, Ethiopia, 1989.
Photo by Liam Burke.

Aengus Finucane with Bob Geldof, Ethiopia, 1985.

Aengus Finucane in Dublin, late 1980s.

Aengus Finucane and Dermot Morgan (aka Father Ted), 1996.

Chantal (15), Diane (12), Angelique (9), Adeline (5) with
Aengus Finucane in Kisangani, Rwanda, 10 June, 1997.

Vincent Browne, Deirdre Purcell, Pat Langan and
Aengus Finucane preparing for Ethiopia, 1985.

Irwin Shorr and Aengus Finucane in Dublin, 1980s.

Somalia, 1993.

Delia Finucane and Aengus Finucane in Limerick, 1980s.

Mike McDonagh and Aengus Finucane, Somalia, 1992–93.

Sally Anne Kinahan, Director of Oxfam Julius Nyere
and Aengus Finucane.

Five CEOs: Raymond Kennedy, Tom Arnold, David Begg,
Aengus Finucane and John O'Loughlin Kennedy.

Michael Byrne, David Begg, Aengus Finucane,
Dominic MacSorley and Anne O'Mahony, 1997.

from many of the weakest and most needy people
in pursuit of 'development' goals which they are ill
equipped to achieve. Materialist rules and criteria have
been brought over from commerce and business in the
name of professionalism.

The development record of governments and of
UN agencies during the two Development Decades
now drawing to a close is pathetic. The development
record of voluntary agencies does not bear too close a
scrutiny, and I say that after visiting voluntary agencies in
seven developing countries in Africa and Asia. In pursuit
of quantifiable results we are in danger of neglecting the
type of personalised welfare work of which we are most
capable. Voluntary organisations have little capacity for
sophisticated development programmes.

His *coup de grâce* was a warning to those back in Dublin: 'There
has been and is a tremendous amount of self-deception.'

It is interesting, in light of contemporary views of
Aengus and his attitudes – and what he expressed in those
documents – that while he is scathing about the aid world's
early attempts at switching much of its emphasis from disaster
relief to development, it was not the issue per se to which he
objected – far from it. Fundamentally, it was that despite many
well-meaning efforts, all this theory, and even groundwork, had
resulted in very little being delivered for his poorest of the poor.
The problem was, as he saw it, lack of insight and general cack-
handed incompetence.

Mark Malloch Brown's take on this debate, as seen through
not only his own experience but through Aengus's lens, is also
of interest.

He was a practical man, a doer.

He would be totally impatient with so much of the
discussion nowadays at board tables of these organisations
I sit on, where now it's all about 'sustainability of the

investment,' and hugely boils down to this overused metaphor of the fisherman and his net.

And behind it does lie this growing and eye-watering body of literature encompassing self-sustaining development, which enables recipients to go on to reinvest on their own in whatever it is, water or power or seeds or finance. Development, more than relief, has become highly professionalised.

But even in the field of relief there are new schemes afoot where people are helped outside camps by cash transfer systems or dry rations for instance, rather than soup kitchens....

Malloch Brown defines the 'Aengus Formula' as:

> Put your money into programmes, don't spend it on all this highfalutin big-picture thinking, this science of measurement and results and all the rest of it.... And when I see big players putting more and more into advocacy and less and less into feeding the poor, down the road I can well envisage a backlash, a reversal in some ways towards this Aengus formula. So I think fashion will not be against him forever.

It is evident that in many ways Tom Arnold has sympathy for Malloch Brown's 'Aengus Formula', but his core view at the time of his chairmanship and his policy review was that his organisation had to keep up with the thinking of its peer-NGOs, and of course with its donors' demands. When work began on that policy review, Arnold says that while the Chief Executive was not happy about it, 'he certainly wasn't' obstructing it. It was later:

> ... when the debate about strategic planning actu-ally got going, he felt himself much more at sea. He wouldn't have seen the real purpose of it: 'Why are we doing all this talking when there are so many obvious

things staring us in the face that we should just go off and *do*?' What he ultimately cared passionately about were the poorest of the poor. He lived that.

During Aengus's latter years as CEO, discussions and attitudes within Concern increasingly mirrored those in the aid world generally, even tending towards polarisation along lines of welfare on the one hand, development on the other. This was of growing significance, and was to be one of the issues later to confront David Begg when he took up office as Aengus's successor.

There were further difficulties. Aengus had begun to struggle with health issues at that time. He suffered from a severe and recurring back problem (Moira Conroy recalls having to organise traction for him), and became very seriously ill following a trip to Africa. Ciunas Bunworth remembers:

On his way back to Ireland he was going home via Nairobi. I had been in South Africa and I was going to be in Nairobi on the way home too, so we were going to go out to dinner. But that night, Aengus was complaining about his hand. He had stuck his pen into it and apparently it was very sore. I said to him he should stay in Nairobi. 'No,' he said, 'get me home.'

There are several versions of how that accident with the pen happened, and it was not as harmless as first appearance might have indicated. The most dramatic scenario, and in a way the most likely because there is a witness, is outlined by Ted Shine, an army man who is married to Ciunas's sister, the Reverend Aisling, a Church of Ireland priest.

Ted Shine is one of those who on the surface seems unassuming, even diffident, delivering memories and views of Aengus Finucane and accounts of his own work for Concern in a modest, staccato monotone. In reality, though, he is another of those amazing people whom Concern somehow gets to work for it. An engineer/logistician, he is a high-ranking army ordnance officer who travels on behalf of the army to test weaponry and then spends all his holidays abroad in very dangerous places for Concern, setting up camps, organising latrines and providing support to anyone who needs it.

During one of his annual leave periods from the army:

We started off working in Burundi because there had been a genocide there the year before, a ping-pong affair. We moved then from Burundi to the Rwanda–Tanzania border, because there were a couple of hundred thousand people moving into Tanzania. The numbers went from 5,000 to 300,000 in a couple of weeks.

I flew into an airstrip on a plateau overlooking the camp, just as Aengus was due to fly out. I looked down and saw two cars stuck in a muddy stream at the bottom. Aengus came up to me, but wouldn't shake my hand because he was covered in mud from pushing and trying to extricate the cars.

Then, on his way back to Nairobi, he was writing his notes on the plane when it hit turbulence. The pen slipped and the nib stabbed the palm of his left hand. And next day, on his way back to Dublin, his hand swelled up completely and then his arm swelled. It was a flesh-eating bug. One cause is dirty water entering a wound.

All who report on this agree, quite graphically, on one aspect of the story: by the time he got from Nairobi to Dublin airport, Aengus's entire left arm was red and swollen right up the shoulder, he was in exquisite pain and Ciunas rightly insisted on rushing him straight to hospital. His sister, Patsy, says that if she had not been so alert he would have undoubtedly lost his arm.

So called flesh-eating bacteria, such as necrotising fasciitis, don't actually eat flesh, but destroy skin and muscle by releasing virulent toxins. They work very, very fast, and can be quickly lethal. What had happened, obviously, is that when he was on the original flight from the camp site to Nairobi, some residue of the bacteria in the muddy water still remained on his hand, enabling invasion through the skin penetrated by the pen nib.

St Vincent's hospital worked fast, inserting intravenous and very strong antibiotics – so strong that, while the arm was saved, between the original infection and side effects from the drugs, Aengus was out sick for a very, very long time.

When his sister, Patsy, went in to see him that first evening, however, she found him sitting up in the bed, tied to drips, 'with a pad on his lap, composing an official letter to some forty-two people, ministers and others about something *very* important ...'. According to Ted Shine, the drugs permanently affected his hearing.

Ted's view of Aengus? 'He was a great character and motivator with a lot of compassion and a simple form of people management: *give people good beds but don't let them sleep in em!*'

Ciunas says that Aengus was physically absent for so long as a result of his illness that 'in a way he lost control of Concern.' She also says that, although on the surface he maintained his usual cheery front, she recognised that underneath he was worrying about his captaincy, and reports the tenor of this worry as he voiced it:

> 'I built up this organisation to what it is today. I joined it for my lifetime, I didn't join to go and enjoy sun-shine in retirement.' I think he was trying to convince himself. 'Lifetime' would have been the word he would have used about his formation as a priest.

Ciunas, herself just about to retire, was beginning the task of office clearance:

When I came to 61, I began thinking, *four more years....*
I don't think that had entered Aengus's head, or if it had,
he was probably ignoring it. When he came to 61, he
was dealing with Somalia and all the other big issues.
Anyhow, priests don't consider anything but a lifetime's
work. It's part of their formation.

And when he did come back into the office, a lot
of people said that he seemed quite negative, but that's
because quite a lot of people were now negative about
him and I knew the word was going round: *well, he is
coming up to 65....*

There you had two completely opposing
viewpoints. Those people waiting for him to turn 65
weren't looking at his lifetime commitment; Aengus
wasn't seeing the retirement rules.

Meanwhile, Tom Arnold had been busy with his policy review,
one of the outcomes of which was a decision to get outside
help for a further and major review on how to implement
the theories and suggestions so far offered about bettering the
structure of the organisation. That outside help was recruited in
the form of a consultation with Craig Gardner and Company.

They would have been the best at the time. We ten-
dered and they came in with the best plan and we went
with them.

Over a period, Craig Gardner [operatives]
interviewed management and council, wending their
way through the decision-making process, and at the end
of it all there was a fairly clear definition of the respective
responsibilities. It could all be summarised into two cores:

Management proposes, council decides;

Management implements, council monitors.

Up to then, he says, there had been 'interminable' discussions
about budgets and finance.

Craig Gardner set up a much more structured approach: set numbers of meetings per year, an expansion of sub-committees, clarity as to what management was to do, a streamlining of work for everyone. And even though there were other changes over the next twenty years, the basic principles still applied, and worked. Both sides knew what they had to do, and the council wasn't micromanaging or intruding on day-to-day work.

This, he says, was a bridge from personality-led to corporate. Not in a negative sense, but for clarity.

It was a crucial development in the life of Concern.

16

*'I knew he was upset, but you're better off moving on rather than
trying to recreate the fun we had.'*

– John Leahy (friend of Aengus and Joe Finucane)

In 1996, Aengus was 64 years of age and Tom Arnold, chairman
of Concern, was still working in the day job as Assistant
Secretary at the Department of Agriculture. He was also busy on
other bodies and committees, including an OECD committee
on Agriculture, which he chaired. But: 'I was coming over to
Concern on a weekly basis to chair meetings about difficulties
between Aengus and his senior management team, trying to act
as referee. That clearly couldn't last.'

Meanwhile, at all levels, management and council, quiet talk
about another issue was seeping through the organisation: its
CEO was coming up to retirement age.

Eithne Healy had been Aengus's secretary since 1991,
having come from the accountancy firm KPMG. She had found
working for him:

> ... very challenging, but in a good way. He was so inter-
> ested in everything, had an enormous capacity for work.
> He never said no to going anywhere or doing anything.
> But when he came up with an idea, he wanted it *now*!

You enjoyed it, though, because you were caught up in the passion he had for some action or other.

(Any flaws as an employer?)

[She thinks, then:]

He found it difficult to recognise that Concern wasn't everyone's *entire* life. He was a bit old-fashioned that way; you stick with Concern, you don't say no, you don't count the hours and everyone should feel the same. He was married to Concern, and expected everyone to be married to it too.

Ciunas Bunworth heartily endorses this:

During the Somalia phase, we were working every hour there was in Dublin, and one time my phone rang at two minutes past three in the morning. [She jumped to answer it. It's a generational thing: *who's dead?*]

But it was Aengus's voice:

'Have you been listening to the three o'clock news on the BBC?'

'Well, Aengus, my alarm didn't go off at three o'clock, so no. Tell me what was on it ...'.

Next morning, he was down to my office. 'Sorry about that!' But he wouldn't really think that kind of thing was wrong.

Eithne remembers, after the poison pen incident, 'that he was very, very ill, lucky that he didn't lose his arm,' but in the first days when he was still in hospital 'there was some emergency running that he was all fired up about,' so she was in and out of St Vincent's Hospital, back and forth, back and forth, as they did different drafts of a letter to highlight the emergency. She really misses his personal touch.

He had beautiful handwriting and a great turn of phrase. Very clear thought processes. We still get briefings, but they're not as personal or self-witnessed. Any time Aengus came back from abroad he'd gather all the staff, anyone who wanted to hear about what was happening overseas. You felt very involved with what you did, that you were part of what was going on in the field.

That 'involving' of the staff even stretched to events like the annual Concern Christmas Fast. 'Everyone, Aengus included, would gather, and we'd all wait for the money to come in and we'd all count it. You felt really relevant to real work for poor people.' After the security company collected the money, everyone would repair to The Bleeding Horse, where inevitably at the end of the night Aengus would look at whoever was left: 'Will we have the one we came for?'

Yet, for all the late nights and gregarious chat, he was quite private. I got to know the public him rather than the private him. But one thing I always admired: he always thought of the poor person, a child, a woman in Bangladesh; people would have all these elaborate plans for advertising campaigns and he'd always say: 'What's in it for the poor person?'

As for the period before his retirement, working so closely with him day after day she was in a good position to deduce, as far as that could go, what he felt about leaving.

He remained very dignified. He'd seen it happen to other people, but I don't think he ever thought it would happen to him. He definitely wanted to die with his boots on, preferably in the field.

In the latter part of 1996, Aengus wrote a carefully reasoned letter to the council suggesting that he should stay on for a further three years to facilitate an orderly transition and to help with his successor's selection.

At the meeting where that letter was noted, after much discussion, sometimes factional, his request was refused, and he was thus informed by letter in return.

'He threw down the gauntlet,' says Evanna Barry Schorderet, a Donegal woman, who is a long-term member of the council. A former volunteer, she is, in her own words a 'pot-stirrer'.

> He challenged us ... well, no. I suppose he didn't challenge
> us, but he opened a path that might have been followed.
> I wasn't happy, and it was very painful, but I did think we
> were doing the right thing. It's a testament to our relation-
> ship as friends that it remained strong afterwards.

As it happens, the vote of Father Mick Reynolds with the council against Aengus was crucial because all the other members knew of the very long and close friendship of these two men. Mick loved his friend dearly, but he was not conflicted about his decision on which way to vote:

> I thought it was time. The great expression is: 'go when
> they still want you.' So many of us stay too long. So yes,
> for me friendship didn't come into it, but for the others,
> the fact that I was a very close friend, and I thought he
> should go, was a factor.

After the council's decision, Tom Arnold was mandated to break the news:

> I just went into his apartment and talked to him: 'This is
> the news. This is how we're going to proceed.' I remem-
> ber the date: it was 21 October 1996. I think he took it
> as well as he could, kept his dignity, as he always did, but
> I could see that it was a very big blow.

Father Reynolds, echoing Eithne Healy, Ciunas, Patsy, Jack and almost everyone else who expressed an opinion, says that for

Aengus, starting with that vote, leaving Camden Street was an enormous wrench.

Mick also agrees with all those others that Aengus was married to Concern, adding, drily:

> But whatever job Aengus had was the most important job. Whether it was cleaning the avenue or doing the toilets or [working with] the Nigerian relief flights, that was all that mattered.

Remember those early Penny Dinners in Limerick?

> He was strange that way, very focused on whatever he was doing. And whatever he was doing was going to succeed. He wasn't conceited, you wouldn't really say that, but he had a good opinion of himself. He couldn't imagine defeat.

As to this last point, ex-volunteer Paula Donaldson, another of Aengus's great friends, said that he did accept the inevitable. 'He wasn't happy, but always liked people to be open and honest, because that's the way he treated others.' She always felt, she says, that in any case he was going to move on to another phase because there was still a lot he could do, and so she was not surprised that he went off to America.

> What was astounding, though, was how he took off immediately. Talk about shaking hands! He had always had a soft spot for America ... always joked that he'd retire to a parish in California. Just not yet.

Could Eithne Healy describe Aengus's legacy to the organisation?

'He left the building blocks. But when the time came,' she adds, 'his tenure ended quietly. He just kind of slipped out.'

Ciunas agrees. He left:

> ... by the back stairs. People were devastated – not all peo-
> ple, but some. We went down to Devitt's and Aengus had
> a big roll, and there were drinks and then the usual stuff,
> but there was no big session here with a proper goodbye.

The take on all of this by Mark Malloch Brown is that, as painful
as it was for Aengus, the council's decision was justified. He is in a
good position objectively to judge. This is a man whose CV runs to
the length of a tome, who has dealt with British Cabinet colleagues,
foreign potentates and despots, and who these days in his 'spare' time
away from commercial company boardrooms, serves on a number
of non-profit and advisory bodies, including the International
Crisis Group, the Open Society Foundation and Save the Children.

Of Aengus's retirement, he says:

> It's hard to be definitive, but all my management instincts
> would tell me the council was right. This dilemma is
> classic, about as fundamental an issue as you can get.
> It's in all the business literature. Organisations outgrow
> their founders, because people can no longer run them
> in the intimate way they used to, the thing gets too big
> and too complex.
>
> The world had changed. The Irish NGO sector had
> become much more tricky and competitive. You had
> the field countries now wanting to do it for themselves.

He is speaking with the greatest of affection and admiration, not
just for Aengus, but for the ethos of Concern and the honesty of
its commitment. Any implied criticism is made in the knowledge
that the organisation would continue to serve its clientele well,
just not quite in the same way.

> For me, what was fantastic about Concern was that here
> was a group who didn't come with problems but who

came with solutions. I think, however, that it was absolutely due a makeover.

Like almost all ex-Concern people, Moira Conroy has kept in touch with former colleagues and the organisation itself, even though these days she divides her time between her two homes in Killaloe and Arusha in Tanzania. She knew, if from afar, what had been going on in her alma mater.

Over the years, right from graduation as a nurse-midwife, she had been in contact with some of the hundreds of Holy Ghost Fathers like Aengus, Jack, the Dohenys and a lot of men who had been thrown out of Biafra. On their return, they were left to mill around in Kimmage with no jobs in sight and the authorities, hapless in the face of this huge problem, telling them to go out and find their own work.

She creates a powerful image of crowds of intelligent, trained and experienced men, seasoned by years of independence, hard work and not-enough-hours-in-the-day, now crowding into the limited spaces at Kimmage with nothing much to occupy their time. After the white heat of Biafra they were physically, mentally and vocationally marooned.

The more she saw of these men, the more she was impressed with their personal courage, including that of Aengus and Jack:

> To think they had the energy to get out there and go with this new organisation, with no idea how it was going to work, or where it was going to go in the future!

Initially, during her first spell as a volunteer in Bangladesh when he was her director, she says she found Aengus 'very forceful,' not only because of his imposing aura, but because of 'the red pen for the corrections, the grammar, the capital letter,' and there were times, she says, when she would not have liked to be on the wrong side of him. Over time, however: 'He made me believe there wasn't anything I couldn't do.'

180

She does understand his reluctance to relinquish the reins of Concern. 'After all, starting with his sojourn in Bangladesh, he had real power to get things done,' with access 'to ministers, officials and celebrities.' But she suspects that, as he got older, his beliefs had calcified.

> They never changed. He began reminiscing about the good times, and it was very difficult for him to take on new things.
>
> If my daughter was working for him now and he said to her: 'Here's what we're going to do, we're going to do this, that and the other,' she wouldn't take it from him. It's all participatory now.
>
> I do think the time does come where you have to let go. Aengus would never say he couldn't cope with something. Whether he could or he couldn't he'd never say it, but he had a great way of getting around it.

For instance, she remembers asking him: 'Are you driving down to Limerick today?' And getting the tart reply: 'I don't have to prove any longer that I can drive. I've been there and done that. I'll let someone else do the driving.' That was his way of coping with the fact that he couldn't drive.

Like Moira Conroy, Ciunas Bunworth had been intimidated during her first meeting with Aengus. (In common with Aengus, this woman carries a whiff of mischief on her person. It was she who divulged that during plenary meetings, when the staff of Concern were awaiting the arrival of Aengus and Jack, and when the footsteps outside the room were heard, the whisper would go round: *Here come the Earls!*)

On her first night in Bangladesh, she was sitting with the other volunteers at the big table in the big room in the Concern House in Dhaka, when 'this man' came into the room and sat beside her.

I thought to myself, would he not have chosen to sit beside someone else? But then this man asks you a nice, friendly question, and you start to chat away to him....

She had been in Bangladesh for two weeks when the man asked her to go and check out a programme in Demra that had just started. So, with her background in catering:

... not knowing anything about slums or slum resettlement, off I go. I saw this horrific displacement of an enormous number of people. Women wanted me to take their kids. There were people injured. There were no hospital facilities. I came back in bits.

I said to Aengus: 'Please do not send me out to anything like that ever again!' And he said: 'I think what we'll do is, if you move a desk into my office, we'll set up a programme.'

So she did. And they did.

He thought I was brilliant if we talked about this number of grams of food per person, and moving that up into kilograms. He thought you were top-drawer if you could say this number of kids at this number of grams per kid ... you're going to need this tonnage in a month. Genius level.

So I was there, he asking me questions, I doing the sums and coming up with the answers, and he assuring me we were writing this proposal together. That was the first time I came under his spell. And I think I still live under his spell. I say good morning to him every morning when I come into Concern because his picture is on the wall of the lobby.

Evanna Barry holds to the view that forcing his retirement was the right thing to do, but she struggled with the decision she made. She was sad for him, but also has an interesting thought about it:

> Maybe it was better for him to feel that we'd pulled the rug. He was proud of us all [ex-staff and volunteers] being on the council, and he had to be proud that we did the right thing.

Even Jack, ever loyal to his older brother and distressed at his hurt, agrees with the thrust of what the others have said:

> In a sense it *was* time for him to go. He didn't see problems; didn't want to hear about them. And although he fought hard against his disabilities, his physical stamina and energy had deserted him.

Concern's response to emergencies is as good as it ever was, as are individual and highly imaginative reactions of staff to what might seem to be relatively minor difficulties.

On that note, this is Ciunas, speaking in 2013 on the brink of her own retirement, remembering when she worked with Aengus in the famine situation in Karamoja:

> We realised – eventually – that there was a problem with the old folk. These old folks, not that old of course, were sitting on the outside of the feeding centres, always on the outside of whatever was going on and not getting any food.
>
> [She approached Aengus]: 'There's something going on with the old folks, Aengus.'
>
> He had read some anthropological study about an area in the north of Karamoja. It had been carried out on a tribe called the Ik, and he was able to refer me to a particular book, which I then read. And this showed that in pastoralist communities like these, the old folks are always the last to eat, because in pastoral communities during famine times, if you bring something to the family pot, you can eat; if you

don't or can't, you don't eat. Here, the land was dry, the old folks had nothing to bring, so they didn't eat.

Aengus had a think, which didn't take him long, and then decided:

> We'll set up an old-folks' programme where they sit and discuss things on a fairly regular basis like grandparents should, and at those meetings, we'll make sure they get a ration. The families will know that they've gone to the meeting where they get a ration, and that they'll bring the ration back to the household and they'll get fed again. You do the logistics on it, find out how many old people there are, work out how much they will need each for their ration, and then we'll go to the World Food Programme and get what we need.

Just another way, says Ciunas, that Aengus always solved problems the practical way:

> I could have been sitting worrying about those old folks for the rest of my life. He had given them something they could do that gave them a social purpose. They could sit in the shade under a tree and chatter away to themselves at their meeting like old folks everywhere: *this famine isn't half as bad as the last one! Our grandchildren aren't half as badly off as we were...!*

For Ciunas, what inspired her during her working life (and which she fears could somehow be lost as the organisation scales up) is 'the Aengus-type thinking. The magical thinking.'

It is clear from what she and others have said that association with Aengus definitely trained his people not only for massive projects involving millions, but small, hugely beneficial innovations for little groups, such as the 'youth club' in Khao-I-Dang, where Dominic MacSorley established the football league

– plus song sessions to distract surly teenage boys and angry young men from hanging around corners.

Dominic, now in charge, broadens this 'Aengus-type thinking' into 'Concern-type thinking', giving Aengus himself a lot of the credit, saying that 'he was always looking at what we were *not* doing, who we *weren't* reaching.'

Some of these ideas were very, very simple, and based on ordinary human observation:

> During one of the mass refugee migrations/returns [either in Sierra Leone or Rwanda – memories differ] there were thousands and thousands of people on one major road, walking, walking, so the route resembled the exodus at the canal end at Croke Park after an All-Ireland final, although multipled by a numerical factor of many thousands.
>
> People were so tightly packed together that if a child who had been holding onto a mother's skirt got tired and fell, or even let go and fell behind, the mother first of all mightn't have noticed until it was too late. And even if she did, she was being carried along in the human torrent and couldn't turn back, so the child was lost.
>
> Concern came up with the simplest of expedients: nabbing both mother and child within the flow while they were still together, tying one end of a little piece of string to the child, fixing the other end to the mother....

We end this chapter with a letter written to Aengus in May 1997, after the CEO's last AGM. It was handwritten by The O Morchoe.

Dear Father Aengus,

> *I did not join the string of oral tributes made to you at the AGM, but that was not because I did not want to – only that I had made up my mind to do so by way of a letter to you. My continued association with Concern has been because I believed that in a small*

way I could contribute to an organisation with which in conscience and in fact I can and want to be totally associated.

To me the work of the organisation epitomises the Christian message totally uncomplicated by denominational differences. And it is that message which has come so clearly from you and which has resulted in real action across the areas in which Concern has been involved.

Your inspiration and your clear-sighted grasp of the fundamental issues has been what has made Concern the much respected organisation that it is — both in the eyes of the Irish public and in the eyes of those who see its work and purpose on the ground.

To me, whatever the difficulties of actually getting there — and there were not a few along the way since I first met you — your conviction that ultimately 'the Almighty will provide' and that in order that he could, leaps of faith and conviction were required, was what has motivated so many including myself to support and be involved in Concern.

Expressions that 'Aengus is Concern' and Tom Arnold's that 'Aengus is irreplaceable' were not made lightly, and of course do have more than a ring of truth. Your inspiration has engendered faith in everyone in Concern that things can be done, that the difficult is not impossible. And that has been infectious throughout for the good of God's most deprived people.

Your appeal at the AGM that the ethos born in the early days and developed and nurtured by you was well made, but I do not think you need worry. Although your 'being Concern' and 'irreplaceable' must be overcome by those who succeed you, I believe that ethos you have engendered will be the one that motivates those who are left to make it work. I think there will be too many of us around who will be saying 'What would Aengus say?' when paths start meandering!

I have to say that, like so many of us, I was very sad that the last year or so has gone so astray. I am sure that all of us realise that it must have hurt you bitterly. I can only say that it was merciful that on council there were no bitter divisions and that what eventually materialised was a consensus view.

I think we understood that at some stage you had to stand down and that your powerful influence had to be transferred to your successors. With the very real difficulties that were there, perhaps it was better for Concern that this should happen as a controlled event at an appropriate time. That may not make sense to you but it did to us, even though we realised the very real hurt it might cause you.

I hope you don't mind my long letter to you but I wanted to say simply how much my life and my thinking on all the issues tackled by Concern has been influenced by you and how grateful I am for that. I felt I had to say everything else I have said to explain that simple fact.

Thank you.

I wish you well and I wish you happiness and continued fulfilment of your wonderful mission.

Yours very sincerely,

David

17

'I fear that much of what was distinctive and valuable has been sacrificed on the altar of progress. NGOs should not allow success to go to their heads or settle for becoming junior members of the major international league. They must regularly go back to their roots and renew their commitment to serve those most in need.'

– Aengus Finucane

The values of Concern:

1. Extreme poverty must be targeted.
2. Respect for people comes first.
3. Gender equality is a prerequisite for development.
4. Development is a process, not a gift.
5. Greater participation leads to greater commitment.
6. All governments have responsibility for poverty elimination.
7. Emergencies call for rapid response.
8. Democracy accelerates development.
9. Environment must be respected.
10. Good stewardship requires good procedures.
11. Experience is the best teacher.

These values embody what David Begg was to uphold and promulgate when he was selected to take over from Aengus Finucane as CEO of Concern in July 1997.

The man who in September 2014 announced his forthcoming retirement from his post as General Secretary of the Congress of Trade Unions – the job he took directly after leaving Concern – moved to the NGO from the Communications Workers Union.

So why Concern? Was that not quite a jump from a trade union?

David Begg has a self-deprecating sense of humour. The word had gone out, he says, that the appointment was going to go to an outside person: 'And I guess all you had to be was ambulatory!'

Seriously, though, at the time he saw the newspaper ad for the job, he had just left the board of Trócaire, having spent 'ten thoroughly enjoyable years of immersion in the world of development and relief. I was suffering from a bit of withdrawal.'

For him, however, the problem with talking about his days in Concern is not having to go back to remember; the problem is memory itself:

> I see all these people appearing before tribunals and not remembering, and I realise I would be an absolute disaster before a tribunal. People who have very busy and engaging careers and a multiplicity of personal involvements in other aspects of their lives tend to move from one aspect to the other.

Well briefed by Tom Arnold, the new CEO was aware that, once he sat into Aengus's chair in Camden Street, he would face a long list of challenges, both internal and external.

For the interim, Arnold had arranged for Aengus's actual retirement date to be shifted for three months into July 1997 and suggested that Begg should join him and Father Finucane on a field trip so he could discover what Concern was all about. Up to then, David Begg's familiarity with the 'dark continent' had been based on a trades union-centred trip to South Africa to support a strike by the National Union of Mineworkers. So if he were now to plunge into deeper waters, he would start briefed and in good company.

So this unlikely trio, Three Men in a Plane, set off together for Rwanda, Burundi and the country now known as the Democratic Republic of the Congo. As an exercise, the journey was an unmitigated success, creating amity, at the very least sincere cordiality, between the Holy Ghost Father and the trade union man. (Bonding would be an overstatement here – the two personality types and proclivities were too far apart – but Begg does use the adjective 'firm' in describing his ensuing friendship with both his travelling companions.)

Anne O'Mahony, the Rwanda country director, hosted them, and she says the pace nearly killed her:

> I nearly needed a month off after they left. If you can't stay the pace you just go to bed – but you're not allowed. And next day you have to be up to face the day with great enthusiasm. I was like a rag at the end of the week.
>
> David would be sitting there and you didn't know whether he was asleep or awake, but every so often he'd come in with a comment and you knew that he wasn't sleeping with both sides of his brain.

'Kisangani [formerly Stanleyville in the Democratic Republic of the Congo] was like the Belgians had left it in the 1960s,' says Begg, 'and it hadn't seen a lick of paint since. The heat … The dim light with hardly any electricity …'.

The first 'social', as it was called in Ireland in times past, was in the Concern house:

> It was like *The Eagle Has Landed*. All of Aengus's aco- lytes came in from miles around. He really was a great raconteur, drinking away and telling his stories. But then, at about 2.00 in the morning, he said: 'I suppose we'd better go to bed, but sure these nights will never come again.' Waiting for someone to disagree with him,

like.... Nobody did. We had to be up early for an early
flight, but what he didn't know was that his watch had
been tampered with!

So it was in reality only midnight as they all gratefully (except
Aengus) went to bed.

The trio became a quartet as Anne travelled with them
through Rwanda. Aengus celebrated a Mass at the kitchen table
of the organisation's house in Kigali, and Begg found this: 'Very
moving; the closest I've ever come in my entire life to pure, raw
Christianity.'

His next most abiding memory of that trip happened when,
after stops at various places, they got to Nyarubuye Roman
Catholic Church, located about sixty miles east of Kigali and
now notorious as the place where the genocide had been at its
most violently horrifying. In effect a shrine, this is where, over
15 and 16 April 1994, thousands of Tutsi who had taken refuge
from the Hutu were massacred.

According to a variety of reports, the mayor of the town, a
Hutu, had encouraged them to seek sanctuary there and assured
them they would be safe.

He then betrayed them.

When the killing started, there were so many inside that,
again according to reports, ammunition ran out and the slaughter
had to continue by machete and club, the killers taking shifts
over the forty-eight hours it took to massacre all trapped inside.

Nyarubuye Church is one of the places in Rwanda that
now accommodate neat, crammed rows of victims' cracked
skulls and hacked bones, offering wordless testimony to what
happened. At the time of that trip, however, no such organised
memorialising had yet occurred; recollections were still too
raw. But Begg learned that, as part of a final insult to the Tutsi
bodies, the Hutus either left them *in situ* to be eaten by rats and
dogs or threw them into rivers so they would be carried 'back
to Ethiopia', from where, contemptuously, the Hutus believed
they had originated.

That scene is indelibly printed on the consciousness of all who saw it. In general, the Rwandan situation was so awful, and the work so stressful for aid workers, it is almost a miracle that they managed to continue working. Which they did.

Concern volunteer Rossa O'Briain was relatively new to Concern and the aid world in general when he was sent there. He remembers being 'on a bridge crossing a river' when he saw the bodies 'floating down ...'. Even now, years later, he gets very upset in the narration. The words cannot adequately convey the images he carries and now projects: tightly packed like log rafts, the bodies of dead men women and children being carried along in the flow. 'There were hundreds and hundreds,' he says when he recovers, 'Tutsis or Hutus – the distinction would have been lost on me, but they were recognisable to each other. Stature and physiognomy.'

Now, David, Tom and Aengus were standing at the entrance to the church where these people were massacred in shifts. 'You could see the pots and pans and cooking utensils that they had used,' says Begg, 'it was really a moving experience.'

While there, he witnessed a moment 'that will stay with me always':

I saw Aengus had gone white, absolutely white, because the tabernacle was open and empty.

It was biblical. The abomination of desolation. Christ defeated. The whole imagery of the thing; the terrible act that had taken place, the open tabernacle. He had to be inured to horrible things, but this had an extraordinary effect on him. Hugely traumatic.

The other thing I remember is from the same trip, but in the Congo. When the Tutsi Army invaded from Uganda, eventually they pushed out the Hutus and a lot of these escaped into the jungles, living wild for months, eventually coming out to where Concern and other NGOs had set up feeding stations, medical aid stations and so on. All suffering from malnutrition and kwashiorkor.

Every day the aid workers, including those from Concern, would come from Kisangani to this camp they'd set up about forty kilometres from the city, but for two days at one stage they were prevented by the Tutsi Army from coming to it. And when they got there on the third day there was absolutely nothing. Nothing.

For David Begg, as Aengus and Tom had known it would be, that trip was a fast track into the reality of Concern fields and the reasons for the organisation to be in them. For someone who presents rather an inscrutable demeanour in public, it is clear that he is haunted by the images he absorbed that, like persistent wraiths, continue to hang about him, and for a few moments while remembering them he is not present in his ICTU office on Dublin's Parnell Square with its high, graceful windows, dark wood, board table and magnificent break-fronted bookcase, but mentally moving again through those unspeakable arenas of carnage. These include the refugee camps where the *génocidaires*, those silent young and old men and women from both sides who had committed atrocities of the most execrable kind, had to wait their turn for the white man's food and medicine along with the mutilated survivors of their guns and machetes. This, he learned – and still believes – was proof of Concern in action: 'If there are people in need, you serve them no matter what.'

As a postscript to that trip, Aengus, say many in Concern, found the Rwandan genocide extraordinarily upsetting, not least because there is irrefutable evidence that some Catholic priests and nuns were in some cases heavily involved, not just in collusion, but hands-on, with machetes.

Begg concurs: 'That got him very deeply.'

For someone who has led such a public life, Begg is shy. In personality, appetites and sociability he is the antithesis of the former CEO: 'Never went to the pub with the staff on Friday evenings, just went home,' or: 'Never went around the country like Aengus did to meet people' were common complaints from those who, nevertheless, in the end conceded that his four-year regime proved overall to be 'good for Concern.'

Eithne Healy, Aengus's secretary, comments on her new boss:

> It was very strange for me to see someone new in Aengus's chair. David was a very different personality, but when it came to a focus on poverty, he had basically the same outlook. His was: 'This doesn't have to be rocket science. You don't have to have a Master's.' That bit would have been very similar.
>
> But he was far more strategic. Aengus went in, justified it later. David strategised first. Aengus was definitely the better politician, but in a sense, in an odd way, both men's work combined in a new and very successful fundraising initiative after David's succession. He invested in it, but it wouldn't have been the success it became without Aengus having built up the reputation of Concern in difficult times.

More crucial than anyone's personal opinions or even gripes about him, however, was how David Begg's ideas about running the organisation differed in such a fundamental way from Aengus's more intuitive, hands-on approach. For example, without in his view abandoning all valid commitments espoused by his predecessor, he decided that under his watch business processes would run along orthodox business lines. He would also use his extensive contacts in Europe to bring Concern online there, to access the vastly bigger funds and operations of well-established funders and NGOs.

As he took over, however, the list of immediate tasks was long. Among these were:

- Sorting out internal relationships and communications issues;
- Salving wounds within the council, 'because all of Aengus's friends who sat on it had voted for the CEO's retirement,

but by doing so had inflicted psychological wounds on themselves – in a sense they were enraged that they had had to do it for the greater good';

- Facilitating Aengus's new role as Honorary President of Concern US by which, based in New York, he would help with fundraising.
- Resolving Concern's financial position – which at that point was shaky – so much so that redundancies were being considered;
- Dealing with internal arguments about whether Concern should move to the Development Model rather than that of Relief; and
- All of this was to be taken into account while simultaneously pursuing his own vision for the future of the organisation.

The debate about development-versus-relief ethos was serious, and Begg knew that he had to set a new strategic course by marrying, accommodating or directing all sides of the increasingly loud debates about it within the organisation:

There were passionate advocates on all sides – for the traditional Welfarist model, for the Developmentalists, and for those in the middle, a large group, whose desire was not to abandon the founders' ethos while trying to accommodate both sides of the argument.

Aengus, he says, interpreted the wishes and mission of the founders as being somewhat different than what he had been given credit (or blame) for. He was committed to both streams: *Respond as fast as possible to an emergency; stay on for recovery and development.* Poverty alleviation – elimination if humanly possible – remains the goal, but in order to travel towards it, its causes have to be tackled and not just the symptoms. It's a much more subtle and nuanced approach than 'the Aengus formula' as defined by Malloch Brown: *Put your money into programmes.*

Sitting in his office in Parnell Square, Begg says that when he joined, the organisation was sitting in the middle of a line. He outlines an imaginary one through the air with his index finger:

> Trócaire was at this end of the line. [He points.] It's fantastic on advocacy and brave in following the advocacy line to the justice element.
> Concern was here. [Indicating the middle.] It's a hybrid, implementation-plus-advocacy, but advocacy predicated on its presence on the ground. Makes it very effective.
> Goal was at this far end here. It's very much, almost totally, welfarist in its approach.

He accepts that, at the time he took office, the international development literature was already running these arguments ('and, by the way, they're still not fully resolved'), but once *in situ* in Camden Street he began to negotiate his way through them. In doing so, given the calibre and heat of the passionate debate, he realised what a unique institutional organisation Concern is:

> The strength of the organisation had always been its presence on the ground.... When *Morning Ireland* called up Concern's Mary Murphy, originally from Dingle but now working in deepest Africa, she was able to describe what was happening there, and everyone at home understood it and opened their hearts, and not only that, their purses. Third World aid organisations have to operate on the basis of trust, public empathy, and willingness to support the 'great work out there, wherever "there" is.' This is very important.

But according to the 'very interesting professional disagreements internally,' one school was very traditionalist, welfarist: *If someone's starving, you don't have to analyse the situation: do something about it.*

And the other was the social justice model. *You might be starving, Deirdre, but I don't want to interfere with your coping skills by giving you some food, because if I don't give you food you might spontaneously start to grow it.*

What can be missed in the general chat about these differences, he adds, 'but was not missed in Concern, is that a welfarist programme or project can include investigation, advocacy, and the all-encompassing Development.' In his interview, for instance, Dominic MacSorley pointed out that, for Concern, while this kind of internal debate rarely gets an airing in public, the 'hybrid' approach is what makes the organisation what it is, and in essence is what Aengus advocated.

Before the poor person can benefit from development, he or she must be lifted out of degradation and destitution into shelter, warmth, health and dignity, otherwise that person will find no pathway towards the ultimate goal of healthy self-sufficiency. They won't even have the energy to take the first step. And without that lift, all the investigations and theories from the best brains on the planet will not achieve the ultimate goal, which is elimination of absolute poverty and human dignity for all.

Understanding the complexities of this debate immediately on taking office, what Begg strove to point out to the advocates of opposing sides was that 'both emphases are actually complementary.'

But during his tenure, he says, there were a lot of people in Concern determined to move this hybrid model to one end of the spectrum or the other, and in his time, 'never the twain' did meet.

Also high on his fledgling agenda in 1997 was the critical matter of the financial viability of the organisation, including the real possibility of the unthinkable: redundancies.

This shocked everyone since this had previously been unheard of in Camden Street, even as a concept. My sense of it is that redundancy sundered a sort of unwritten contract: *if you completely commit yourself to Concern, Concern will look after you.* This was a very personal organisation, with a lot of personal commitment to Aengus.

During the Rwandan crisis, he says, Concern had done extremely well in terms of publicity and fundraising as a result of Mike McDonagh's CNN broadcasts from the field almost every night – which led to the dollars 'rolling in' from America. The New York office had opened on foot of expectations that this would continue, 'but when the TV pictures ended, so did the money':

> The whole organisation had been over-extended, based on those huge amounts of disaster money and, save for the Tarbett affair, probably for the first time in its existence there was a major financial crisis. You had Concern groups around the country raising money. These were the backbones of the organisation. A lot of the people running those events were returned volunteers, very committed. But to be honest, the amount of money raised through fasts and so on was small in the scheme of things and was very costly to organise, consuming a large amount of resources.

He does concede that within Ireland, though not specifically designed as such, these traditional, voluntary schemes are good marketing and consciousness-raising tools. And without abandoning them, he very quickly sought an additional, more thrusting and modern way of bringing in money by persuading Sally Anne Kinahan, an expert fundraiser, then head of Oxfam Ireland, to join Concern. 'And when she came in she instituted the street collections.'

This practice, known as 'chugging', though reviled by many, who resent being accosted by cheery, Duracell-bunny types in the streets, has proved hugely beneficial to Concern.

Jack's twin, Jim, has an opinion on this:

> I had a lot of friends who contributed by Standing
> Order every month. But when it all got too professional,
> a lot of them became very annoyed about [receiving
> circulars containing such questions as]: *Have you thought
> about your will?* To fellas that weren't thinking of dying!

Jack himself, while agreeing that the practice is unpopular in
many quarters, says that it works, guaranteeing steady cash flow
in lean times. And Begg, although understanding the pushback,
remains unrepentant:

> I know it's persecution, but it's incredibly successful. We
> got first-mover advantage and built up a huge database
> of subscribers, which was independent of peaks and val-
> leys, so it allowed for much more effective long-term
> planning.

All of Begg's business instincts, he says, would have led him
to close this loss-making US operation that, for many on
the council such as Evanna Barry, should never have been
set up in the first place. But he had heard Tom Arnold's
instruction loud and clear: for Aengus, he had to get America
off the ground. 'Whatever else I did, I had to ensure that the
American operation became viable.'

No easy task.

There were, in addition, all kinds of other hurdles to clear in
the donor arena and in recipient countries:

> Donors now expect 100 per cent western accounting
> standards as to how their money is used, but if you
> work entirely with partners, it can be quite difficult
> to demand those standards because of a whole variety
> of reasons attached to patrimony and so on in those
> countries.

One guy came to me one day and said:'I became an accountant because my whole family clubbed together to pay for my education. Now they expect me to look after them.'This is a realistic difficulty.

What did Aengus himself think about Concern's journey into the future?

Two years before he retired, in a deeply knowledgeable – and prescient – fourteen-page paper entitled 'Framework for Survival', he wrote trenchantly about the evolution of Third World NGOs and aid organisations, touching on bilateral giving by governments and regimes within recipient countries. He offered his views on the entire international bureaucratic development spectrum, setting everything not only within his own experience and perspective as a participant via Concern, but also as an observer of the entire assemblage of multinational organisations and systems that had burgeoned between the first major disaster to explode onto the world stage, Biafra in 1967, and that in Somalia in 1992, a span of twenty-five years.

He dealt with what was at the time the most recent big wave on the restless sea of discussion: a recipient country's record on human rights. This goes right to the heart of Concern's foundation ethos of dealing with the poorest of the poor, whoever they are and whatever they've done. 'If a clean human rights record was made an essential criterion for receiving aid,' he wrote, 'there would be a very short recipient list.'

He also dealt knowingly with the growth of those organisations that survive and grow after the crisis that led to their being set up – with the erosion of idealism that tends to go hand in hand with the growth in scale. 'Small is Beautiful' is an attractive concept, but it is difficult to uphold in the real world in the face of the enormity of needs.

And, as he did publicly from the field in a TV interview during the Somalia crisis, in his document he tears into the inadequacy and delay of the international response to the horrors in that country, which served to worsen them.

> *There wasn't a will in Somalia until very late, and even then it was lukewarm for far too long. One can only be cynical about what have been rightly described as the 'pathetic and uncoordinated efforts' of the superpowers and super systems. In the twenty-five years since Biafra, we have launched satellites into space, put people on the moon, made all manner of technological advances. And at the end of July 1992 [while the conflict in Somalia was raging] there were twenty-five million metric tons of cereal in European Intervention stores alone. Given these facts, how did the world community cope with the shame of watching hundreds of thousands of people die of starvation? It was not that we did not know.*

He handles difficulties encountered between some NGOs and their beneficiaries:

> *Third World recipient governments can become resentful at being bypassed by NGOs and seemingly not trusted. I have experienced such reactions in Ethiopia, in Sudan and in Bangladesh. They will often vent their frustrations on the NGOs, placing almost unbelievable constraints on their operations. Indeed, these NGOs, sometimes because of their insensitivity, arrogance and even incompetence, deserve any backlash they receive.*

And he remembers visiting a conference about Somalia in the Kenyan capital, Nairobi, in July 1992 at the height of the crisis:

> *... it was like visiting Cape Canaveral. Somalia was very remote from the twenty-fourth-floor conference chamber where I counted fifty-five heads discussing it. A few had been in*

201

Somalia for substantial periods. A greater number had had brief exposure. More had read reports.

One of the great tragedies of disaster situations, he wrote:

> *… is that those who learned in earlier ones have moved up the ladder or left Third World activity. A new generation is left to reinvent the wheel at the expense of the unfortunate disaster victims.*

And at the end of his fourteen pages, he concludes:

> *As NGOs become more professional, handle vastly increased budgets, manage enormously bigger and more far-flung organisations and support heavier structures and bureaucracies, their real strengths have been severely eroded. These strengths include commitment, ethos, mission, caring and flexibility. I fear that much of what was distinctive and valuable has been sacrificed on the altar of progress. NGOs should not allow success to go to their heads or settle for becoming junior members of the major international league. They must regularly go back to their roots and renew their commitment to serve those most in need.*

Does Begg think Aengus's influence, and/or the ethos he espoused, will continue?

He does. 'I think the ethos will survive':

> All organisations develop their own culture, and they operate in a path-dependent way; we're doing it this way because we've always done it this way. That's not always negative. It can mean resistance to change, but not necessarily so.

But one thing he has noticed: 'If you interrogate those who are quoting him, they could be quoting things he never said!'

His assessment of his own relationship with Aengus?

He thinks for a bit, then: 'Maire [David's wife] loved Aengus. She loved to cook for him. You didn't have the sense that he was a picky eater! But seriously, for me, he was one of those people you always feel better for having known them.'

And David Begg's feelings now about Concern, sixteen years after taking office there, twelve years after he left?

'Concern forever!' He adds wryly: 'It's the Hotel California, isn't it? You can never really check out.... Well ... you may check out, but you check back in again immediately!'

18

Do all the good you can. By all the means you can.
In all the ways you can.
In all the places you can. At all the times you can.
To all the people you can.
As long as ever you can.

– Preacher John Wesley

U p to mid-September 2014, the origins of Aengus Finucane's most well-known mantra *Do as much as you can ...* has remained obscure and speculative amongst those of whom the question was asked.

The riddle is solved during an interview with one of his senior management team. Almost casually, Howard Dalzell, who is a Methodist, mentions that, although adapted by Aengus, the broad concept, as quoted at the head of this chapter, comes from the exhortations of John Wesley (1703–1791), priest, theologian and evangelist preacher, and one of the founders of Methodism.

The Reverend Ivan Biggs, a Methodist minister, was one of the co-founding directors of the ecumenical group who set up Africa Concern in the late sixties alongside the Supreme Knight of Columbanus, the Holy Ghost contingent and others, including lay people. Although we will never know for sure, his influence on the founders – and his own founder's principles

and sayings – may even have somehow prompted, consciously
or by osmosis, Aengus's adaptation.

This would be logical. The Reverend Wesley never actually
left the Anglican Church to which he had been ordained, but,
according to the literature, within it developed his own doctrine
of 'pure' Christianity, personal accountability and (see Aengus
Finucane) social justice. Throughout his ministry, he preached,
for instance, in favour of prison reform and abolition of the slave
trade. (See Aengus again….)

'He clearly identified with it, with that social thing,' says
Dalzell about the late CEO of Concern.

> He was passionate about doing good for poor people,
> as happy as [that pig simile!] when standing amongst
> poor people in the slums of Bangladesh or in the vil-
> lages. Not in a voyeuristic way. A bit paternalistic – he
> thought he knew what was best for them – but he was
> genuinely interested and concerned about them, so that
> should never be forgotten. 'Concern' is a word that fits
> him.

Although retired now, Dalzell continues to work as a consultant
in the agricultural-economics arena, and not just directly for
Concern. On the day of the interview in his granite-walled
cottage amongst the hills of deepest Wicklow, where his terraced
back garden is lush, as might be expected, with a mesmerising
and densely planted display of variegated greenery, he is just
finishing a document for presentation at an international
conference.

Originally from Belfast, Howard spent seventeen years in
India as an NGO volunteer, but came back to Ireland in the
mid-eighties because he and his wife wanted to provide an Irish
secondary education for their three teenage children, and places
had been secured for them in Wesley College.

When they got there, however, times were tough and jobs
were hard to find, and seventeen years spent volunteering does

not allow for nest eggs, so with those three teenagers to provide for, their father needed work quickly.

As an aside, he mentions that the period in question gave him quite an insight into poverty – not absolute poverty, as in Concern's client countries, but poverty as has existed in Ireland in the past and again in the present austerity regime amongst some of the affected population: 'Burgers and bread-only type poverty.'

Ironically, although Concern did not know him, Dalzell knew Concern. He had gone to the subcontinent from England, where he was then working in 1968, just as Africa Concern was being formed. He had been, he says, 'a "Biafran Activist" ' in the period just before he left. So, when he got back, he applied to Concern in the normal manner, but officially was told that, although his agriculture-development work in India was very much in the Concern mode, there were no vacancies for people in his area of expertise at the time. Nevertheless, he was advised (by Mary Humphreys, who had interviewed him) to contact the CEO, Father Aengus Finucane.

At their first meeting, Howard Dalzell's impressions of Aengus, like those of everyone else encountering this priest for the first time, were of size, charisma and warmth. He was also struck by Father Finucane's compassion – not just for Concern's poor, but for the family plight of the man sitting in front of him: a man who did not own a suit, and who had cobbled together some sort of interview outfit from his well-worn collection of Indian garb. After quite a bit of 'enjoyable' discussion, Aengus offered Howard a job as an adviser on agriculture.

Very quickly, however, he promoted Dalzell through the administrative ranks until the Belfast man eventually became Head of Overseas, one of three senior managers layered just below the role of Chief Executive in the three-member Senior Management Team. So he is in a good position to speak on the achievements of Concern through the final eleven years, 1986 to 1997, and of his superior's sixteen-year tenure.

Right through that period, he says, the organisation, enthusiastically pushed by its CEO, went through massive development and expansion. When Dalzell joined, five countries were served by Concern programmes. By 1999, just two years after Aengus's resignation and his replacement by David Begg, the organisation, with that wind of momentum still behind it, was operating in twenty-two countries with 2,500 staff.

David Begg continued to steer that expansion throughout his own term of office. It was in turn then taken on by his successor, Tom Arnold, so that at one point in 2006 the totals were thirty-two countries with 3,750 staff, and as more and more nations, particularly in Africa, begin to build capacity to take care of their own citizens, the flexibility and reaction speed of the organisation has also come to the fore.

Back in the Concern headquarters of the mid-nineties, confirming what David Begg has mentioned – the spiky professional relationship between Aengus and his senior management team towards the end of the CEO's official leadership in Camden Street – Howard Dalzell says that, at times, his own liaisons with his boss were 'extraordinarily difficult. Unprintable.'

He is at pains, however, to point out that he owes Aengus a lot:

He gave me a job when jobs were thin on the ground, partly from compassion for having come back to Ireland with little capital and three teenage kids, but also because he did recognise that I had a lot of very valuable experience.

It is not often, he chuckles, that an agronomist walks into your office offering seventeen years of experience in all types of agricultural fieldwork, including forestry, in a place like India. And after he started work in Camden Street, he says, 'within Concern, Aengus also imparted recognition to me as a Methodist amongst Catholics. He knew a lot about Methodism, he had worked with Methodists early on.'

Personally, they got along fine most of the time. They had a lot of similar interests, including sports, for instance. 'And at times I had a brilliant relationship with him – I enjoyed his humour, his generosity his love of sport, his consideration for others …'.

He gives examples of the latter:

A lot of people fell out of the Catholic Church in Africa. Aengus would get to know about them, get them to do a year's diploma in Kimmage or something like that, and he'd look after them, make sure they were all right.

Within such care, was there perhaps a subconscious motivation to get these dropouts back into the fold?

No. Definitely not. He knew they were gone, but they needed assistance, both material and physical. He employed a lot of them too – to an extent there were accusations within Concern along the lines of: *It's not a remedial hospital we're running here.* And for sure there were people who could not have competed in the jobs market. But Aengus would say: 'They can contribute and we can use them. If we don't, they'll be out there on the street.'

   An interest in people – that I would say is his defining positive characteristic. And, you know, a lot of people in aid hate poverty, but they don't have much interest in poor people!

Still on Aengus's plus side, like many others, Howard credits him with the saving of Concern from the depredations of Alex Tarbett. 'There is no doubt about that. It could have, maybe would have, gone under without him.' And after the crisis was over and the organisation was again in 'normal' mode, he says that the CEO remained zealously alert in ensuring that such a situation could never happen again, separating out the trusted staff who would open incoming mail, for instance, to make sure that no cheques, postal orders or any form of donation could be purloined: 'All mail was opened. Except for letters marked *personal, private and confidential,* I don't think I ever got a letter that wasn't.'

He also instances the priest's continuing and huge rapport with the Irish public: 'Through the seventies, eighties and early nineties, he understood the Irish people. He understood the influence an Irish priest could have, and he built us into Ireland's premier aid organisation.'

Financial heft was, necessarily, being added to the expansion of theatres of operation outlined above. At the time Dalzell joined, Concern was largely a volunteer organisation in the field, raising money in Ireland both north and south:

> ... although a bit *ultra vires* in the north because the company hadn't been properly registered at the time. [It has been now for many years]. Turnover was between three to four million, Concern wasn't well known inter-nationally. Overseas they knew about 'Irish Concern' and so on, but as an organisation at a European or UN level it didn't really count.

But by the time he retired from his post as Overseas Director in 2008, the number of countries had increased (from the six Concern was working in when Dalzell joined) to twenty-five, all glaringly poor: 'The Somalias, Rwandas, Mozambiques, Haitis, all those from the real bottom forty,' and the organisation's fundraising reach was now not only in the Republic but in the UK, Europe and the US. Its budget by then had gone up to fifty million, which, even allowing for inflation, achieved a real increase of 10 per cent every year. (As of February 2014 it was €165m, with 3,500 staff working in twenty-seven countries.)

During the same period, Concern's public profile had increased enormously. According to Dalzell, it had become one of the top UK agencies – 'top five in overall volume,' and with its membership of the Disasters Emergency Committee, as we heard from Rose Caldwell of the London office, it was very well recognised, not just by its peers, but by the British government, both for emergency response and development work in civil society.

And he gives full credit to Aengus for establishing the basic momentum, which resulted in getting the organisation into those positions and which continues to this day.

So much, so positive, so sincerely offered.

To be fair, what follows next is sometimes hesitant, but there is no gainsaying Howard Dalzell's firm view of the difficulties he experienced at the top of Concern in outlook, in analysis, and particularly in management style towards the end of Aengus's tenure.

When David Begg took office in 1997, a major component of what has been presented in the previous chapter as one of the primary problems with which he had immediately to deal – *sorting out internal relationships and communications issues* – had its roots in the strain that had developed between Aengus and his senior management team. There were differences of opinion on many matters, not least methods of fundraising, but in chief, the way the organisation should be run. It can be encapsulated thus: Aengus believed that when he returned from illness he could simply carry on as before, but there had been a fundamental change in his absence.

On fundraising:

> ... he thought we had reached the limits in terms of raising money from the public in Ireland – and we certainly had in terms of church-gate collections and the roadshow that went around promoting the Christmas Fast and so on. But he had begun to lose touch a little bit – and he also didn't realise that the church was no longer the good fundraising base it had been.

One of the interesting points that Dalzell makes on this score is that local fundraisers in Ireland – whether in parishes, villages, towns, townlands or cities – are vocational. While they

will organise fundraisers for Concern, they will do so too for
Trócaire, Goal, the Lifeboats, the GAA, a child facing treatment
for Leukaemia – all sorts of continuous good causes: 'It's the
same people all the time.'

But during the growing economic boom, he says, Aengus
could not see the latent opportunities for less traditionally
personal forms of fundraising, 'for instance this face-to-face
on the streets,' the highly successful and lucrative chugging
adopted by his successor, David Begg, with Sally Anne
Kinahan.

> This was just being developed in the UK at the time,
> but he couldn't see it as a possibility here. He couldn't
> see that, in Ireland, there were now lots of young and
> youngish Irish people doing well, who now had money,
> and were idealistic enough to donate.

And tolerant enough to pause and listen to the spiels of Duracell
Bunnies that were stopping them in the street with their bright
smiles and cheery: 'Do you have a minute?'

With the growing and diversifying international operations of
the organisation making more demands on its spending, however,
Dalzell says that the senior managers did recognise this at the time,
and in fact were already leveraging the inflow of funds:

> By the early nineties we were using the money that was
> being raised within Ireland to lever more, so much so
> that Concern's Aid programme was now bigger than
> the Irish Government's. There was money available
> from the UK government and from the EU – and we'd
> absolutely moved into position for that.

By the mid-nineties, therefore, just when Aengus Finucane had
perforce to be absent, a high percentage of Concern's funds were
coming from EU/UK/Irish government and UN bodies, so that
leverage of the Irish money was not just a possibility, but a fact.

Howard Dalzell's description of the professional and interpersonal difficulties that arose around differences of opinion on matters such as this between the CEO and the other two members of the management team is bracing.

If once again a cliché might be permitted, there are two sides to every story, and although he has a staunch battalion of fervent and loyal defenders, Aengus is not here to give his side about what happened during the very personal 'troubles' within the top echelons of Concern in the two years or so before he retired. As we already know, these seem to have peaked around the time that he returned to his desk after that severe brush with illness arising from the 'poison pen' incident.

What 'tipped things over the edge,' he believes, was that that his six to nine months' absence had coincided with that time of enormous growth when the three senior managers had simply stepped up to the concept of 'Just do it.' Therefore, when he got back, things had moved on, their tails were up and their leader's management style came into sharp focus when he attempted to re-establish control in the way he had always so successfully done before.

> He tried to regain it without realising Concern hadn't done that badly in his absence. And he didn't realise that he could have regained that leadership by working through other people, but he just didn't know how to do that. Aengus was a very charismatic, very energetic leader, but he liked To Be In Charge.

Dalzell's tone inserts those auditory capital letters with bell-clear emphasis – and with them, we're back to the *was Aengus an autocrat?* debate. Dalzell is in no doubt regarding on which side of this he sits:

> I think he felt he could do everybody's job better than they could themselves. He might have been right, but he couldn't do them all at once. And if something didn't go exactly as he would have done, he would let you

know. He wouldn't tell you exactly what he would have wanted you to do, but you did get clobbered.

Dalzell's considered opinion is that Aengus:

> ... stimulated the organisation to grow, but in some ways he didn't grow with it. He kept going at his style of management, but as the organisation continued to grow, it needed a different style.

Insightful, imaginative entrepreneur as he was – and acknowledged as such by all, he had been a terrific manager in the old-fashioned, traditional way when he had undisputed control. But Aengus was by nature and training essentially a leader from the front. Again and again people said he was 'a born leader.' That judgement is absolutely authentic. And yes, his quality of leadership was innate.

But ten years of priestly and teacher training was followed by ten further years during which, starting at the relatively early age of 28, he enjoyed sole authority as a missionary and held sway over throngs of people. Then there came Biafra – dangerous but exciting – with action at its core.

These experiences culminated in Aengus's stewardship during his first major field appointment for Concern in Bangladesh, where he could shine, and did shine – a guiding star to his corps of young, impressionable volunteers, able and qualified in their respective professions, but in many cases only beginning their careers. As *paterfamilias,* he led very confidently and with conviction from the front, and could make undisputed decisions based on his own judgement. So his modus operandi was set, was in its time very successful, and was given a high degree of respect.

Now, however, he was faced with a very different scenario. His beloved organisation had become a highly organised business, staffed with opinionated people qualified and equipped to argue with him about methods and even core values. For him this was difficult because he had hired a lot of them, including Howard Dalzell.

The best manager he ever worked with, says Dalzell, once told him:

> Efficiency is organised laziness.... If you can get some-
> one else to do it well, a lot more will happen than if you
> try to do it all yourself. If your definition of manage-
> ment is working through other people, Aengus didn't
> normally have that trick, although at times he did.

For the latter, he instances the CEO's deployment of Mike McDonagh, 'one of the best assets Concern ever had. When there was some disaster, Mike didn't worry about the finer points of detailed management, he got on with it, driving people.' Aengus instinctively recognised the advantages of the way Mike worked: We would be discussing Somalia and Rwanda and so on, and he would say to me: 'I think it's time to play the McDonagh card.'

Mike was a very cute manager in some ways: he would pull good people from everywhere, not paying any attention to administration. Aengus knew this, but he also knew that in agreeing to deploy him I would say: 'I'll send in the vacuum cleaner in three months' time and we'll clean up afterwards, but we should let him manage the disaster. We can't mess about getting the administration right while people are dying, starving, being abused ... we need action.'

That, of course, was music to the ears of both McDonagh and Aengus Finucane. So it's clear that, while delegation was an arrow in Aengus's quiver, it was deployed when he himself was the initiator.

Like many people predisposed towards action, he was suspicious, even dismissive, of the modern business strategic concepts of Mission Statements, Core Values and all the rest of it, instinctively believing that relying on concepts and conceptualisation created 'paralysis by analysis' in organisations. As Eithne Healy has remarked, he would consistently demand of strategies presented: *What's in it for the poor person?*

From 1994 onwards, Dalzell says, an additional stress for Father Finucane was the apparent loss of ground by the

Catholic Church with regard to its laity. 'Plus the fact,' he adds, 'that purity welfare money was getting harder to source because donors were thinking harder about what they were giving money for.'

This was particularly evident in the struggling US setup. This, cannily, had been instituted by Concern's CEO in the wake of the Rwandan crisis (where Concern did develop a US profile, as we know) as a way to secure not just personal contributions from a hinterland of forty million Irish-Americans, but as a conduit to USaid.

'But,' says Dalzell, 'yes there were forty million Irish-Americans, but there were 160 million other Americans who were not, and the Irish card does not work with them. The Irish card works only with pockets of Irish America.'

The vast majority of US citizens, therefore, were sceptical about donating to a small Irish aid organisation – albeit with a US office – operating in countries overseas, many of which they could not pick out on a map, and could even have been, for all they knew, inimical to American global or domestic interests.

So these potential personal donors and philanthropists across the Atlantic, who might have been persuaded to part with their money for Bangladeshis, Haitians, a panoply of starving Africans, Afghans or North Koreans, were asking probing questions about how their money was being administered, and on whom and what it was being spent – and, crucially, what forms of tax breaks were attached to it.

All the difficulties and stresses coalesced around the mid-nineties, which made life very difficult for Aengus Finucane, who was returning to his big chair in Camden Street with spirit undiminished, but physically not having fully recovered from the disastrous accident with his pen – he was also in pain from increasing back problems.

He was by nature a great networker, but according to Howard Dalzell there were limits to his networks. He didn't want to get involved, for instance, with government officials:

> We had realised that there was an increase in finan-
> cial allocations to the Department of Foreign Affairs
> and that, given our credibility, mission and reach with
> the Irish public and ability to deliver programmes effi-
> ciently, we should have been able to apply for the lion's
> share of the funds in its aid division.

But they had difficulty in persuading Aengus that a direct
request for such a lion's share was the thing to do. 'He would
rattle about the government every so often in the media about
this,' but when it came right down to it, seemed reluctant to
engage forcefully. There was a lunch arranged, but, according
to Dalzell, Aengus remained as charming as ever, but on the
subject at hand, curiously far away.

He contrasts this with David Begg's attitude to the
department, whose largesse he felt was seriously lacking: 'We're
now flying a much bigger flag than they are in aid funding –
we're going to get a much bigger grant from them …'. So he
requested a meeting, got it, and with Jack Finucane, Howard
Dalzell and some other seniors, apparently lost no time in laying
into officials and demanding bigger and better funding.

All of the above being said, Howard Dalzell does
acknowledge fully that without the personal vision, utter
commitment and energy of Aengus Finucane, Concern
would not have risen to the level it did in any sphere –
including fundraising, and that its guiding principle and ethos
– that all efforts were fundamentally to be directed at the
poorest of the poor – may not have been so unwavering. (In
the context of Aengus's commitment, another thing Dalzell
says is that he believes the priest was so psychologically
bound up with his organisation that, in his mind, he and it
were one and the same thing, which made any challenge to
him, or to Concern, very difficult for him or anyone else
to handle.)

Howard also fully acknowledges Aengus's post-retirement
contribution to the entire Concern effort via the US. It was

successful, because that Irish–American cohort saw him not just as a trustworthy figurehead, but as someone lovable, with a marvellous personal history and a talent for storytelling. They marvelled that the 'fire in his belly' still blazed as brightly as it had at the beginning of his career in the aid world, and respected him because of his evident spirituality. He was also a repository of that great Irish quality, a sense of fun. For them, he was the best of Old Ireland.

Howard Dalzell remembers with affection a lot of genial social interaction, sports chats, stories and laughs. The breakdown in communication towards the end was unfortunate, but after he himself retired he went to visit Aengus in Kimmage. 'We made our peace, and I think mutual respect was restored.'

19

'I would be very happy to be named as a patron of Concern Worldwide USA.
I simply cannot see myself refusing to do that.'

— Seamus Heaney (15 February 1996)

The involvement in Concern of Michael Lally began with a trip to Ethiopia in 1986.

After the 1984 famine, he had been assigned by RTÉ to 'take a look' at the farming/agriculture situation, with the Irish Farmers' Association as sponsor. Before he left, he asked for advice internally in the station about who to talk to get an advance feel of what he should be looking for. He was told to 'avoid the Finucanes' and to work through the channels of another agency. So he did.

> But I didn't find the person I spoke to all that convincing. I had always thought that Third World agencies would be centres of love and fellowship and all of that, and this was the first glimmer I got about the extraordinary rivalry between them. That first agency I had approached had been very condescending about Concern.

Being the good journalist that he is, Lally went along to Camden Street to find out for himself. He met Aengus and Jacqueline Duffy, and was not to know right away, but that 'bit of a chat' meant he had checked into the Hotel California. The approach took place on a Sunday afternoon. 'I was travelling the following day. Aengus's opening line? "You've left it a bit early, haven't you?" '

Why was he advised to avoid the Finucanes?

'Too much to the fore. Very strong with opinions, and seen to toe the Church line.' That was the attitude within RTÉ at the time.

Some time after that first trip, Aengus and Jacqueline came to him with a request. Father Michael Doheny, who for many years had faithfully film-documented Concern's activities at home and overseas, had suffered a stroke. Aengus and Jacqueline were 'just wondering' if there would be 'any chance' that he could get a camera crew 'free gratis' who could carry on the work. 'And of course you were expected to get it broadcast as well.'

The result was a further ten or twelve trips abroad to film documentaries, 'to Vietnam, Cambodia, Bangladesh – Aengus's biggest love.'

This priest had snagged him so closely that later, in America, Lally felt he could broach what initially he saw as the incongruity of someone of that size stumping on behalf of famine victims: 'This doesn't look good with Americans, Aengus ...'.

His friend's response was a defensive: 'Everyone is fat here!'

On that score, it would be a mistake to think that Aengus was insouciant about his weight. He did attempt to control it, many times. His family constantly badgered him about it, and he had on many occasions attempted the cabbage soup diet (Patsy), the grape diet (Brigid Ryan and Ciaran Kitching), and many other regimes, exotic or otherwise. And just as in the overseas fields, many of the 'clients' readily accepted his size – 'it's what we aspire to' – Lally eventually did too:

> The bulk became part of his personality. It was the whole package. If Aengus ever gave you a hug, you were *hugged*! This man was enormity in every sense

219

of the word and I think at the time I was just being politically correct.

As for that warning within RTÉ that the CEO of Concern (as he was then) toed the Roman Catholic Church line, Lally, who is in a position to know, draws the distinction between the public and private priest. 'Publicly, he adopted a certain reserve when it came to certain areas. He was afraid that things he would say would be construed as Church policy,' for instance in the matters of birth control, divorce, abortion and the promulgation of condoms to counteract Aids.

In conversation, however, and even in private correspondence, he was, for example, highly supportive of Ursula Sharpe's campaign in Uganda to promote condom use, where publicity and education methods employed included having vans driving around displaying in large letters, the legend: *It's Not On If It's Not On!*

There were times when he encountered challenges to this private support and was not found wanting. Many altruistic Irish–American funders and donors in the States lived in the conservative wing of Church teachings on sexual morality. One, a hugely and repeatedly generous donor, wrote to Aengus expressing serious disquiet, even alarm, about the notion of Concern advocating any policy except sexual abstinence in the fight against Aids.

Aengus's reply was long, thoughtful, diplomatic and conciliatory, but nonetheless firm. Although it is too long for quotation in its entirety, it is worth conveying its flavour, if only to show that while he was indeed conservative, he was far from toeing the Church line. It is also very interesting because of its subtle revelation of the steel underpinning the cheeriness for which he was so well known.

Greetings from Sandymount in Dublin, where I am killing two birds with the one stone! First of all I am responding to your letters of Dec 15th and 19th. At the same time I am practising my typing and letter-writing on the computer. This will be the first time you have had a typed letter from me. This is progress as I head towards 72, isn't it?

In your letters you make some very good points. My priority in identifying projects which I will propose to you is to ensure they are truly addressing extreme need in a meaningful way.

Frequently, there is a certain leap of faith called for. We may have to knock on many doors. Not too many are interested in funding dire poverty needs. Concern certainly always endeavours to build up the self-respect and self-reliance of those assisted. But we try to be realistic in our expectations about what can be achieved. And we approach the search for funds in a spirit of confidence knowing that God never closes one door without opening another.

Quite often, however, I could not absolutely say that something would not be done if a particular funder did not support it.

When I was CEO I sometimes upset the board of directors by my readiness to take risks and spend any funds in hand to meet urgent needs. I keep a letter written to me by a board member after I retired as CEO. I got from it: 'ultimately, the Almighty will provide', and that in order that He could, leaps of faith and conviction were required.

In the context of this overall thinking, your very generous contributions have made a huge difference for great numbers of very poor people.

Concern first began addressing the Aids scourge in 1989. An ex-Concern volunteer nurse had joined the Medical Missionaries of Mary. She was posted to Uganda and became very involved in addressing the Aids problem in that country. Indeed, she has now become somewhat of an authority in that whole sector at an international level. Sr Ursula Sharpe requested me to send Concern personnel to Uganda to work in her area of operations. We did so, focusing our efforts principally on caring for the huge numbers of children orphaned by Aids. In many cases we were supporting grandparents who were caring for ten to fifteen children whose parents had died. We supported *schooling and youth activities. Educating young people about the dangers of casual sex was an important part of our approach.*

Aids in Africa is spread through heterosexual activity. Uganda was one of the first and hardest hit countries. In Africa, attitudes to sexual morality are very permissive and women have virtually no hope of saying 'no' to advances. This is particularly so in marriage. I see the education of girls as the single factor most likely to change that situation. In Concern-run or supported schools – and there are very many of them – we endeavour to ensure that 50 per cent of those being educated are girls. Medication alone will never solve this terrible problem. Abstinence, it is true, is the only certain way of avoiding infection. This can be advocated and this is being done, but the likelihood of universal heeding of this advice is very remote indeed.

I look forward to meeting you while I am back in the US and would be delighted to discuss the foregoing and the many other issues which are so central to the work of Concern.

May God bless you and your family and grant you a truly Happy and Peaceful 2004.

Steel hand in God's velvet glove?

In any event, it is a measure of the respect in which this donor held Aengus that he responded with a rather moving letter, illustrative of the sincerity of religious faith in an entire generation of Irish people, and the esteem in which they held its clerical practitioners. His letter was short, but in it he wrote in essence that he trusted 'Father Finucane', wished God's blessing on the work, pledged support and over the next few years, continued to pour his money into the coffers of Concern.

Basically, his letter said, if Father Finucane thought it was okay, then that was good enough for him.

Michael Lally, (no longer a humble journo but Leader of RTÉ Regions Project, Head of *Nuacht* RTÉ/TG4 and president of the Circom alliance of thirty-eight regional broadcasters in Europe) is no shrinking violet. He and Aengus had vicious rows about the latter's switch, or not, from private to public views on Aids matters, birth control, abortion and divorce. 'In social areas like that, when speaking one to one, no problem. But it was different when the red light went on.'

Aengus's public conservatism extended to his organisation. At one point, during a filming expedition, he expressed serious misgivings about the way some aid projects – and not just Concern's – were being funded and run. In his opinion they were not up to scratch, but he would not say this on camera and, despite arguments, remained adamant:' "No! I will only say what would be the current view of the organisation." We were dug out of one another for ten days, it nearly destroyed our relationship.'

Their last documentary together was during Aengus's final field trip to Haiti in 2008:

> We were filming the women's projects, and there was nothing there he had a basic problem with. But when things began to go further, very graphically promulgating birth control, Aids population control, sexually transmitted diseases – I noticed he was hanging back. I asked him afterwards if he was uncomfortable and he said he wasn't personally, 'but I'm conscious of the collar and all the contradictions.'
>
> He was very good at knowing his constituency - nuns, fundraisers, [older Irish-American donors] – and while in that context he did wear the collar in every sense of the word it wasn't even mentioned if he thought it wasn't appropriate.
>
> He loved being a priest, but there was an innocence about him.

In the last years of Aengus's life, Michael would bring an Indian or Italian takeaway meal to the Sandymount apartment every second Monday. Sometimes joined by Tom Arnold, they would eat, shoot the breeze and frequently argue, but on more than one occasion the priest, having read a newspaper report of a court case involving sexual abuse, would ask his guest to explain certain phrases being used about some of the more deviant sexual practices alleged.

Wearing the collar, though, was a universal calling card. 'It was simple and back to basics, this notion that if someone had a heart attack in the street and needed the Last Rites, how would they know you were a priest?'

The changes coming for Aengus were already evident, according to Lally, the second time they went together to Bangladesh in 1990. As stated many times by many volunteers and others, he had always based his management of Concern's fields on the missionary model, where the workers lived together and were taken care of in the community.

> Now they were all moving out into different houses. Aine Fay was the field director at the time, and despite her 'gently explaining' these were the changes that were happening because of the need for privacy in the staff's own relationships, he was very taken aback. As CEO, he had been mostly deskbound in the previous few years, and hadn't realised the extent of change afoot, although in reality, it was minuscule.

Despite Aengus's written support of the Aids prevention campaign being run by Ursula Sharpe in Uganda, at one stage, according to Sister Ursula herself, he 'was not happy' when there were decisions made in some fields that, because of the spread of Aids, condom dispensers should be installed in all bathrooms in Concern houses.

To Lally, Aengus's reaction to these changes 'manifested itself as the beginning of it being the time for him to move on.' In the period just before he did:

> ... he'd come through a very bad period of ill health, back, hip, knee, the blood poisoning thing ('Imagine! Finucane survived Somalia and was killed by his own

pen!' had become another of the mantras.) I would always have argued that his exit should have been a managed one.

He had brought the organisation as far as he could, and it was time to hand over to someone who could bring it to the next level, with a package giving him a role as the Arch Fundraiser. Which, of course, was what he did end up doing.

Anyhow, Lally, having accepted the invitation to go to New York (armed with the vaguest of instructions: 'talk to business people, talk to Michael Smurfit') was, along with Siobhan Walsh, struggling with his brief to rescue the US operation. He hit a beneficial bend, too early and gentle to call it turning a corner, at an American-Irish Chamber of Commerce dinner.

Former Taoiseach Albert Reynolds was guest of honour at this do, and before going out to the States, Lally, having spoken to Reynolds's government press officer, ex-RTÉ colleague Sean Duignan, had an invitation for himself and the new honorary president of Concern US to attend. 'And I also got Diggy to ask Albert if he would mention Aengus in his speech.'

The two of them sat anxiously, along with 'the six or seven hundred biggies' in the room, while Albert gave a long, long speech, 'all over the place, round the kitchen and mind the dresser,' until finally the Taoiseach said: 'but here tonight is a man who has done more for the world ... I want ye to dig deep ...'. He paused to take an envelope out of his pocket, peered at it, then said: 'There are two guys here tonight. I want them to stand up. Aengus Finucane and Michael Lally!' They stood up.

> I want ye to know Michael Lally – he's a journalist and you might get to know him. But the most important person here is Father Aengus Finucane. And I just want to tell ye – ye meet a lot of hucksters in this world who

come and go. Concern is the best organisation, they're starting up in the States and I want to ask the Irish-American community now to stand behind Aengus Finucane!

Lally's view is:

That just opened things up. All the state agencies were there that night. The IDA was the one that opened the doors for us: *Albert says we've to open doors, we'll open doors.* With the IDA on board, now it's kosher.

At the end of the dinner, Michael Smurfit came up to Aengus and myself and said: 'I'll give you free advertising for Concern in every publication I have – weekly or whatever it is, from now until the end of February. Whatever you want, it's all yours.' And as he walked away, he said: 'I'll have someone talk to you about this.'

And then Aengus said: 'Who's that?'

Smurfit Kappa Group? 42,000 employees? Biggest packaging manufacturing group in the world? Builder of the Smurfit Graduate School of Business at UCD?

That's who 'that' had been – one of the wealthiest men in Ireland, whose origins were from the world of publishing.

That was on 13 November. Smurfit was as good as his word, and the pair, now a trio with Siobhan Walsh, then began to work, 'kind of at arm's length at first,' on relationships with other 'biggies' in the States. It was a steep learning curve. Although he was clutching a cheque ('This is an F-off donation'), Lally was shown the door of the office of one *really* big Irish-American player because: ' "You came in here and you didn't know your ask." He was dead right: I didn't.'

Lesson learned, sort of. They were attempting to identify other potentially big donors when they got a tip-off from the vice president of Chemical Bank, Jeremiah O'Leary, that Tom Moran was the man to track down. Now follows a picture of how the Irish network operates in the cities, and even the states, of North America.

Gerry Morrissey of the Irish state's Export Board *Córas Tráchtála* and Eamonn Ryan of Ireland's Industrial Development Authority, the IDA, were on a working group with Niall O'Dowd of Irish Central.com, *Irish America* Magazine and the *Irish Voice* newspaper.

Jeremiah O'Leary was a cousin of Bart Cronin, ex-Aer Lingus, and at the time press and information officer at the Irish Department for Tourism, Sport and Recreation.

This group agreed that yes, Tom Moran should be the target. Born on Staten Island, with an Irish father and Italian mother, he had been second in command to Bill Flynn (the same Bill Flynn who would later be associated with the Irish peace process) at a huge corporate entity called Mutual of America. Flynn was moving on and Tom Moran was now taking over.

> Tom Moran was one of the biggies out there who hadn't been tapped yet, so Niall and Jeremiah invited me to a dinner of the Friendly Sons of St Patrick.

The dinner was attended and the introduction was made. Aengus came out from Ireland for a consequent lunch at Gallagher's Steakhouse with Moran and his deputy, Ed Kenney, a former head of counter-insurgency for the FBI. The lunch was less than productive. Moran, knowing all too well what was afoot, made sure to dominate the conversation, even at one stage opening up another line by showing Aengus where his name was located on the wall of the restaurant. Lally saw what was happening and was getting progressively madder with Aengus, who seemed to be decidedly unimpressed with the plaque on the wall, and was not behaving as though this was the critical event it undoubtedly was:

> 'I have one of those in my office,' he said, and then he made a smart comment about the old tradition in the Catholic Church whereby people who had enough

money would buy seats in the chapel. I could see Moran
looking at him and I was thinking: *Bye Bye, Tom!*

Tom kept talking; Aengus kept being, well, off-form, and Lally
was almost catatonic with embarrassment when, out of the blue,
there was a spark of redemption. On being offered an Irish coffee,
Aengus said it was a sinful thing to ruin good Irish whiskey by
putting coffee into it. 'And that's where the relationship started.'

Ed Kenney, Tom's deputy, then prompted Aengus and Lally
to make their pitch. At the end, he said to them: 'Well you guys
didn't get much time to talk!'

Ed, interviewed in his office down the hall from Tom
Moran's, is still chuckling about that first meeting with Aengus.

Afterwards, Tom got me outside: 'Don't you *ever* do that
to me again. The *reason* I talk like that is that I don't want
to give those guys the chance to ask any questions!'

No, that meeting didn't go well for Concern....

Mutual of America has always been identified with Irish causes
because of Bill Flynn. He had been invited to the north by
Mairead Corrigan, came back and dived into the peace process
with people like Niall O'Dowd and Chuck Feeney, who were
taking a page from the Tip O'Neills and Ted Kennedys. Ed
Kenney explains:

So these fundraisers look around and they say to themselves this Mutual of America seems to have a green
tinge, and we're deluged. At social events, people come
up and try to head Tom off....

Next thing we're in Dublin. Clinton is in town and
we're at a social event in Dublin Castle, and who's there
but Aengus and Siobhan. They had had her hidden away
in the office during that first lunch. We meet at the dinner,
and in those days we used to stay in the Berkeley Court,

and we all go back to the Berkeley Court for Irish coffees at three o'clock in the morning. Siobhan is at Aengus:

'Aengus, we have to go …'.

'I'm fine, I'm fine, these nights will never come again …'.

All was well in the end. Siobhan and the two Irish-Americans attended Aengus's convent Mass next morning, and from then on there was no breaking apart the personal bonds tying Aengus Finucane and Tom Moran together as buddies.

There was, however, one more thing to do. 'We still hadn't consummated the donor side of the deal when I got a phone call from Ed Kenney,' says Michael Lally, who then relates how that was facilitated.

Bill Flynn, who was still the chair of Mutual of America, had been asked to deliver a memorial at the anniversary of the death of Bobby Sands. Would I be able to help?

So there I was, sitting at the top of the Mutual skyscraper on Park Avenue with Bill Flynn and Tom Moran. It wasn't an oration they needed, thank God. They wanted me to read only for fact and tone, wanted it to be accurate, and the facts to outweigh any emotion he might feel, pro or anti.

At the beginning of the relationships with Tom and Ed, Aengus hadn't paid due homage, but he was learning. He had a unique trick: when a big donor would ring him to say he was very worried about Concern's funding of operations in Pakistan ('I've just been reading about what they're doing to convents over there'), he could play the traditional Irish priest. With Tom, he was on another level. He flowered.

Doors opened for him, and the Americans loved him. One of his sayings that Tom understood was that when you sup with the devil you need a long spoon, but he never said who the devil was.

Tom Moran coming on board was key.

20

'I drank the Kool-Aid.'

– Tom Moran (chairman, Concern US)

Let's deal first with Tom Moran's business credentials as they stand at the time of writing.

Thomas J. Moran chairs at least six boards, including his own at Mutual of America and that of Concern US. He serves on at least seven others, including the Taoiseach's Economic Advisory Board, Aer Lingus and the Ireland–US Council for Commerce and Industry. Having graduated with a degree in Mathematics, he has been awarded four honorary doctorates, including one each from UCD and Queen's, is a trustee of the Citizens Budget Commission in the US, and has been honoured with (at least) six major awards, including the Calvary Hospital Medal of Honour, New York City Fire Department Humanitarian Award, the Commissioner's Award of the New York City Police Foundation and the Ellis Island Medal of Honour. He has presented at the World Economic Forum and at the Petra Conference of Nobel Laureates. His company supports 15,000 charities, and is affiliated to 45,000 more. In the day job at Mutual, he is responsible for the management of $15bn worth of assets.

We are meeting in his office in the Mutual Building on Park Avenue on a crisp November morning. His expanse of windows frames not only other emporia of glass and steel across the street, but Saint Bartholomew's Church, which, jewel-like, nestles quietly between 50th and 51st Streets. He is very proud of that view, as he ought to be. The church is one of New York's landmark buildings, with a history of musical excellence. One of its former choir directors, brought from Europe by Saint Bart's, was Leopold Stokowski.

Tom wears a Concern lapel pin. He carries two business cards: the first notes his chairmanship (et cetera) of Mutual; the second reminds the world about his chairmanship of Concern US. 'I always carry two cards; I'm trying to get 'em put onto one because I get tired of giving out two.'

He has checked in to the Hotel California. 'Yeah. I drank the Kool-Aid.'

Indeed, there is a photo of Aengus Finucane and other mementos of Tom Moran's 'dear, dear friend' very much in evidence in this office along with a portrait of Jerry Garcia, late and still revered lead singer and songwriter of the band, The Grateful Dead. Broad-bodied, with a thatch of hair and a friendly, open expression, he is, or seems to be, a relaxed kind of guy, the antithesis of the go-getting, driven personality his extraordinary CV might seem to indicate.

Quickly, with entertaining side excursions, he rattles through his life story.

> I grew up on Staten Island. When I was 8 years old and my brother was 10, my mother would give us enough money to come in and ride the subways all day. That's when I fell in love with New York City.

Tom started work when he was 14, working as a janitor in his school, followed by a fast-food joint, where he worked his way up to be a French Fries man. Then a short-order cook in a factory, a cemetery and, for years, a cab driver. 'My entire life was within five boroughs.'

> I had no opportunity to travel, so I made the opportunity. I saved up 800 dollars and travelled around Europe

for two months – pretty hard on 800 dollars – but if I
hadn't done that I would have been like so many people
here; when you watch the main news here, it's embar-
rassing how little we see of the rest of the world. Ireland
is different because it's small and the rest of the world is
overwhelmingly big....

In December 1941, when America entered combat in World
War Two following the Japanese attack on Pearl Harbour, with a
number of his buddies, Tom's dad, who grew up in New Jersey,
rushed to enlist in the navy. They were too young and needed
their parents' signatures, so they ran home.

> My dad was the first one back; the others never showed
> up because their parents wouldn't sign. So he ended up
> in the navy by himself. Iwo Jima, Okinawa and all the
> islands ... never spoke about it....

He becomes visibly upset. This is to become a feature of this
interview. Each time, this grandee of business (and of humanitarian
philanthropy) apologises for showing emotion, as he does many
times, particularly when the name Aengus Finucane is mentioned.
In mitigation, he cites his mother, who was of Italian descent.
He talks about a big party in Atlantic City for his mother's 80th
birthday. Tom was determined that, although his father was in the
last stages of illness, he should be there:

> My brother was upset with me; he didn't think my
> father could make it; he was at death's door. He said
> to me I'd had a lot of bad ideas, but that was posi-
> tively the worst idea I'd ever had: 'What you gonna
> do if he dies down there? You really want he should
> die in a casino?'
>   And I said: 'Don't worry about it. Ed Kenney has
> already spoken to friends tied in to the police down
> there. If he dies we get him down to the car and we give

him a police escort to get him home. We'll put him in bed before anyone knows he's dead.'

Mutual of America went into business as a company designed to help workers who retired with no retirement plans set up for them by their former employers, but morphed into what it is today in 1978.

> Our family is cursed to be in insurance. My grand-father was the first Italian-American to become an officer of Marsh McLennon, my father worked in insurance, my brother now works for an insurance broker and so does my niece. When I got out of col-lege the only thing I was sure of was that I would not work for an insurance company; I'd heard enough insurance talk to last me a lifetime.

When he joined Mutual of America it was known as National Health and Welfare Retirement Association.

> I must have asked them five times: 'Is this an insur-ance company?' If it had been I wouldn't have taken the interview. And they said: 'No, no, we're a retirement association.'
> So I started in 1975, and in 1978 we converted and became a mutual life insurance company....

15,000 charities directly on the books and an affiliation with 45,000 more? Does he actually enjoy all these charity connections?

> One of the great benefits of working with NGOs is that you get to work with some of the nicest people in the world. You also get to see organisations that are well run and well managed by very good people. And some ones that maybe are not so good. But you become quite well trained in saying no in nice ways....

He launches into his version of the sequence of events that culminated in him becoming chairman of Concern US. It echoes those of Ed Kenney and Michael Lally, but is replete with Tom Moran flourishes, social occasions and stories. Lots of stories. Tom Moran could rival Aengus in that department.

What is astonishing, though, is not just the speed with which he and Aengus bonded, but also the depth of human warmth, generosity and respect for others that philanthropy generates in this extraordinary man.

> We had lunch, and I made a point of doing most of the talking so they could not get to the asking. I made it through that lunch, so they never got to ask. But then I was at a black-tie event in Dublin Castle one night, and Aengus and Siobhan Walsh came over to say hello, and I invited the two of them to join us afterwards at Dessie Hynes's pub [O'Donoghue's on Merrion Row]. We all went over and had a wonderful, wonderful night. Then we went back to the Berkeley Court, where they would always wait up for me with bacon sandwiches and Irish coffees because they knew I'd always bring back a crowd. Siobhan kept saying: 'You're meeting the president tomorrow. You have Mass in a few hours' time!'
>
> 'Ah, Siobhan! Nights like these don't come round again.'

And we know the rest. Tom Moran had already entered the Hotel California and had partaken of the Kool-Aid. But when did Concern actually get around to doing the asking?

> It was probably the next trip over. We stayed in touch. They had asked if I would consider joining their board, but I'd explained that at that time I was chairing the US board of the Smurfit Graduate Business School and a number of other boards, and that I just wouldn't have the time, but I would certainly support them financially as best I could.

At this level of business, however, contacts are more valuable than bank balances and an invitation to have lunch at the 21 Club is rarely without a subtext. Tom's friend and fellow Irish-American, John Scanlan, invited him to lunch at that famous eaterie with Aengus and Siobhan Walsh.

Scanlan was 'a player' in the bear-pit of New York Public Relations, having represented, for instance, Ivana Trump in her divorce fight with her former husband, Donald. He was now the Chairman-designate of Concern.

At that lunch, he told Tom that he really needed him on the Concern board.

> He asked me to join as a personal favour, so I agreed. And it was just a few weeks after that, poor John, God rest him, had a massive coronary and passed away, and then Aengus came to see me. And I agreed to be chair out of respect for John, and also for Aengus and Siobhan.

Is it still the case, as we've heard, that in the States, board memberships for charitable organisations involve the donation mantra: *Give, Get, or Get off?*

> That's a theory that some people put forward. It is the responsibility of the organisation to engage its board at a sufficient level that its members would choose to give or get. But I've never participated in a board where there's a minimum requirement of $10,000 or whatever. I think you should give of your own free choice because you care about what the organisation stands for. If you're not giving, it's probably because you don't believe what the organisation stands for and would want to get off.

Tom certainly leads by example. This author has lost count of those who, in the States, extolled Tom Moran's personal generosity to Concern. As for his board members, he has no compunction about laying his cards on the table. 'If I'm going to support something, I like to believe that the people around the boardroom table feel strongly enough about the organisation that, no matter how difficult it is, they find a way of supporting it:

> One of the fellows here said to me once that he went to his priest and said: 'How do I know when I've given enough?' And the priest said: 'When you get a pain in your stomach or your chest, when you get that uneasy feeling, you've probably just given the right amount.'
> So I said to my officer group at one point: 'The choice is yours: you can either have a pain in your chest from giving too much or from having a heart attack – which would you prefer?'
> I think it's important to have that level of commitment. We certainly see that for our Seeds of Hope dinner.

This prestigious black-tie event, held in early December every year, is the single biggest fundraiser for Concern US, and on behalf of Concern, the organisers approach the people who knew Aengus and who knew Siobhan.

The Seeds of Hope Dinner (held in the Grand Ballroom of the Waldorf Astoria when it is available), he says:

> … is our chance to make a statement and to show how good we can be.
> (Aengus would have shone?)
> Oh absolutely. We try to keep the dinner itself very tightly run. At my request he would do the invocation every year and then say a few words. Siobhan would pre-edit to keep it tight, and she would sit across the table and give him hand signals, hand-across-the-neck if he was going on too long.

It was always people together to tell the story of Concern. Aengus was at his best for the afterglow. If you met him, you could feel the spirit.

Tom has travelled extensively with the organisation, and has never been less than impressed. 'When I tell people about the travel I do with Concern and the kind of places I go to, people are shocked. *Is this an insurance executive?*'

He is up to speed on the work, and can certainly talk the talk – and not just from briefings or papers:

We can now track malnutrition as it begins. We can see the effects of a bad harvest. In Niger I saw a warehouse and a station that had trucks in and out all day long delivering to remote parts of the country so a woman doesn't have to walk for a week. We still have feeding centres, we still have critical care units, we still have sudden famines, but thank God, the numbers that have to be cared for are far fewer, and it's much easier on the people themselves.

I went to Sierra Leone and met people who had been hiding in the bush for two years, eating berries off the trees and insects off the ground, and when it became safe enough had returned to their village to find everything had been destroyed.

One woman told me they were certain to have died, but someone from Concern came to ask them if they needed help, gave them a loan to buy seed and the equipment they needed, so that they were now growing rice for harvest twice a year and as a result, no child in their village goes to bed hungry.

By the time I got there, Concern had helped them form a women's village cooperative. These women had sold their excess rice, and so had repaid their loan with interest, are now saving up to buy equipment to refine the rice so it will sell for a higher price in the markets, and there is even hope now that one child in that village will go to university.

In the meantime, that original money had rolled on to the next village, and then the next, and so on: 'I tease Concern – which they don't like much – about teaching capitalism in the poorest places of the world!'

What impresses Tom Moran the most, it appears, is that:

... when you go to places where after a crisis things have calmed down a little, you'll see where Doctors Without Borders used to be, where the International Red Cross may have been, but you'll see that's where Concern still is.

(Personally, how much does he miss Aengus?)
'Every day!'

(If this is too upsetting, we won't go on about it.)
'Don't worry, I'm part Italian, I get upset a lot.'

(So, specifically, when Aengus comes into his mind what does he see or hear?)
'A great laugh, a twinkle in the eye – and great wisdom.'

(He wore his wisdom lightly?)
[He can only nod.]

The US operation is very heavily involved in Concern's work in Haiti, which is logical because the desperate needs of that country are by far the closest within reach of its New York office.

And mention of Haiti of course brings up one of Concern's board members. It is not an exaggeration to say that Denis O'Brien, who gets mixed reviews in Ireland, especially in the Irish media, is one of the most highly valued and respected members of Concern in the US.

For Tom Moran:

Denis is a real quality guy. Most of what he's done you never hear about. He's done so much for Haiti and the Caribbean generally. He has a great reputation throughout that region; they all know how generous and philanthropic he is.

He has been accused over there of wanting to be grand with his generosity, but most of what Denis does with his money never gets talked about. Ireland never shone brighter than it did during the Special Olympics there.

Tom's view of another of his board members, Jack Finucane, 'whose secular passion is golf', accords with the general view expressed by everyone interviewed that he and Aengus could not be more different, bar the passion they both felt for eliminating poverty. 'We used to say to Aengus that with the number of women who wanted to spend time with him, we should have all taken vows of celibacy!'

He tells a story about a woman named Marilyn Lownes, British, long-time married and a 'very nice person' who came to Concern via her close friendship with Patricia Harty, the editor of *Irish America* magazine and a devoted supporter of the organisation. Now in her mid-sixties, Marilyn was particularly interested in their work with women and attitude to their betterment and empowerment.

As Marilyn Cole before she married her husband, Victor, a *Playboy* magazine executive, she had worked as a bunny girl in London in the 1970s, had been chosen to be a *Playboy* magazine centrefold and was at one stage Playmate of the Year. Ed Kenney and Aengus, Tom says, always vied to be the first to greet her at functions. 'They were like two little boys,' and Tom remembers that at the last Seeds of Hope dinner Aengus was to attend, ten months before he died, he saw him 'swaggering' ostentatiously back to Ed while tapping a spot on his cheek where she had bussed him: 'Right there, Ed! Right there!'

(Was it that childlike quality that made him lovable?)

I think the sincere honesty of the man, and that he was never judgmental. In a strange way, he was never a priest from Ireland; he was a priest from everywhere else. And yes, I think it was also his childlike innocence, mixed with a very worldly sense of human beings. What people loved about him was he was a man's man, but also a woman's man. You just wanted to be around him.

In Tom's opinion, the core ethos of Concern still belongs to Aengus.

The poorest of the poor, yes, but how can we be most effective with the poorest of the poor? The reason it will survive is we will go into the emergency situations and we will be asking people what they need and providing that – if we're the right people. Aengus always emphasised that there had to be someone still there when the emergency was over and the mayhem subsided.

Innovation is part of it. One of the things we're doing over here is we're working with people in Boeing Technologies who have geniuses all over the place. We're working with them to try to develop predictive technologies that will tell us where the greatest need will be so we can set up with greatest efficiency in advance. It's to be a combination of satellite surveillance, climatology, harvest predictions; it's still at an early stage, but the intention is that we predict events before they become critical.

Is he conscious of how much good he's doing?
'I always say that the number-one beneficiary of Concern's work is me.'

Our allotted ninety minutes is coming to a close, and although he remains relaxed, focused and attentive (and charming, it has to be said), he must have many, *many* other things to do and people to see. It is very quiet and still. No external sound seeps through the door of this vast office. No phone has rung, no one has knocked. Courtesy to visitors, even hacks, runs deep here.

Is there anything he wants to say that has not come up?

Aengus is probably a saint, but I don't know if he ever wanted to be Mother Teresa. Remind people that he was a human being. As you write this book, put a bit of fun into it.

21

*'What a lot of people don't know is that Aengus's favourite
movie was* Babe –
I don't know how many times he watched that!'

– Siobhan Walsh (former Executive Director of Concern US)

Father Mick Reynolds was delighted to witness Aengus's
successful transfer to the United States.

Would it not have been only human for him to have flashed
a metaphorical two fingers at Dublin from across the pond?

'No. He never lorded it. Never the two fingers. Lodging
with the Christian Brothers was a great way of staying grounded.'

As we know, Tom Moran had constantly badgered Aengus
to stay in more materially comfortable accommodation than
the ten-dollars-a-night room with the CBs, but his loyalty was
steadfast: ('200 years ago when we were an illiterate crowd, the
nuns and CBs came in and lifted us out of it.')

'The Irish-Americans loved him,' confirms Mick Reynolds,
'even those who'd had no previous experience with Concern.' Most
were second- and third-generation Americans of Irish immigrant
stock who had maintained a very strong identification with Ireland,
and this had now expanded to include 'Father Aengus':

They were very interesting people, and with them he
was back in his heyday in the 1970s and all that. It also

really suited David Begg to have him out there doing what he did. Begg hated that glad-handing role. He's profound, a very private person, but has to overcome a fierce shyness. Small talk? No!

Aengus, on the other hand, 'was in his element,' says Father Reynolds. 'All he had to do was show up and be himself, with his stories about Burren stones and the Irish famine and Limerick and all the rest of it. It was great to see.'

There was, however, a certain amount of practical adjustment the new honorary president of Concern US had to make in fulfilling his new role. He had been accustomed to a spacious, airy office with its good, if well-used, furniture and with skilled assistance to hand during every phase of his working day. For Eithne Healy, his former secretary:

> ... there was a certain culture in Ireland where women treated priests differently. You'd have all these people who would offer to do things for him, serve him. He'd always take help offered, he'd assign the help. He could even charm you to go down to the clerical outfitters to buy him a black shirt for a wedding.

'In fairness to him,' she added, 'every so often he'd say: "I suppose I'd better go and make you a cup of tea or something?" He was aware.'

When he got to the States, Siobhan Walsh, now gone from Concern, was the new woman in his professional life.

She had gone to New York in 1994 with the aim that she would stay for two years to help set things up. She didn't leave Concern until 2012, remaining because:

> It was the biggest, most exciting chapter of my life to date, because it was a fight, a struggle. Because it was a mission I absolutely believe in. Because I wanted to prove that we could build an organisation in the US.

243

Because we secured a nurturing board who supported us the whole way; because Aengus and I were on that road together for so long, and because I had earned his trust.

This woman was far from behaving as Aengus's secretary or assistant at the beginning, later, or at any time. Before coming to New York she had spent three years in the Dublin office, where, as CEO, he had been quite a distant figure:

He didn't know me from a bar of soap. And when he came over, there was nothing or nobody special to assist him. In New York it was: *I know you were CEO of the whole group, but now you're starting all over again. This is it, Aengus, you're just one of the gang here.*

For instance, he had to learn how to write emails, how to use a computer, share an office. There was no Eithne outside the door. No 'Eithne would you do this for me? Eithne could you do that for me?'

At the beginning, he did try, instinctively, to rope her into that role, but she cut it off at the pass: 'No. I'm not your assistant.'

Tom Moran and Ed Kenney saw all this. They used to laugh at Aengus in the shared, overcrowded little room. At the end there were three in our tiny little office. But both Tom and Ed had incredible admiration for the fact that he was willing to start again from scratch. Tom said to me that he could never have done that. And as for the people Aengus met in his ambassador role, you could see the real love and friendship they developed for him, and very quickly.

Tall, willowy, exceptionally elegant, she is speaking in her parents' home in County Limerick. It is coming up to Christmas and the room is snug, warmed by a coal fire in the fireplace. When contacted she had been more than willing to talk about Aengus and Concern, but a date and venue had been hard to pin down.

She herself is hard to pin down, physically elusive, draped over her chair, body perpendicular to the tape, answering questions as if they had been asked from outside the room. For someone so obviously accomplished she is inexplicably nervous.

Best to tackle it head on. Does she miss the job? Miss Aengus?

'Leaving Concern was a much bigger thing than I thought at the time it would be.'

Her feel for and grasp of strategy is instinctive. Quite early into her occupancy of Concern's New York office she had divined the need for a US board of directors to function in the tradition of many, if not most, 'non-profits' in America.

Her breakthrough, when it did come, was initially a slow burn. Aengus was still CEO in Dublin, and in her opinion his asking Michael Lally to go to New York as his special representative turned the tide in the fortunes of Concern US.

> Michael was the one who negotiated with Ed Kenney to get that lunch with Tom Moran. But for Ed, and him connecting with Aengus, we would never have got any-where. That connection was the second, and definitive, turning point.

Only too well does she remember the Ireland–US council black-tie event at Dublin Castle when the Clintons were in town, and what followed in O'Donoghue's pub and the Berkeley Court Hotel.

> Tom Moran was certainly not hard work. He was fun. And he himself said later that it was because I had been honest about being in trouble that he had taken us under his wing. He appreciates honesty and the direct approach. But after he had agreed to join the board, he had a condition: 'I can build you a strong board. I can bring people, and I can fundraise.

Don't ask me to do anything else. The rest, to use the cliché, is history.

There were a few minor speed bumps, mere wrinkles, in Aengus's settling-in period. He had been accustomed throughout his working life to dealing with officialdom and other NGOs, and in his new role in the States, for a while, was not comfortable with the straight-talking way of doing business with straight-talking corporate business people in America.

> He wanted someone there with him to do the dirty money talk, while he would lend his august presence. Tom Moran was the first one to turn around and say: 'Sorry, Aengus, you're in it with the lot of us. You have to do it. We're all grubbing together; we'll grovel and do what we have to do.'

Before any event or meeting involving the direct importuning of a potential donor, quite aware of the incongruity, she would sit with the honorary president of Concern US to rehearse with him how to behave, what to say and to whom:

> Okay, here's where we're going to be tonight, here's who we target. So, what are the asks?
> In the early days, he and Jack had been accustomed to touring Europe, successfully seeking financial support from large non-profits and even governments in places like the United Kingdom, Germany and Holland, but this was a completely different ball of wax.

Nevertheless, he listened to his new colleagues, overcame his distaste for this overt money-grubbing approach to mega-rich individuals, private boards and bosses of private corporations, and over the next period, aided by the contributions from its own board and its fundraising events, the gains for Concern, although slow at first, began greatly to increase.

For Siobhan Walsh, although they quickly became friends, and although he was not permanently *in situ*, Aengus was there a lot, and there were some disadvantages about having him at such close quarters in the tiny office:

> There was nothing I did that Aengus didn't know about. Even after one of my phone calls, he would often turn around and go: 'Mmmmm! You might have handled that a little more delicately than you did.'

So yes, he could be 'teacherish' with her, but on the other hand, 'in the main he could pass on lessons from his own experience – and wisdom – without being didactic.'

He could also be quite pointed, though. At one stage she was busy and exhausted when someone in the office asked her if she was going to take a vacation. 'No,' she snapped, 'I haven't time to take a vacation.' Aengus turned around to her, drawling: 'Siobhan, you might not need a vacation, but did you ever consider people might need a vacation from you?'

She got the message. 'It was his way of telling me to take one.'

It was not all desk confinement with black-tie break-outs for her. She made sure to keep her passion for the organisation alive, not only by going into the field but by volunteering in the soup kitchens in the Bowery, 'when I could. I wanted to stay connected.' This Bowery stint, she says, was partly spurred by Aengus's daily dismay about his regular encounters with a homeless man who, for heat, slept on a sewer grating on the street outside the Christian Brothers' lodgings. 'He was very troubled by that, especially during the winters.'

After a while, however, she had to give up the voluntary work. The day job was so demanding she became unreliable, 'and there is nothing worse than an unreliable volunteer.'

She went on field trips, 'so I could see what Aengus saw through his lens, and could then speak with authority from my own perspective.' For instance, she visited Rwanda. In a feeding centre there, one of the incidents she cannot forget is sitting with a mother who had reached it too late with her twins, 'one breathing very heavily, the other already dead.' It haunts her.

> It is only when you have experienced that, seen it and smelled it, you make a true connection. I tried to keep what I was doing very real, so I was able to communicate to people what I'd seen and felt.

Tom Moran was entirely *ad idem* with this approach.

> He had a condition for board members: they had to go out and see the fields for themselves too. He went himself. He's pretty impressive. In fact, it's a pretty impressive board.

When interviewees were asked if they missed Aengus, everyone did. Family members, of course, still grieve; in response to the question many volunteers adopted an affectionate, almost faraway look as though they were seeing something huggably lovable in their minds.

After four years, his passing is still raw for Siobhan Walsh, who is a very private person. It is probably torture to her to reveal any life other than the professional one.

> Do I miss him? I miss Aengus very much. And he was my teacher, he taught me an awful lot. People don't normally describe him as a businessman, but he was one, a very shrewd one. He was a very, very good friend. We spent a lot of time together, so much we came to behave like ... I don't know ... I don't know whether it was like brother and sister or husband and wife, because we used to get on each other's nerves. He used to press my buttons and I used to press his.

They were sometimes together even at weekends. Thursday or Friday would roll around:

> What a lot of people don't know is that Aengus's favourite movie was *Babe* – the one about the talking pig who wants to be a collie dog so he can herd sheep. I don't know how many times he watched that!

Frequently, her then husband was roped in too, for meals, for excursions. 'Mike [the NBC News foreign correspondent Mike Taibbi] had a boat, and often took him sailing. He loved that.' They had meals together: 'Aengus was famous for his Peking Duck.'

Then there was the time Siobhan's mentor got to bless the first ever smoke-free ship, the Carnival Cruise Line's *Paradise*, first of its kind, with a large 'No Smoking' sign welded to its bow. The American Cancer Society was thrilled, especially when it was given the free run of the vessel for the launch night.

Since that shipping line was owned at the time by an Israeli company, the launch was to be conducted by a Rabbi – but Tom Moran and Ed Kenney, never missing a trick, got wind of this and managed to convince everyone involved in the event that an Irish priest involved with a small Irish-founded aid NGO that included, for instance, Pakistani Muslims in its ministry, would be a much better person to do the job.

In an email, George Barker, one of those who had been convinced of this by Tom and Ed, remembers that evening:

> We escorted Father Aengus to the barge floating under the bow of the ship and he departed to join the gathering. His grand entrance included shaking hands with everyone in sight. In other words, he took over.
>
> As I shook his hand, I knew I was meeting a very special individual. The barge included many celebrities, politicians and members of the Carnival

Cruise Line. But for us, the most important person was Father Aengus. There were a few speeches, and at the conclusion Father Aengus stepped up, blessed the ship and all assembled.

The Irish priest and the wife of the shipping line's Israeli owner then took unto themselves a bottle of Dom Pérignon and swung it at the bow of the huge ship.

And missed.

There is a postscript to the event. The singer Michael Bolton (multiple Grammys, 53 million albums and singles worldwide, hit duet with Luciano Pavarotti of 'Vesti La Giubba' from Leoncavallo's opera *Pagliacci*) was one of the major attractions of the entertainment laid on for guests on board that night. He and Aengus were introduced, shook hands warmly, had a lovely chat, and as he moved away with Siobhan, Aengus whispered: 'Who's Michael Bolton?'

Equally endearing in one sense, maddening in others for Siobhan, she says, was that when tension was high in the office, Aengus used to go around reciting: 'Lord, make me an instrument of thy Peace. Where there is hatred, let me sow love …' et cetera. 'Aengus, would you cut your prayers?'

'Siobhan, this is why you need people like me in this office!'

For all his sophistication, he was very childlike. There's a photo of him wearing about seven ties, where he'd sing his party piece: 'Goodbye Johnny Dear'. *Just twenty years ago today, I grasped my mother's hand. She kissed and blessed her only son, going to a foreign land….*

He couldn't sing. He hadn't a note in his head. But he loved and really needed company. Any time he was left on his own he wasn't comfortable. I often wondered if he was afraid to be alone.

Aengus finally left New York in 2008, but not before taking one last field trip to Haiti, despite his seriously deteriorating health. He and Siobhan had talked about the prospect of his final leaving.

> He didn't mind talking about it. When I'd say I didn't know what I was going to do when the two of us were not here to make decisions together, he'd say things to me like: 'Siobhan, you have it. Would you stop worrying about things like this? You know exactly what needs to be done.'

During his last couple of years in the States, the priest's family worried that he was still commuting transatlantic, still working, entreating Siobhan and others: 'Would you stop asking him back? Would you be sensible and let the man slow down?'

> But the man didn't want to slow down. He needed this. He needed to be in that energy and that environment. It was all young people, all of them with so much energy. A room full of kids – and the thing he did was to inculcate the culture and history of the organisation within every young kid who came through that door, telling them stories. They realised it afterwards. How many people get the chance to sit with a guy who had been on the front line since almost the very beginning, but who was also open to new experiences?

She, like almost everyone else, talks about Aengus the Diviner: his uncanny ability, in the guise of friendliness and chat, to draw newcomers out and thereby uncarth hidden abilities and latent talents. After he finally left, while she knew intellectually that he wasn't coming back, 'that was one thing.' His death was another:

> The first year after he passed was very lonely. He was much more than a colleague to me. Part of my life. Even at Christmas, when we'd come home he used to

come out here and sit at the table with my parents. He had a big family of his own, but he became part of my family as well.

But then, at his funeral, came the realisation that he really was gone. I found being in New York after that very, very hard.

22

'*Don't be looking for your effect on the global statistics!
Just come back to the effects on individuals.*'

– Aengus Finucane

A ine Fay, another lifer for Concern, and since 2013 operations
director in New York for Concern US, graduated as a nurse
but went into administration in Limerick instead, working for
NIHE, later Limerick University. She comes from a family
densely woven with vocations, however, so the urge to 'give
back' was inherent, and one day in Dublin, finding herself with
time to kill and with Concern's offices nearby, she walked in.

Within an hour she had her application form completed, had
been interviewed by Mary Humphreys, and had been offered a job
as Jack's secretary in Bangladesh. 'I didn't know where Bangladesh
was, but if she'd offered me a job as a cleaner there, I'd have said yes.'
Even on such short acquaintance, she had been really impressed
with the atmosphere and ethos of the organisation.

At her induction course, one of the first things Aengus
mentioned to her group was the Alex Tarbett affair:

He told us that once we said we were working for
Concern, inevitably people were going to ask us
what had happened to that money. He told us what

had happened. It was very Aengus. He confronted.
*Here's what's going to happen. Here's how we're going to
deal with it.*

Aine's job in Bangladesh had as much to do with high-level
administration as much as acting as someone's secretary. As her
contract was coming to a close, she got an urgent phone call
from Aengus, who 'desperately' needed a secretary in Dublin.
She accepted.

On the day before Christmas Eve, her new boss, who was
driving home to Limerick to celebrate with his family, offered
her a lift since her family comes from the same neck of the
woods.

> When we arrived at my house, it was, 'Father Finucane'
> this, 'Father Finucane' that. He had a whiskey, my father
> had a whiskey, my mother had a sherry, and then she
> said to me:
>> 'There's orange juice in the fridge.'
>> 'No. I'll have a whiskey as well.'

The mother said nothing. Poured the whiskey. Didn't bat an
eyelid. But as she saw Aengus out the door:

> 'Father Finucane, there is just one thing I'd like to say
> to you.'
>> 'What's that?'
> 'My daughter left here two years ago to join your
> organisation and she was a teetotaller, what have you
> done to her?'
> I can still see Aengus standing there. Then he threw
> his two hands in the air: 'Mrs Fay, it's my brother you
> need to speak to!'

Having worked for both of the Finucane clerics, Aine is another
of those in a position to contrast their styles of managing their

charges: 'To some extent,' she says, 'each acted like a house mother but with different approaches':

> Jack could open a conversation with the dreaded: 'So what happened in your house last night?' That meant that he knew. He just wanted you to confirm. Whereas with Aengus, if there had been something going on in your house, he would have been part of it.

It was now 1984, and she was working as secretary to Aengus in Camden Street.

Secretary Schmecretary: 'You did everything that was thrown at you. The famine was raging in Ethiopia and that was huge, really huge. I ended up writing proposals for projects.'

She moved wholly into the project side of the organisation pretty quickly, proving again everyone's categorisation of Aengus as The Diviner. It's one thing I would always credit him for. He put his confidence in your abilities.

> I see the whole management thing now, and you sit down with people and you ask them where do they think they're going and all that. With Aengus there was none of that. It was just: 'I think you could…?'

'Jack has a lot of the same qualities, she says, 'but in a very different way. For him there is definitely a right and a wrong way to do things; for Aengus it was definitely ad hoc.'

Her career in Concern could have foundered early as she did not find it easy at the beginning in Bangladesh, to the extent that after less than three months there, she offered Jack her resignation: 'I couldn't hack it. I wasn't enjoying it, it was: *I don't know what brought me here.*' So she went to Jack and confessed how she was feeling, how she hated the climate, the heat, everything.

> Jack's solution was for me to take my holidays early and to go somewhere slightly cooler. He suggested Kashmir.

255

'And when you come back from your holidays, if you still feel the same way, I'll accept your resignation.'

This solution proved to be very wise because here we are, sitting in a New York neighbourhood restaurant on Lexington Avenue just across the street from her office in the Big Apple, with her marvelling at her 'amazing thirty-year journey' and giving credit to both Finucanes.

> Working with Concern introduced me to a whole new world. Parts of that experience I honestly feel I could have done without; being in situations where the problems seemed so many and so insurmountable that you wondered what could be done.
>
> But coupled with that are experiences that have filled me with joy, hope and a belief in humanity, in particular a belief in the power and dedication of women to fight for a better future for their children.

Since Bangladesh, she has lived and worked in Ethiopia, Uganda and Afghanistan. She has been country director in Pakistan, and has led Concern's responses to difficulties in Indonesia, Ethiopia, South Sudan and Haiti, where she saw the Denis O'Brien operation at first hand. In general she thinks that he is one of the best 'joined-up operators' that she has encountered.

He himself is interviewed while sitting not behind but in front of the desk in his Dublin canal-side office. (Original art; brilliant flowers.)
Why did he get so heavily involved with Concern?

> I'd read a lot about Concern, including a book about it [Tony Farmar's *Believing in Action*], and it wasn't just the work, although that was key. There was a sort of Roy of the Rovers feel about the organisation, especially as it came out of the Biafran conflict.

256

At the time, he says: he had: 'made some money out of the sale of Esat Telecom, so I rang Tom Arnold and asked could I meet him.'

(And of course Tom said no?)

He laughs, then: 'I said to him I'd like to fund some projects.'

So, in January 2003, Arnold organised a field trip for Denis O'Brien and his wife, Catherine, to Ethiopia. They landed in Addis Ababa at six in the morning: 'When you land in Addis and the sun is rising, it's like a lunar landing: it's a beautiful place.'

> We chartered a plane and flew up into the middle of nowhere, over all these valleys. We had farmers telling us about all the problems they had with irrigation. So we funded wells. Because when you spend the time and see all those Concern people working in the field, you say to yourself: this is a fantastic organisation.
>
> Sometimes, when people look at a not-for-profit organisation, they say that their management skills wouldn't be great – this was the total opposite. Concern is the Smurfit of what it does. If this was a for-profit organisation it would be one of the biggest companies in the world.

By the time the ultimately ill-fated Celtic Tiger was on full rampage, Denis O'Brien had not only drunk the Kool-Aid, he was fully immersed.

> I said to myself: things are going great in Ireland. There are a lot of very wealthy people here, so why don't I grab them all up for Concern? At that stage I'd bought a plane. So, I thought, I'll get them and we'll all go but let's make it to somewhere where we can really make a difference.

He rang his nearly-best-buddy by now, Tom Arnold, who came back with the suggestion that South Sudan was the place.

So I rang the lads up. Bernard McNamara? You wouldn't believe how generous he is; he even helped me with the Special Olympics. Anyway, they were all really interested.

He widened the invitation list to include anyone he felt could be talked into contributing. They left Dublin Airport and flew to Lokichoggio - a remote airport in northern Kenya.

In Lokichoggio they all boarded a Russian plane, and carrying barrels of fuel with them, headed to the state of Western Bahr el Ghazal, bordering South Darfur. They landed there 'in a field,' an airstrip near Aweil, the state's capital. 'And there was this hut. And as always in Africa, there was one little naked light bulb and a lot of flies.'

'You have to hand it to them,' he says, 'they were all game.' And little naked lightbulb and flies notwithstanding, the evening took off.

> The guy who ran the camp was a Bengali. He [Saddiqur] had worked for Concern for twenty years, tremendous guy. He started singing. And we were up until two in the morning. The stories were fantastic. The discussion for a whole hour was about animal husbandry; I had only limited knowledge of farming although when I worked for Tony Ryan I ran his farm, but the builders on board were very knowledgeable. We were all discussing what would be the best breed of cattle to bring down to South Sudan.

The projects they actually planned before they flew away again included a medical centre, an agricultural training centre and a school, to run on a three-year, multi-annual funding basis. According to O'Brien, they returned every year for the three years to check on the projects, and 'the project management in the field by Concern was fantastic. To the penny. They brought everything in on budget.'

At the time of writing, Concern is again heavily involved in South Sudan, an independent state since 2011, but again embroiled in conflict and the very real prospect of yet another widespread and devastating famine caused in many ways by the extent of the fighting.

Given the cynicism with which Denis O'Brien is frequently regarded in his birthplace, even if a lot of his involvement is with the US side of the organisation, why is he really so engaged with this Irish-originated and Irish-based NGO?

He answers this by comparing his own role unfavourably with, for instance, 'people like Anne O'Mahony and other people like that.' He absolutely admires the work that Concern has done since 1994 in Haiti ('they're the most successful NGO in that country'), and while he didn't know Aengus Finucane all that well personally, is familiar with his pushing and widening the spread of that work. Haiti, deemed hopeless by many commentators, held a special place in the priest's heart.

When, worldwide, he sees the scale of poverty, does O'Brien personally ever despair? Will Concern and colleague agencies forever be like Sisyphus, pushing the boulder upwards and having it roll back down again?

He remains upbeat, and not just because of the practical efforts of Concern and other specialist NGOs, but because of the work of huge international bodies such as the One Foundation, which are influencing governments and powerful politicians in the global humanitarian area, and in the newly urgent area of climate change.

He gets back to Concern. 'There are very few top ten world lists in which Ireland features – aviation yes, universities no.' For O'Brien, however, the position is nuanced: 'We're talking about the shifting economic development of the world, and Concern would be in the top ten *influencers* [he emphasises the word] in that world.' He believes that if Concern markets itself better, and makes use of the internet, there is no direction but upwards for it, and of course for Aengus's poorest of the poor.

How would he characterise Aengus and his role in the organisation?

Galvaniser. Talked to anyone and everyone. Tremendous with young people, prolific in fundraising, using every big name he could find to raise money. The whole North American side of Concern is down to him and Siobhan and Dominic, mainly him. Aengus was able to adapt how he did it in Ireland, move it into America, and he did it brilliantly.

Why do Irish people have a good calling card in Africa, Asia, South America, Fiji, Trinidad, Samoa – *you're from Ireland? You're in.*

It's because the top civil servants were educated by Irish priests. That's the forgotten bit about the Irish DNA. Concern, with no proselytising, has taken over from the missionaries. Even that Bengali guy in South Sudan? Celebrating the Irish way, singing around a campfire.

Where does he get the philanthropy gene? It's obvious that while he enjoys making money and is very good at it, he also enjoys using it.

'I do. I get a great kick out of it. Having the means and opportunity to use it like this.'

He grew up with a Roman Catholic father and Protestant mother. One person who obviously influenced him was a lady whose home, with her sisters, was just four doors away from the O'Briens'. Miss Elizabeth Ferrar was a Church of Ireland lay missionary and teacher in India, serving her church 'faithfully and forcefully' according to a reference to her in a eulogy to deceased members made by Bishop Walton Empey to the 2001 Church of Ireland Synod, of which she was a 'valued member'. She came home annually, and was always invited to dinner in the O'Brien household – where, as a result of involvement with Miss Ferrar, the whole family was 'always collecting for India.' So the habit of giving was learned early:

We're [Digicel] going to make a lot of money in
Haiti and in Jamaica and in Papua New Guinea, so
we need to do a disproportionate amount of activity in those places; we're going to put a percentage
of our profits in Malawi into projects there. Because
if you're taking money out of a country and you're
not doing something to move the economic needle
in that country....

[He stops and sighs:] Oh God, I'm spouting now!

We work with the locals. It's a different form of
capitalism, a better-sleep-at-night kind of capitalism. That's
the drum that Clinton has been trying to beat, with some
success. We're not talking huge amounts of money to be
transformative. You need advocacy, that's the bow end
of things. You have the doers, that's Concern. You have
governments who do step up. And countries are stepping
up. Even Ireland stepped up, and we're bollixed!

23

'I am walking in the footsteps of a giant. In 2008, Haiti was the very last country that Father Aengus Finucane visited in his remarkable lifetime, and his legacy was unmistakable in Concern's work there.'

– Tom Moran (chairman of Concern US)

Aengus Finucane's influence is very evident in Haiti, the last field he set up as CEO and the last he ever visited. There is no need to worry about his legacy being lost amongst the Concern people working there as they toil against tremendous odds in his name, and that of his organisation. 'Brave' is an overused word, but it is appropriate here.

Reacting to a round of criticisms in the media about development issues in Haiti, Joe Cahalan, CEO of Concern US, released a document about these workers and what they do. And perhaps a few extracts might illustrate not just what was on his mind about that country, but the synchronous nature and thinking of Concern operations worldwide.

In some quarters, Haiti has become a convenient lightning rod for all that's wrong with humanitarian aid and development assistance. You've no doubt heard it all: the problems are too complex and intractable; another example of the developed world forcing solutions on the developing world; fraud,

Kelly McShane, Aengus Finucane and Seamus Heaney marking
Concern's 40th anniversary, Royal Hospital Kilmainham, 2008.

Commemorating the introduction of wheat to Bangledesh,
30th anniversary of Concern's foundation in Bangladesh, 2002.

Aengus Finucane with President Mary McAleese, 2008.

Saidpur, Bangladesh, 1998.

Malachy McCourt, Aengus Finucane and Frank McCourt.

Martin McGuinness, Aengus Fiuncane and Ian Paisley,
5 December 2007. A historic day at the Nasdaq when Northern
Ireland's government declared:
'Peace ... we're now open for business.'

Famine memorial, Battery Park, NYC. Opened in July, 2002, the park is designed to be 'a comtemplative space, devoted to raising public awareness of the events that led to the Irish Famine'.

Aengus Finucane and Hillary Clinton.

Aengus Finucane and Sarah Finucane.

John Hume, John Scanlon and Aengus Finucane,
New York City, 1998.

Abdi Rashid, Siobhan Walsh, Aengus Finucane, Mary McAleese,
Tom Moran, Anne O'Manony and Ed Kenney Snr in Dublin, 2008.

Aengus Finucane with Mark Malloch Brown, Seeds of Hope
UNDP administrator, 2001.

Siobhan Walsh, Aengus Finucane and Dominic MacSorley,
New York City, 2006.

Gabriel Byrne and Aengus Finucane, New York City.

Toireas Ní Bhrian, Aengus, Noel Maloney, Siobhan Walsh and
Dominic MacSorley.

Tom Lavin, Tom Arnold, Caroline O'Dowd, AF, Ger Farrell,
Ciunas Bunworth, JF, Phena O'Boyle, Mayor Michael Hourigan,
Evanna Barry, Kay Walsh, Fr. Ciaran Kitching, Mary Humphreys,
Anne Cummins, Toireas Ni Bhriain, Cleo O'Reilly, Brigid Ryan.

corruption, and mismanagement siphoning much-needed resources; quick fixes that are fleeting and unsustainable; and on and on and on. There's truth in that story line, of course, but it's only part of the story.

While the public may perceive that the majority of those who lost their homes in the earthquake are still living in camps, the reality is something different. Just after the earthquake, some one and a half million Haitians called camps their home. That number has already been reduced to a quarter of a million – a number of course that is still unacceptable, but progress is being made, camp by camp, family by family.

... Since 2010 Concern has developed and operated a 'Return to Neighbourhoods' programme, facilitating the movement of people into permanent homes via rental subsidies and small cash grants.

Each of these families – 2,700 in total – will soon have a new home, a year's rent paid up-front, and a $150 stipend to ease their transition. If history is a guide, the stipend will be used for education. Yes, that's right: parents who have nothing will invest their small windfall in their children's education

Meanwhile, in Saut d'Eau, a rural area, Concern:

... organised 300 mango and avocado farmers into an asso-ciation that has doubled their production and increased the price of their goods fivefold. In partnership with the Haitian government, we've almost completed a nearly eight-mile road to the ominous-sounding area of 'Montagne Terrible', the most isolated part of the commune. In a few months, the road will link another farming community to the cooperative and improve the quality of life for another 1,400 farming families.

But possibly the most daringly ambitious of Concern's Haitian projects is an attempt to jump-start a fledgling tourist industry in Saut d'Eau, based on two of the district's major attractions: a magnificent waterfall, and a culture where Christianity and voodoo live side by side.

(Aine Fay says that her experience in Haiti was that, when they fell ill, Concern staff, educated and sophisticated as they are, frequently consulted the voodoo doctor before the medical one.)

Cahalan's document continues:

Each July, tens of thousands of Haitian pilgrims descend on Saut d'Eau to celebrate a major voodoo holiday. Sadly, they leave little but garbage behind. If the nascent local tourism board has anything to say about it, soon they will be leaving money.

And he concludes:

We tend to focus on what is wrong with relief and aid, and in some cases it is justified. But it is time we recognise the people who are dedicating their lives, long after the world has moved on, to chipping away at the work that remains to be done in Haiti. It's a story of commitment and resilience, of hope and promise, of people who want and deserve a chance for a sense of normalcy.

It's not the stuff of headlines, but it's inspiring nonetheless.

The headline over this document is 'Haiti's Unsung Heroes.'

Peter McNichol is in charge of the Haitian operation and, during conversation in his office situated behind the high steel fence of the Concern compound in Port-au-Prince, he confirms that the programmes mentioned in Joe Cahalan's document are still running, albeit with setbacks expected, such as the next hurricane, or periodic withdrawals from the more dangerous of the programme sites when staff are victims of stonings, or threatened by gang members with worse.

To keep going, he says: 'you have to be dedicated to what the organisation is all about.'

He needs every fibre of dedication in his body. To the untutored eye, much of the infrastructure in the Haitian capital is still devastated after the 2010 earthquake and the infliction of four major hurricanes since, resulting in, officially, ten million cubic metres of rubble from collapsed buildings, roads, hospitals and schools.

There is a new paved road from the airport to Pietonville, where McNichol's compound is, but for many of the other thoroughfares in the city the surfaces are pitted with craters so deep, and so close to each other, that riding in the Concern jeep is akin to being in a fairground dodgem, zigzagging, swaying, jolting and crashing, all at speeds somewhere between one and ten miles an hour.

The camps – including a vast sprawl along the perimeter fence of the airport – consist of closely packed shelters, some made from perhaps just a sheet of corrugated iron swathed with pieces of plastic, fabric and all kinds of different materials, there are even front porches: little roofs of plastic or other stuff propped, or strung, on or between tree branches. Without making light of what all this means for the residents, a huge number do resemble an Irish child's play-tent in a back garden where a demented mother threw out a few tatty blankets or sheets and ordered her giddy offspring to: 'Go out and play!'

Cheek by jowl, washing lines flutter and overlap. At first glance the sprawl seems random, even shambolic, but there is evidence of a degree of organisation. There are rudimentary avenues and open spaces here and there, although many are dotted with smoking fires, great piles of rubbish and broken machinery. Wheel-less vans and rusted wheelbarrows jostle with mysterious bundles of wire and cable, jerry cans, dust-streaked barrels. At a safe distance from the residents, dogs with ribs like spindles root for scraps of food in the dust.

Security considerations are paramount. The first item handed to a visitor in the Concern office is a mobile phone, with emergency numbers already programmed in.

Discussions about the security of staff are frequent; they are driven to their programmes always by official drivers, and always walk accompanied, even to a coffee shop only yards away. And there is now cholera: a frightening disease that was never endemic to this country. There are well-documented public allegations that it arose because raw sewage was discharged into a stream in the hills above the city. Those responsible, according to received wisdom, belong to one of the groups who came in to help with the aid effort after the quake. 'Poor Haiti can't catch a break, a major earthquake, four major hurricanes, and now cholera,' says [young] Ed Kenney, Communications Director of Concern US and son of Tom Moran's deputy, [older] Ed Kenney. In these circumstances, McNichol says, what helps him get up in the morning is to know that multitudes in Saut d'Eau are dependent on Concern for cholera treatment. The Returns [to Neighbourhoods] programmes with its 10,000 clients – of which, more anon – are expanding into new areas. And then there is the permanent work with schools, women who have been assaulted or raped, potential women entrepreneurs being trained for business, fisherfolk – and mango farmers:

> Haiti supplies the US with 4 per cent of its mango requirement, but the farmers were losing a huge amount of produce because of lack of proper storage facilities and transport to the port. So we built a storage complex, trained people in its use and taught them how to experiment with new varieties.

When schools were investigated it was found that 28 per cent of children were being beaten with sticks, many teachers and most children spoke only Creole (Kreyol) while the curriculum was in French. And of the 366 four- to eight-year-olds tested, only ten could write a sentence in any language. 'We badly need training for teachers.'

Customarily, Concern's definition of extreme poverty had been based on measures of paucity, or complete lack, of assets. Added to that now, however, are risks, vulnerabilities and inequalities. In Haiti, the organisation is involved in aquaculture conservation, setting up public–private partnerships to help with fishing.

It is also trying to improve the breeding stock of goats – 'we're buying stock from the Dominican Republic' says McNichol. It has set up a rubbish collection and disposal service in some of the slums and camps, and, since the island of La Gonave receives less than a fifth of Haiti's rainfall, it is installing rainwater cisterns there to conserve what does fall.

In all cases, it tries to work in conjunction with Haiti's state authorities, who are themselves, to put it mildly, struggling in many ways.

'Politics in Haiti is like a soccer match without a referee – everyone fighting for the ball,' says Najac Jean Linz, one of the organisation's Haitian employees. He is project manager for a peace-building programme in Grand Ravine.

Grand Ravine is an enormous slum where the 'houses' cling to the walls of a steep canyon, where the living space for each individual is approximately 1.6 square metres, and where you have as many as ten people sleeping in a room the size of a bathroom in many houses in the western world. It is also cursed with gang culture. A visit to the project there was on the schedule for this book, but on the day in question Concern had withdrawn its workers, who had been threatened with attack. They will go back the next day. It's what they do.

Najac's mission is to build peace between gunmen and the Grand Ravine community – and while he is at it, between members of rival gangs. He is wearing a natty shirt today because it is his birthday. He is 39. He also reveals that four weeks after this interview he will leave Haiti for New York, to which he has already sent his wife and two children.

They Skype every night, but that gets him only so far. It is not hard to deduce that the work here has burned him out.

> If you have money you can construct a church, a school and a latrine, especially if you have the technical experience. That's easy. What is not so easy is working from the inside out to change the minds of people.
>
> Sometimes you see progress, sometimes it goes backwards. Like a bicycle, you have to keep it going. Keep pedalling. If you stop, the bicycle falls over.

Najac has been with Concern for nine years, starting as a civil engineer in 2004, and then, like many another, adding community work. He was constructing latrines and laying paving in the St Martin district of Grand Ravine, but while working there recognised that he could do additional and maybe more significant work, 'if I understood the community.'

St Martin and Martissant in Port Au Prince are two of the most problematic districts in Haiti; armed gangs, not loth to rob, kidnap or shoot, rule with ruthless ferocity.

But Concern found symbiosis here. Like Haiti, Ireland has its own history with hardship – including famine, terrorism and war, both colonial and internecine. Although the conflict and violence in St Martin is gang ('Baz') related, Najac instinctively grasped the premise that the art of resolving most trouble is seeing the other guy's point of view. In other words, dialogue.

Ireland's International Centre for Peace and Reconciliation (Glencree) grew out of the Northern 'troubles', and is now operating internationally.

So, in 2006, Concern asked the organisation to help, sending Najac and others on courses there to learn the process of using dialogue to ameliorate extremely challenging circumstances. 'And since then,' he says, 'I never stopped.'

After his training, he began the formal peace programme with an invitation to the community through the multitudes of different churches, health and education groups, to meet with him, simultaneously offering the same invitation directly to gang members.

> (Stupid question of the day: how does he identify the gang members?)
>
> [He laughs.]
>
> Not difficult: guns. And we work in the communities. People will tell you: 'Look, there is the leader!'
>
> We said to them: 'Concern is not the police. We are not going to block the police from doing their job or protect you from your wrongdoing, but when our organisation goes into a community, we work with ALL in the community, we are non-judgmental. You are part of the community, part of the change, and we don't want to work without you. We are not going to give you an amnesty, but we want to engage you, with us, in the work.'

A man named Nasson had been gang chief in Grand Ravine since before the earthquake.

> The first time I met him I explained to him what Concern wanted: to create an atmosphere where, in peace, people in the community can send their children to school and that kind of thing.
>
> That first time, Nasson said: 'I will go to the meeting, but if the police harass me, what will you do for me?'
>
> 'It's just an invitation, and if you do go, we're sure you will listen and transform. That's the reason I invite you.'
>
> 'All right, I'm coming.'

The meeting is set up in a mountain area, far from Grand Ravine. Nasson does arrive, with others.

> We spend five days with them to show them what they could do for their community – how their children can go to school. 'You are a leader of your gang, but you can

be another kind of leader in your community,' we show them how they can do that. We do Mediation training for them, Group Facilitation, Conflict Resolution in the community. How they can call the police about their guns....

As is only to be expected, all is not over after five days and a descent from the mountain.

Afterwards you need to support and accompany these people. They are used to the power and the money, and now you are asking them to be a true leader without the force, and this is where the bicycle comes in, you have to keep up the support.

Does he ever get frustrated?

Sometimes, but I think it is possible to transform people in six years. Peace-building is a long process. And when I see the change in Nasson and other gang members, to me that is a big success. He still lives in Grand Ravine. He works with another group now, Lakou Lape, 'the back garden of peace', with the support of Glencree. He is now Christian. He goes often to church, where he is like a pastor. He has completely reformed.

Despite this major success, minor in the context of poor Haiti's multi-stranded travails, Najac is not optimistic about his nation's future.

It not easy to change the country towards the positive. Personally you can do things in Haiti, but in community you can't. Not easily.

He takes a breath. He has obviously prepared something he wants to say.

One thing I would like to tell you. Haiti needs support to change. Not just money. We need respect as a nation.

We need experts to come in, people who are charismatic enough to change the mindsets of neighbours fighting against neighbours, these people who are a lot of egoists, very, very selfish. I'm not sure that the problem is just poverty, although relieving it could be a start. We should change the way we build a community.

He goes back to the statistics, the 1.6 square metres per person for those living in Grand Ravine, the eight to ten people sleeping in a few square metres.

The houses are too close together, there is no space to pass through, many are just one room, no parks, no recreation facilities, no fields, no nothing. When you have this situation, people have trouble.

He finishes with a courteous, and affecting:'I hope I have assisted you, and that what we discussed will have some circulation.'

He has.

And it will.

We hear something similar from Jean-Frenel Tham, assistant country director for Concern in Haiti, another extraordinary, dedicated and impressive man, who was a central banker before he joined.

He knew Aengus:

He came in 2008, and my first impression was he was old and not full of energy, and I was asking myself why was someone of that age flying to Haiti all the way from Ireland?

Susan [Finucane, one of Aengus and Jack's nieces who was in Haiti at the time] said to me, 'That's my uncle!' And then I realised that Haiti really does

271

come under a global vision that Concern has. That
makes us unique in what we're doing, working in
the most difficult places and with the poorest. I
understood then that it's what he wanted. Actually, I
have to make an effort not to become too passionate,
because you have to retain some rationality.

The tenth of eleven siblings, Tham comes from a rural area in
the south-west. He started work at 14:

> Everyone in my family has now left the country, all
> running small businesses in America and Canada. I'm the only
> one left. On my phone, I can call only people from Concern.

After his education, he joined Haiti's Central Bank, then
switched to a commercial bank, where he was involved in the
piloting of a micro-finance product, and in that way came into
contact with entrepreneurs and women, which in turn led him
to answer an ad wherein Concern was looking for a facilitator
to run a micro-credit programme in Saut d'Eau.

> It was a very big shift, very difficult to turn my commer-
> cial banking mind to the NGO mind, but it was a very
> good experience. My first day, still in my banking mode,
> I showed up at the office with my nice tie, nice shoes –
> everyone started laughing at me.

Twelve years later, the benefits of working for Concern are
many, primarily the influence he feels he personally has on the
lives of the people he serves. The physical results are obvious.
Then there is the choice the organisation makes to work in the
most difficult places – Grand Ravine, St Martin.

> When I told my Haitian friends I am going into Grand
> Ravine, they think I am insane. Those are places people
> don't go. But that's where I'm working.

You see changes in communities and people's lives – and this is what keeps me committed. Grand Ravine is like a small kingdom controlled by the gangs. It is very difficult for any organisation to go there and work without paying these gangs.

We changed our approach completely. They sit and work with us now, so that means a lot. When the gang members see me passing by they don't insult me.

Do the people in those districts appreciate what Concern is doing? The courage involved? Tellingly, he hesitates.

For sure you will have some people complaining that we're not doing enough: 'we need electricity' and so on. People confuse you with the government. We have to clarify very often how limited our resources actually are.

The extent of the general level of poverty in Haiti seriously depresses him. 'Investment is what we need. We're hoping that people will see what we're doing. Dialogue is good, yes, but people need to eat.' At some point I am asking myself if it's possible to solve this; to have something to live for.

When I see the poverty in the eyes of the people in the street when I'm walking past, and I have a job, this makes me feel very vulnerable. You live amongst them, these young men sitting around with nothing to do. They know that you are feeding your family and they are not. The first opportunity they have to do something to you, to get some of your wealth, they will do it. That's human nature.

How does he cope with this constant feeling of unease, even low-level guilt, at being a 'have' in a land of 'have-nots'?

Good question – it's being humble as much as possible. You don't express any arrogance, even if you've been

273

working so hard you'd like to reward yourself. My strategy has always been, if possible, not to put any barriers
between myself and the people in my neighbourhood
who have no means. Moving house doesn't solve anything except my personal worry.

One evening, he was coming home from work when eight
men, dressed in police uniform stopped him, told him to
get out of the car and then locked him into the trunk. He
could hear them discussing what to do with him because
they had discovered that the fuel gauge showed hardly any
fuel; some were arguing that if he couldn't afford to buy
fuel: 'We're not going to get anything from him.' Obviously
having fuelled up, these men drove around from six o'clock
until eleven.

All I was worried about was that they would tangle
with the police, because I would probably be killed in
the crossfire. I started to pray. I asked God to forgive me
my sins. I was getting ready to be killed.

But then, at about eleven o'clock, the chief of these guys came around
to him and said: 'We're going to let you go. Get out of the car.'

I did not believe him; I thought *this is where they'll kill
me*, and stayed where I was. And then I heard a lot of
talking, and after a while I just put my head up a little
bit, and they saw me, and the chief said: 'Are you still
there? Why are you still there?'

Tham is not the only one in from the Concern office who's
been through this, 'our accountant has too.'
The security situation in Port Au Prince can change
suddenly with no notice, and it is worth noting that the aid
workers are not the only ones at risk; the Concern drivers too
face danger.

Meanwhile, at the start, both Tham, as Najac's superior, and Najac himself were facing a significant credibility problem around their infant peace-building project within the slums, especially since they suspected that at the highest level, it was seen as 'promoting impunity' – and that the gangs guessed this.

Their fear proved well-founded when they went to the prime minister to explain that this was not the case and that the model was legitimately from Belfast, the Irish organisation Glencree, which had success with the conflict situation in the North of Ireland – and the Irish aid organisation, Concern, which had a good reputation with the authorities.

> 'Okay [said the Prime Minister], arrange a meeting for me with all of them together, and I'll come with all of the police and we will get all of them.'

They explained again, in detail, which proved to be 'a big shock' for the politician because of Haiti's long tradition, not of negotiating, but of violence and revenge.

This is dangerous territory, and Tham knows it. Does he ever feel like just giving up, and taking a rest from all this struggle and worry?

> I still have a lot to do in the development world. I still don't feel it's difficult to get up in the morning to come to work. That for me is where the signal is: I wake up happy to start a new day, and what keeps me in Concern is its flexibility. I have the opportunity to make sugges-tions, to make change.

Building physical bridges can yield visual evidence of progress. Yields from the peace-building process are slow and psychological. And these days, he says, some of the gang members who have been through the Concern/Glencree process are actually acting as 'consultants in peace-building, and if we need to have them as consultants we do a contract with them and we pay them.'

Let's finish with an article of faith as expressed and lived for so many years by Najac Jean Linz, whose dogged persistence is typified, by not just by his striking bicycle metaphor but by this: 'People need to find a way to wake up the good in them.'

24

'When the going gets tough, you have to have a reason to be there.

– Aengus Finucane

Following retirement from Camden Street, as we know, Aengus jumped with his customary joyful gusto into his new post as honorary president of Concern US, making new friends and conquests, not immediately and not all at once, as that first lunch with Tom Moran, Ed Kenney and Michael Lally has shown.

As it happened, as the years passed, four of the most generous of Concern's US donors were named 'Tom'.

One of them, Tom McCauley from Chicago, died suddenly from an aneurism in December 2003. Aengus, in Ireland at the time, immediately hopped on a plane. On it, he took out his trusty pen and pad and spent the flight musing and writing about his Four Toms. Always one to title his pieces, he called this one, 'Thoughts on a Flight'. It is lengthy and has been cut down for print.

> I have spent a few months in the US each year – for a few years – promoting Concern … Fulfilling years. Made many good friends and worked with wonderful colleagues.
>
> During the years, Four Toms stood out prominently, very good friends of mine and great friends of Concern.

I first met Doctor Tom Durant from Boston in the Kampuchean refugee camps on the Thai border in 1978, working with the thousands of refugees who had fled the killing fields of Pol Pot.

I met him again in 1992 among the displaced and famine-stricken people in Somalia. Then five years ago in 1998 again, when he was attached to Massachusetts General Hospital. His mother's people were from Galway.

He died in Boston in 2001, and I was a concelebrant of his funeral Mass with another concelebrant, Father Felix Ojimba, who as a senior seminarian had worked with me in the parish of Uli during the Biafran war and famine in the late 1960s. Felix headed a team of twenty-three junior seminarians to prepare any food they could procure and to distribute it to feeding centres in the four towns that made up Uli parish. And it was from operations like this in Biafra that Concern emerged.

Ojimba, now ordained a priest, was a chaplain in Mass General, and with me visited Tom Durant during his last illness. And it was Tom Durant who introduced me to the second Tom on the list, Tom Flatley.

A man of substance in Boston and well beyond, he had Mayo roots. Tom left Ireland in the early 1950s, but has always endowed not only causes in the US, but charities and institutions in Ireland.

And each year since, he has supported the organisation, and in 1997 was the driving force behind the erection of the Irish Famine Memorial in Boston, unveiled in 1998 in the presence of the Jewish, Asian and African communities, signifying the universality of the immigrant experience and in tune with Tom Flatley's global thinking. He also funded the erection of a famine memorial in Kiltimagh.

I gave Tom a small piece of stone from one of the famine roads of Clare, broken by our ancestors for a road going nowhere as a work-for-food scheme, an alternative to giving handouts of food to the feckless Irish during the 1840s. The wages for a full day's work were a handful of grain.

Tom McCauley in Chicago had quite a lot in common with Tom Flatley. A daily Mass-goer, he too had left Ireland in the early 1950s. We were close in age. He was from Cavan, and during our first meeting we began to discuss the All-Ireland final between Cavan and Kerry, played in the Polo Grounds in New York as part of the Commemoration of the centenary of the Great Irish Famine. As a schoolboy I had collected photos of the players of that era for a scrapbook, and McCauley was impressed by my recitation of the names of almost all of the Cavan team. As a young lad, Tom was brought to New York by his uncles for that famous match.

Tom and [his wife] Mary were strong supporters of Concern from the get-go. They provided free office space, put me up in their home and they went to Haiti to see the work for themselves.

Tom was a steelworker on the Manhattan skyscrapers, but invested his earnings in a bar, did extremely well until he owned several, bringing singers and Irish musicians to the pubs. Then he again moved, into building and property development, and became very prosperous.

He was an usher at Masses in Holy Name [Cathedral]. He was the strong, silent and unassuming type to the end. I had a great evening with him and Mary just ten days before he died.

Tom Moran is one of the best known and deservedly admired philanthropists in New York. He has a global vision, but never lost the common touch, and wears his loves on his sleeve.

It was a good day for Concern when he joined the board of Concern US and brought with him a host of friends from Mutual of America and many of his other spheres of influence. When he became chairman of the board, Concern became the envy of many worthy organisations. I cheerfully concede that their envy was justifiable.... He has attracted to the board an extraordinary array of talent. He is not above arm-twisting when recruiting 'volunteers', and his own generosity knows no bounds. He is a practical Christian, in gratitude and appreciation for the blessings we enjoy and in the readiness to reach out and share with those who have much less.

Thomas the apostle is sometimes referred to as Doubting Thomas. This epithet would not sit easily with any of the Four Toms of Concern US. All four knew where they were going and steadfastly pursued their goals. Ten years on from setting up operations in the United States, Concern is garnering a fruitful harvest for the poorest in developing countries.

You get the picture. And by the way, Aengus always attributed Cavan's famous win by four points at the Polo Grounds that day to the fact that the team flew to New York, whereas Kerry had to travel by the rougher and longer passage by sea.

Tom Flatley from Boston was of the first-generation, Irish-immigrant-makes-good school. A legend has grown up around how his friendship with Aengus came about, and like most legends involving Father Finucane, the substance and tag line of the story is accurate, but it's how we get there that differs in various people's memories.

What is not in dispute is that Aengus and Tom Flatley first met face to face when Aengus went into the little diner/restaurant where Tom was having his regular breakfast after Mass one morning.

There are those who say that he knew who he was targeting when he 'just happened' to walk in.

There are those who say that, having learned that Mr Flatley attended that early morning Mass without fail, Aengus arranged to give a powerful sermon at it that morning, laying it on about the Irish famine in his dramatically graphic terms.

But his brother Jack knocks this one on the head.

Whatever the details of the arrangements surrounding that first meeting across the table, Tom Flatley asked this impressive Irish priest to meet him again at breakfast for a second time. At this second breakfast he handed Aengus an envelope. In the envelope was a cheque for a million dollars.

This proved to be the precursor for similar generosity to Concern from Tom Flatley and his family, even after the deaths of both Tom and Aengus.

Tom Moran we have met. Tom Durant we have encountered only in Aengus's Four Toms musings, but to Aengus he was very important. From Dorchester, a suburb of Boston, he was a friend of the Kennedys, Ted in particular. He was assistant director of Mass General Hospital, but, as is evident from Aengus's piece, spent a great deal of his life rushing to disaster areas to offer his help and expertise.

This brings us to the late Tom McCauley. On a cold Chicago morning, his widow Mary and his daughter Kathy order coffee for the three of us in a downtown coffee shop.

Kathy, a realtor, is living proof that devotion to Concern can move down the generations as she is now one of the younger Concern Chicago queenpins. Because of her mother's devotion to Aengus, even posthumously, and to Concern in general, she had been attending Concern events since she was very young.

As for Mary ('I'm an old lady – I'm all paint and putty now!') she relates how the organisation's fundraising arm in the second city began in the first place.

> Ten or maybe fifteen of us sat around my dining table asking what should we do. And Fergal Mulchrone said: 'We can all sit around and go to meetings, but let everyone here actually do something?' And I said: 'I'll have a black-tie.' I had no idea how I was going to do it. But my son Michael had said: 'If you make it black-tie, people behave better!'

In the annals of Concern in Chicago, that event is legendary: everyone interviewed in the city remembered it and brought it up, talking at length about the Irish and Israeli bands, the food, the glamour, the sudden, monsoon-like downpour at 2 a.m., and in most opinions, although there have been other stellar events, this one wears the crown. 'We danced until four o'clock in the morning. The police were called twice,' says Mary happily.

They raised $30,000 that night.

This event took place before Aengus arrived in their midst, and when he did, like all the other Irish-American philanthropists, the McCauleys fell for him. He and Tom sat for hours in their house talking about Gaelic football and all kinds of sport. Mary set aside 'the Aengus suite' in their house, 'with a lock on it so no one else could use it.'

Tom, one of nine siblings, had no truck 'with all that *Erin go Bragh, Kiss me, I'm Irish* stuff,' says Kathy – and according to Mary, the sentiment included Ireland itself. Son of a farmer, he was beaten in school because his hands weren't clean, so he left education and came out to America as an ironworker on the Prudential Building. Then one day, says his widow, he 'threw his tool-belt into the lake, went downtown and got a job behind a bar.' He ended up owning a chain of bars and a construction and development company.

She smiles reminiscently: 'I got to see the beauty in him the longer we were married. People thought he was such a toughie, but underneath he was a cookie ...'. He went back to Ireland only once.

For Kathy, who was very young on first acquaintance with Aengus:

> We'd pick up this priest guy from the airport, and he'd come in and he'd have his hot toddy or something and a bit of apple pie, and he'd regale us with the stories. He was Granddad to the world....
>
> Yeah, [Mary chimes in], the kids loved him. And he'd say Mass for us. We can put fourteen around my dining-room table and we'd have the best time. He was like an old shoe around the house. He was there for one Ash Wednesday, I remember. I'd got in all the Irish stuff, and I'm there in the kitchen doing breakfast for him and frying up the eggs and

sausages and everything, and he goes: 'I'll just have the eggs please, Mary.' What a sweetie! *I'll just have the eggs! Such tact.*

What always struck Kathy, she says, was that for Aengus the money wasn't going into being picked up at airports in (Lincoln) Town Cars, but that it all went where it was supposed to go. He'd be at our house getting ready to meet donors for dinner and he'd say: 'Gotta put on the gear,' and he'd go out to do battle for the money with the donors. Then he'd come back in and he'd stop being 'that priest guy'.

What is striking about this conversation is that both mother and daughter integrate what is virtually Concern jargon throughout their conversations about the organisation and Aengus: 'Yeah, Concern will go in where no one else will,' or 'The best thing about Concern is that Concern never gives up ...'.

Why is it that wealthy, even just comfortably off Americans are so philanthropic?

'Are they?' Kathy seems genuinely surprised. She thinks about it. Fundraising is no cakewalk, and not automatically successful. She understands why this would be so for an organisation like Concern, admitting that it is difficult to expect people not connected in some way to give money for people 'millions of miles away' with problems they cannot comprehend and have barely glimpsed in the media.

'But I'm connected. Every time I have a glass of water in the middle of the night I think about it.'

Her mother's take on this is interesting, and perhaps illustrates the reason for at least some of the Irish American philanthropy. 'Where do you get your conscience from but from your parents? A child is not born with a conscience; goodness and kindness is passed on.'

These two women have visited Haiti; a trip that had served only to deepen and solidify their commitment.

Equally so for Jim and Kelly McShane, a couple whose commitment to Concern is, if not fathomless (because they do ask questions for themselves), very deep. They too have been to Haiti, as well as to other places, including Ethiopia and Bangladesh. 'We're trying to understand the donor of the future,' Kelly says, over dinner in a downtown restaurant.

> We're in an information era. Why do people give? Because someone asked them to. Because their fathers used to donate. Because there has to be some sort of personal connection to make it stick. [Mary McCauley's 'goodness and kindness passed on.']

Jim is a civil engineer, founder and CEO of various interrelated development, construction and investment companies, he puts his money where his mouth is in the service of Concern's poor. At the time we spoke, Kelly was preparing to go again to Ethiopa to have a look at more of the Ethiopian programmes, including water projects she and her husband have funded in memory of their deceased son, Michael. (And on a personal basis, the couple appreciate very much that for a long period after their son's death, Aengus rang them 'every single week.')

Frances O'Keeffe, at the time the chair of Concern in Ireland, was her escort on their visit to the former camp area of Harbo, the women discovered that 'every second person there' remembered Jack and Concern. One man, well into his seventies, whose wife and a couple of children had died in the famine, particularly appreciated the two Concern nurses who had sat with him and cried.

During their tour of the water projects, Kelly met an old lady with a thirty-litre container of water and asked her what difference the project had made to her. And the woman said back:

> I can sleep every night now. Before, when we went to collect water at night, many of our women were attacked and raped. Now I can sleep, get up in the morning, meet all my friends at the water and go home safely.

We then met an 11-year-old with a twenty-litre container and Kelly asked her the same question. 'I can get to school every day.'

'All we needed to know,' Kelly said to me at the end, 'was that we have changed people's lives.'

Jack had been their escort on a previous trip to South Wollo province. This is Jim:

These women, about thirty of them, wore these blue burkhas. They went to the elders and demanded that no girls were to be married before the age of 18, and they got that law passed in that community. And now they were going out to other communities to try to enrol them too.

And then Jack asked one woman how old she was when she was married. She was 11. She had her first child at age 12. These women had no chance for education.

Now, her children or her children's children may have a chance. Kelly and I have a foundation, and education is a big part of it. Aengus said that: 'to lift a culture you need to educate the girls.' That rang a bell. Seeing that in Ethiopia made me very, very proud of what Concern is doing.

Jim then recites again what so many have said in connection with the organisation to which they are now attached: 'Once you see or experience it, you get hooks into your heart that don't let go.'

When the name 'Aengus' is mentioned, what does it mean to the McShanes? For Jim:

He was very graphic when he talked. He opened our eyes to the poorest of the poor around the world.

25

*'From being overseas, I realise now what Aengus and Jack did:
they sacrificed their entire lives.'*

– Susan Finucane

Aengus has starred in many people's personal memory-movies, but did you know he played a small but pivotal role in a novel? It was written by no less a collaborative pair than the ex-mayor of Boston, Ray Flynn, and Robin Moore, author of *The French Connection*. This tidbit comes courtesy of Dan Casey, of the previous chapter, when he could make his voice heard above the din.

The novel is called *The Accidental Pope*, and the writers' main character is a humble fisherman, married with children, who becomes Pope after his wife dies. Following his elevation, the new US ambassador to the Vatican is on an aircraft bound for Rome when he finds himself sitting beside an Irish priest, a Father Finucume (*sic*).

Over four pages, this 'old priest' (wouldn't Aengus have loved that!) fulminates passionately about famine and poverty in Africa, and bats away criticisms about the operations of his humanitarian organisation in countries ruled over by corrupt despots, tyrants and other unsavoury types. He tells his American seat companion in no uncertain terms that who rules where is not his problem, just the plight of 'God's children' in their territories. He drops broad hints to the ambassador that he would like a personal meeting with the Pope to expound on this – and in fact, the writers do give him that opportunity, letting him ride with the fictional Pope Peter the Second, who is on his way to Dublin Airport after a visit to Ireland.

Remember Mary Pat O'Connor, who by calling the meeting in Chicago with Don Mullan set the whole Concern ball rolling there? That Women of Concern luncheon was her idea. She had noticed that Irish Institutions in Chicago were dominated by men, and 'was noodling that around for a while.'

She mentioned the idea to Siobhan Walsh, who passed it on to Aengus, whose response, predictably was: 'Anything to do with women is OK with me.'

We catch up in Dublin on a dreary January morning in a coffee shop in Terenure. Over a Full Irish, she talks with insight, love and some humour about the decidedly real Aengus. She was with him one time in Palm Beach, Miami:

> ... where the parking meters have gold studs – and he was doing what he did best: shakin' hands and kissin' babies, telling me out of the side of his mouth: 'I know who this is for!'

She and her daughter went to visit him during his last illness, and when they walked into his room, opened with the usual: 'Aengus! You look great!' The quick riposte was, 'You look disappointed!'

'He was so quick.'

She will never forget, she says, the expression in Siobhan Walsh's eyes when the suggestion was made that Chicago should set up its own office: *God, I can barely keep New York going*:

> ... and she says: 'Let's do one thing at a time.' Then Bob goes: 'Well, how much would it cost?' and Siobhan goes, real quick: 'A hundred thousand!' and he says back:

'Okay. That'll be our goal.' Everyone else was saying: 'Let's go, let's get going.' The whole thing escalated. It was hysterical.

And once she became embedded in Concern, she says:

I ended up meeting Aengus in New York; we went to dinner. I fell in love with that man. I'd never met anyone like him, so kind, and he was just so much fun. And boy, could he tell stories! And he always said how important it was, wherever he was, to get the women involved because of their eagerness and ability to do anything.

Flattery had carried Aengus many, many miles.

Being involved with Concern, for her, does feel like having fun, but also like being a member of a family. She instances this. Shortly after the Concern venture took wing in Chicago, her daughter fell off a cliff in Killiney in Dublin, broke her back, and was hospitalised for quite a long time in St Vincent's Hospital. On hearing the news, Mary, of course, flew immediately to Ireland but with no real place to stay:

… and one day I was in there visiting with her and Aengus and Siobhan arrived. They were great together, those two: a great dog and pony show!

He was on his way back to the States, and he just handed me the key to his place, which is in Sandymount, walkable to Vincent's. I was able to stay there for the duration in that magical place, surrounded by all his icons and stuff. It saved my sanity.

There were a few wrinkles to be ironed out before that first women's lunch. For instance, the organisers felt they needed to secure the involvement of the board and parishioners of Holy

Name Cathedral, many of whom fall into Dolores Connolly's 'well-heeled' category.

> So we go up there, and I do this presentation to the board. I'm not really a holy Catholic, so I was nervous.
>
> The Monsignor, Bob McLoughlin – four foot nothin', cute as a button – introduces me to the board, and I give my spiel about maybe co-hosting because I knew that nobody in Chicago knew much about Concern at that point.

She then faced searching questions, including some about this new [to them] organisation's attitude towards and/or advocacy of birth control:

> I got frustrated, but the next thing, [Monsignor] Bob jumps up and says: 'Look, justice is never pretty and those people need justice, so whatever it takes to give them a chance at life, that's justice. And number two, my niece works for Concern in Africa, okay?'
>
> Nobody had known that Bob McLoughlin's niece was working for Concern in Africa, but then he went on and on about what an incredible organisation it was. It was one of these wonderful *Ohhhhh my Gaaaawd!* moments. And the board women bought in and they were just rocks.

Of course she, like most of the other Concern supporters in the US, travelled to Haiti. 'That country is always in emergency.' But she went to other places too, including Cambodia, where her mission was to view Concern's forestry programme. 'That was on the development side. It was so successful, all the other agencies wanted to get in on it.'

In Cambodia, Concern people had noticed the ravaging of beautiful old forests. In one region the organisation's workers brought in all the schoolteachers, monks, villagers, everyone who lived on the periphery of the woodlands who were willy-nilly taking what they needed for firewood, but not reseeding. 'And there were a lot of problems with the Vietnamese coming in and taking their teak.'

Concern took these problems in hand, devised a programme and asked Mary Pat to organise a brochure about their plans for reafforestation. As research:

> They took me all over so I could see what was happening with this project. They were training people to use the forest for a lot more than charcoal, using seeds to replant and even for food in some cases, weaving baskets, even making clothing from the foliage. It was a huge, cooperative development effort with monks going around teaching people how to plant little saplings and take care of them.
>
> Women were getting into it. There was a school for orphan girls who had started their own little orchard. We're talking mindset change here, and really it was magical.

She was upset, however, on finding a man in his thirties noticeably hunched over his Concern Office desk as a result of very severe scoliosis.

Lest we forget, Pol Pot's regime, the Khmer Rouge, dictated that the country should become solely agrarian. Education and urban living were banned, schools closed, teachers shot, and anyone who wore glasses condemned as part of the intelligentsia. Urban dwellers were sent en masse into the rural areas to work in the rice paddies.

This man, the sight of whom so upset Mary Pat in that office, had been only 2 years old when he was thus displaced with his family. Even at that age, however, he had been put to work, bent double in these fields for long, long days, and his little 2-year-old spine had grown and solidified into an inflexible 'U'.

26

'Aengus was a natural-born leader who didn't like bureaucracy, and wasn't he right?'

– Michael D. Higgins (President of Ireland)

Yes, great memories – that little grandniece of Aengus had showed foresight beyond her years. Memories and reminiscences of Aengus's life and work spiced the winter air within the surrounds of *Áras an Uachtaráin* in January 2014 during the ceremony when the award in his name, the Aengus Finucane Humanitarian Award, was being presented to President Michael D. Higgins in recognition of the president's lifelong work for social justice on behalf of the poor and the marginalised.

In an atmosphere of affection and tangible warmth, the award was presented by Jack and was attended by the Finucanes, along with grandees, a large number of former volunteers plus present staff of Concern.

Mary Finucane, the eldest and now the matriarch of the Finucane family, agrees with the rest of the family that Aengus made his mark early. 'As a child,' she says, 'he was full of fun and energy, always in good humour and a great confidant.'

Now well into her eighties, but still playing bridge twice a week, she trained as a nurse in Baggot Street. Following graduation in 1952, she established the family tradition of adventure and travel, taking a job in Newfoundland, then moving onto the main Canada landmass, then down into the States. Wanderlust sated, she returned to work as a district nurse in various areas, including Kerry and the Midlands, before finishing up in Limerick, where, long retired, she now lives in the family home on Shelbourne Road, surrounded by 'all the stuff, my mother's, father's, even my grandmother's, all the things from our old home.'

She is giving her interview in one of the splendid reception rooms of the *Áras,* where the president has just received the award. In the course of the event, a video about Aengus had been played in which all aspects of his own services to humanity were covered. Through the loudspeakers his great laugh rang around the room, infecting the distinguished audience who could not help but laugh along. But with the relay of his anger and indignation about the ineffectual response of the UN to the situation in Somalia, the mirth trailed away.

Mary admits that seeing her brother once more in full flow was very emotional for her, adding that she 'misses him terribly.'

Two weeks later, President Higgins gave a private interview for this book. Whatever about accepting his award from Concern, he is constrained, naturally, by not seeming or being seen to favour one Irish development NGO over any other. And so, probably to keep a watching brief, we were joined over lunch not just, happily, by Sabina Higgins, but by Wally Young, an army man, well seasoned in media affairs from his days acting as spokesperson for the forces and now adviser to the Áras communications team.

The president, as he had said in his speech a fortnight previously, was familiar with both Jack and Aengus:

I met them at conferences and so on and at meet-ings of agencies when I was on the Foreign Affairs

committee. Aengus would have given the overview;
Jack would have presented the information from
the field.

His impression of Aengus was that he was 'a natural-born
leader who didn't like bureaucracy.' Then, with that lopsided,
mischievous (and rather twinkly) smile, Michael D. added, 'And
wasn't he right?'

In Michael D.'s opinion, Aengus displayed the same type
of character traits in espousing his issue (the poor) as Bishop
Eamon Casey did, in his day, about his: housing in London.
These traits, which he seems greatly to admire, coalesced in
both clerics as:

> ... kind of unstoppable forces, seeing no such thing as an
> unsolvable problem. Whether one was right or wrong,
> get on with it and do something, and do it now. There
> was a sense of immediacy, and a kind of raw human-
> ity. People who aren't like that don't understand people
> who are.

Like the general population of Irish people at the time, Aengus
Finucane burst into the president's consciousness during the
period of the Nigerian civil war.

> I heard of him first during the early stuff on Biafra
> and so forth. What was extraordinary about this was
> this larger than life character avoiding the bureaucrats
> and responding very vigorously to the demands on the
> ground.
>
> I remember seeing images of him being very
> distressed. The unorthodox ways of delivering food off
> the planes at night, not doing it the slow, bureaucratic
> way, but done in the way that it would work.
>
> For these Holy Ghost Fathers, there wasn't the
> sophisticated storage for aid that you have now, ready

for quick responses, no NGO structures or Irish Aid or any of that, so all of this was new ground.

Curiously, my view of the two brothers was always that Aengus was doing the work of pushing the governments to have capacity for humanitarian response, whereas Jack was on the ground putting in the structures.

Michael D. Higgins travelled through the famine fields of Somalia at the peak of that country's troubles in 1992, spent time in Mogadishu, and was accommodated in the Concern compound when it was coming under attack. 'Nothing fatal, just the usual crowd of young men, teens and early twenties. The gates were locked, and they would be trying to get in, rattling them.' Scholar that he is, before he left for Somalia, Michael D. researched its social system:

... which is clan-based. They're a pastoral people with a very oral culture, full of ritual.

When someone dies, they stop all the animals and change their clothes before moving on again. So many died in the hut beside where I was staying, the Somali rituals of death couldn't prevail. You'd look in and the bodies would all be in corners. They'd come in wearing masks to remove them.

These death rituals were specific. The deceased must be buried on the day of death. To encourage the spirit to pass, the Koran is read over the body by a family member while another one prepares and washes the body, a man for a man, a woman for a woman. Then, after a service in the mosque, the body is covered with a green cloth embroidered with gold, leaving the face uncovered to enable direct contact with the earth and other natural elements, including grass, leaves, sawdust and wood. In Somalia, the cause of death of a loved one is apparently usually cited by family as the Will of Allah.

For the dead in this place, Michael D. saw merely: 'A huge mound of sand being made, and they'd a big machine that poked holes in the sand and they'd just push the bones into them. It was the death of a culture as well.'

Frances O'Keeffe, who is now a public health nurse in Dublin's inner city, spent twenty-five years working for Concern in different fields. When she gave her interview, she was the then chair of the organisation.

She explained that there are a lot of rituals surrounding burials in different parts of the world, and that those who work or volunteer in these fields are always made specifically aware of the importance of the differing cultural practices.

> We would spend hours and hours talking to chiefs and elders and God-knows-what musicians under trees, making sure we were doing what they wanted.
>
> It would be one of the first things we'd do, to know if we were being culturally appropriate. I think that comes with the missionary history – they lived with the people.

During that lunch in the Áras with Sabina and the diplomatically tactful Wally Young, President Michael D. Higgins continued to relive his time in Somalia. A veteran of many difficult experiences in many different conflicts, what he witnessed in Somalia at the time was:

> ... desperate. Not just the mothers and children, but a huge proportion of the general population in a dreadful condition from disease and malnutrition, Somalian bodies being routinely collected each morning by huge trucks....

He talks then in a semi-whisper about 'the most harrowing part' of his Somalian trip: the time when, with a local bishop, he was on the road, watching the relentless flow of people:

> ... an enormous number of people, walking and walking. And there was this mother who had been

walking for 200 kilometres. Walking. She had twins. One of the twins had died; the other twin was very dehydrated....

They took the mother and twins into their car, rushing them to the next medical station. 'But there was a big, long queue.' They did manage to get the mother up to the top of this queue, 'and the bishop handed over the [living] twin, and didn't the child die.'

He stops. He has to. He and Sabina have four children: Alice Mary, John, Michael Junior and Daniel. John and Michael Junior are twins.

He could not shake that image, he says, after a bit. It haunted him for five or six weeks after he got back. Sabina, who is across the table, looks compassionately at him: 'I remember that!'

He doesn't say any more. None of us says any more about that.

Michael D. then recalls why we are all here this day around the lunch table, and whom we are to talk about: 'When someone comes along who is a great force of nature, he can make a difference.' And he quotes part of Aengus's most famous mantra: '... as much as you can for as long as you can', adding: 'and then you leave.'

Even as he says it, it is clear that he is still seeing that particular horror of horrors he encountered during the trip to Somalia.

Sometimes, the human psyche cannot easily deal with such disturbing matters. In compensation, it latches on to peripheral details. One of the president's abiding memories of that trip is that, having left Mogadishu during his stay in the Concern compound in Baidoa, with Mary Robinson expected, the place swarming with reporters and accommodation tight, he had to share a room with Vincent Browne:

There were three beds in the room, I remember. He had the largest mosquito net. I remember saying it to him afterwards, but he never acknowledged it. He had a four-poster bed so the mosquito net could hang properly.

It's nearly impossible to get mosquito nets to hang properly, unless you have hooks in the wall.

President Higgins is possessed of a wicked sense of humour. The very first overseas country he visited was Tanzania:

> And the local people in Tanzania told me that the attitude of many NGOs to Africa could be very patronising. They called them 'The Whenwees.'
> (Sorry, President ... 'the Whenwees?')
> 'The Whenwees!' When we were in India we had this, when we were in Sierra Leone we had that....

27

'Concern did an amazing job putting an Irish African charity on the mainstream of US donor philanthropy, and not just on the usual Irish-American circuit. They succeeded at the very higher levels.'

– Niall O'Dowd (Irish Voice newspaper)

Sarah, one of Aengus's and Jack's nieces, works in a bank in Dublin, although in personality and presentation she is a million miles away from the besuited and be-shiny-shoed image the word 'banker' conjures. She is tall, blonde, striking – and very much her own person.

She believes this trait came early, necessarily so because, when her mother died: 'I had to take charge.' Of Aengus and Jack's nieces and nephews (there are fourteen), Sarah is still, she believes, the 'contact cousin'; she certainly was when Aengus was still alive. 'He was always saying to me: "Well, Sarah, have you been in touch?"'

In her day job at the bank, the environment:

… is less than eccentric, and I used to love evenings with Aengus and Michael Lally. Mick is mad in a Connemara way, like fireworks, you start something, then you think of something else and you go off on it. It's so entertaining.…
And when himself and Aengus got together it was like:

'Sarah, I have to write a letter to get a million quid, so cook us something nice?'

'Would you like an omelette?'

'Er … will we share a fish and chips?'

'Okay.'

'Ah, sure, if you're going, we'll have the full fish and chips, will we? But don't tell Jack …'.

And I'd go down to Borza's on the Green [famous throughout southside Dublin] and get the fish and chips for us all, and that was his favourite thing.

After our mother's death, as girls, as nieces, we ended up with three fathers in our lives: Aengus, Jack and Dad.

Between them, she says, these three Finucane men instilled in the girls, and in Jack, their brother, that there should be balance in all areas of life: work, play, friendship, enjoyment, altruism, kindness, discipline, tenderness – and a little bit of mischief; but also that it was okay to enjoy what the Lord has provided, like good food and wine, good whiskey, nice shirts and decent shoes. 'They would always believe that you don't have to save the world in bad sandals.'

For her, her uncle was ever the optimist. Having just been diagnosed with the illness that proved to be his last, just before going into treatment where he fully expected to become bald, he came in to the apartment holding three hats: 'Which hat do I look fat in, Sarah?' But he never lost his hair.'

For the wall of his hospital room in Kimmage, she made a map of the world. He had a notebook in which he had written the names of all involved with his treatment and welfare, and from where in the world each had come. Along with the map, she gave him a set of pins so he could red-dot everyone's home place:

… from the home of the lady who used to bring him his cup of tea, right up to the top. This is something he has given to me and to us all: to have great respect for people and who they are.

I think that comes across in all the jobs that he
did. He was very practical and in the moment: chicken
wings with the company, solemn head when out and
about. He was all those characters. He had friendships
from young to old, from top to bottom, the secretaries
in Concern who would still want to meet one of us
when they're over. No matter who you were he had
these individual relationships with everyone: everyone
was Aengus's best friend, and in a way that was true.

We are meeting in the Radisson Hotel. She talks about the size
of his loss to her life, how much she loved him, how much she
misses him, how Dublin is a poorer city for her without him:

> He was my sense of place in Dublin. That view of the
> [Poolbeg] towers from the corner of Aengus's block is
> my favourite view of Dublin. He was my slippers. You
> just hung out with Aengus....

She chokes up.

Despite his gregariousness, conviviality and practicality,
the spiritual side of Aengus was never far from the surface
– for instance the 'intimate' Masses he celebrated around
kitchen, dining and other tables which had such an effect
on so many people of little or diverse faiths, his wearing
the collar in public going about the streets of New York in
case someone had a heart attack and was in need of the Last
Rites, *and how else would he or she know there was a priest at
hand to administer them?*

Aengus was called upon to give Last Rites in a very tragic
situation in Somalia. Out of the multitudes who served as
volunteers during some of the most volatile conflicts in some
of the most dangerous places in the world, to date the only
person killed in action has been 23-year-old Valerie Place,
who was shot in a car while travelling in a small convoy

between Mogadishu and Baidoa in Somalia. Aengus was with her. And the image of this experienced priest kneeling beside the car to administer the Last Rites to a dying girl, in a dusty Somalian roadway so far from home, for both of them is vivid, and telling.

'People ask you what was the toughest place you worked in.' This is Frances O'Keeffe, the organisation's chair. 'It was Somalia.'

Concern had 1,000 staff in the country, and she was in charge of a feeding centre in Mogadishu, 'feeding God knows how many thousands.'

Valerie Place, a 23-year old staff nurse in St James's Hospital in Dublin, was one of the volunteers in Mogadishu. Before signing up, she already had the giving gene. She had been involved with CASA (Caring and Sharing Association, providing respite and social care for people with disabilities) and with taking people with learning difficulties to Lourdes.

'She was the youngest volunteer at the time,' says Frances; 'she'd never been to Baidoa, and really wanted to go.' As it happened, Aengus, as CEO, was in Mogadishu at the time, and acceded to her request: 'I think you're ready.'

And so, on 22 February 1993, she set off down the road as part of a small, security-protected convoy that included Aengus. They were ambushed and she was shot.

> That was the one time I saw Aengus cry. And every time Valerie was mentioned since, no matter how often she was mentioned, he'd cry again. He felt responsible, so did Mike McDonagh.

Prior to Valerie's remains being brought back to Ireland, her father and sister flew to Frankfurt, the staging post to which the body had been transported with the help of the American military.

Frances accompanied the Places on the flight to the German city; burned into her brain is the question the dead girl's father asked her: 'I'm just wondering, Frances, is Concern going to leave Somalia?' She told him that the organisation had not even thought about it. 'And he said: "I hope they don't, because poor Valerie would have died in vain." '

Frances, who like others interviewed has worked with both Finucane brothers:

> We worked in very dangerous places, but with Aengus and Jack, you just found the bravery. A great strength, no fear. I never once doubted the decisions made. With Aengus there was no discussion: 'This is what you're going to do.'
>
> With Jack, people's worries were taken away. You'd tell him what the problem was, he'd take it away and come back with a solution.
>
> They just worked differently.

Perhaps because of their initial training as missionaries, in their private and Concern lives both brothers insisted on the tradition of open hospitality. Patsy has already talked about all the young people, nieces and their friends, who treated Aengus's Dublin apartment as a crash pad. Jack continues to host ex-volunteers and Concern friends who come to Dublin in his.

Frances has some surprising – and jolting – juxtapositions to offer, such as: 'Somalia is beautiful, like Kerry; beautiful people too, but no one, no one, should ever have to see murdered children.' She saw many corpses in that conflict, not all of them children.

> 3,580 people buried in the first few days I was in Mogadishu. These were adults. Nobody was caring for them. I rang Mike McDonagh: 'We have to do something.'
>
> Mike was very busy with his own programmes: 'You come up with a plan!'
>
> So we opened up a feeding centre – a hospice, basically. There were three governing principles:

One: Everyone would have a wash;

Two: Everyone would have clothes: 'They were dying with no clothes on. God, there's nothing worse!

Three: No one would die alone

Within a very short time, people were living. And the reason was that someone was caring for them.

Bananas were big. Working with Frances was a girl called Mary Considine, who was in charge of supplies.

> She was called 'Mary more bananas' because she was always screaming down the phone at the suppliers: 'More Bananas! More Bananas!' The suppliers couldn't keep up with the demand.

On an inspection trip to the field in Wajid, Jack found that his workers, including at that stage Frances herself, 'were living like camels,' as he said in disgust. What is more, they were getting sick.

> He took one of us off in a plane with him to buy supplies, then got Phena [O'Boyle] to come in so there was clean water and proper food. God, if I had seen one more plate of spaghetti with red sauce!
>
> But she'd get a bit of garlic and a bit of salt and a bit of flour and make a different kind of sauce, and it changed our lives. We'd been sleeping on these awful beds, but she got pillows for everyone, and very quickly people stopped getting sick. We were sleeping better at night; we weren't all like zombies during the day.
>
> Poor Phena, she was working her socks off and he was: 'Do this, do that,' but he was right because everything was much better for us all. Every cook was trained in how to do the water, how to cook properly. People were trained how to change and clean the linen. These things really made a difference....

There then arose the matter of the potatoes:

> There were pilots coming in at all hours of the night
> bringing food in for the feeding centres, and we used to
> have to go to the airport because otherwise the pilots
> would be shot – ridiculous carry on – but when they
> saw we were with them they wouldn't shoot them, blah,
> blah, blah....
>
> Anyway, one of them said to me one night: 'Is there
> anything ye'd like?'
> 'Oh my God, we'd love potatoes!'
> 'Anything else?'
> 'Any chance of a bit of butter?'
> So every time they came in after that, they brought
> two bags of potatoes and butter. And the other girls
> were saying to me: 'Could you not have asked them for
> brandy or something?'
> 'I will in my foot,' I said, 'I'd rather have potatoes.'
> That's the kind of thing Jack would never mind.
> Anything that would help people work better.

Frances was in Baidoa, one of only five workers there until
the danger became such that it had to be hurriedly evacuated.
Before that happened, she was puzzled by the number of times
Aengus telephoned: 'Are you all right, Frances?'

After the evacuation, she discovered that every night they
were there he had telephoned the parents of all five individually
to tell them that they were safe: 'I was talking to Frances again
today. She had a very busy day, but everything's fine.'

> Baidoa was bad, and they [the families at home] were
> seeing terrible things on the television. They all waited
> for that phone call. It was an extraordinary thing to do,
> and we didn't know about it. He didn't tell us, so we
> never felt under pressure. My parents are simple people
> from west Limerick; they really appreciated his kindness.

Frances is one of the many nurses who went into Public Health rather than face the wards after she left her service for Concern. Her base now is behind high barbed wire in one of the most deprived areas of Dublin's inner city – no big deal for someone who has been through the worst of the Somalia crisis.

> I worked in a lot of dangerous places. We knew there was a high risk of dying. South Sudan was very dangerous, for instance, but when Jack and Aengus were around, you just found the bravery. Those Finucanes, they were never 'risk averse'. Now everyone is risk averse.

Frances thinks it is 'really interesting' that the Spiritans allowed these brothers to be members of Concern and for so long. 'All of their lives, really':

> Yeah, those Finucane brothers were strong, brave men. You'd say to them: 'Ye were fine men in ye're day!' Aengus'd go: 'In my day?' Jack'd just look at you. Our task in Concern now is to preserve their legacy.

Sarah Finucane too is in a good position to have dealt with the differences in these two personalities.

Her view coincides with that of Frances O'Keeffe about the Finucane brothers' differently shaded attitudes about the issue of clerical child abuse. Aengus, both say, was very uncomfortable even talking about it. In ways, he was indignant about the way it made him feel: 'Look at me with my nieces and nephews; I can't even give them a kiss now in case someone thinks there's something wrong with me!'

Jack's attitude, said Frances, is a simple: 'There is no defence.'

How does Sarah feel about her fun uncle's departure from Concern in Camden Street when he had to retire?

> He was very sad. I know that. And I'm sure there were a few people who weren't on top of his best friends list,

but I would have got a reality check with Jack who has gone off and done his own thing. There does come a time. I was being protective, but really, Aengus didn't want the protection, and now I've come very much full circle.

At some point during this period, she realised that Aengus saw himself as 'a mascot of Concern. He *wanted* to be rolled out.'

Towards the end of his life, Sarah's uncle spent many hours sitting on the balcony of his rented apartment with hands folded, watching the *Paseo*, the passing parade, and the way sunlight and shadows increased or decreased the presence of the twin Poolbeg chimneys, quietly mouldering but still marking the entrance to the Great South Wall, landmarking the port of Dublin for those approaching from the sea.

Until, that is, the urge to pick up the phone and summon company got to him.

Over and over again, between the lines or overtly, throughout all these interviews it became clear that Aengus did not relish unbidden solitude. Dominic MacSorley, who knew him very well and is an astute observer, wonders, like some others, if he was actually lonely.

Everyone on earth experiences lonely moments. And yes, because of a spate of oral evidence (especially from interviewees quoted within the pages of this book) it is demonstrable that Aengus loved company because he enjoyed and loved people.

At the risk of sounding like a pop psychologist, many people who surround themselves constantly with friends, who go to such lengths to keep in touch and who set so much store by the objects that represent their friendships, often are. Once the party is over, the sound of your own footsteps rings hollow.

Of course, hands up, this is pure speculation by an author who encountered Aengus rarely, and never one-on-one. To come clean, the most important interaction with him was when he agreed, when other clerics would not, to impart a blessing at her wedding. But even on that occasion, Jack and a hundred others were in the tent. Busy as she was that day with guests, she was struck that the people he talked to most were his brother and Jacqueline Duffy, with whom he had maintained a close friendship since her days as his press officer in Camden Street.

'There were great depths to Aengus,' says Jacqueline, who adds that everyone thought of him as a *bon vivant* because 'he adored parties and was always the last one to go. But that is to underestimate him. The private person was far deeper than most people saw.'

And Patsy, his sister, has also wondered: 'Was he sometimes lonely? Lonely in his world of vast horizons, huge dreams, limitless possibilities, incapable of being really understood by most of us?'

28

'Irwin? Seven months and forty years with Concern!'

– Evanna Barry Schorderet

Discounting family, even counting family (who feel entitled to cavil a little no matter how beloved the relative), Irwin Shorr has to be by far Aengus Finucane's most passionately vocal advocate. He spent only seven months in Bangladesh as a volunteer before going back to his own world, but this brief, hands-on involvement with the organisation resulted in a type of devotion to his mentor rarely encountered. This devotion has, unabated, survived Aengus's death.

A nutritionist from Woonsocket, Rhode Island, he is now a wealthy entrepreneur as a result of his invention of the 'ShorrBoard', a weight and measuring device developed to measure children and thereby nutritional status. Flexible enough to measure adults, it is now in use worldwide by all the major humanitarian agencies including those of the UN and Concern.

Irwin is Jewish, from an observant, although not strictly orthodox, family.

When I told Mom and Dad that I was going to Bangladesh with Irish priests, it was: 'You're going with who? To do *what*? *WHERE*?'

And I remember when I got back from Bangladesh after travelling with Aengus through Europe and Israel, my parents came to pick me up: 'Well, Irwin, now that you got this out of your system …?'

'Oh, Mom, this is just the beginning!'

And it was. Irwin's desire to talk about Aengus Finucane is an imperative. He travels constantly and confirmed he would be available at 8 a.m. on a specified date at Dublin Airport prior to a flight to the States.

At 7.01 a.m. that morning, he calls to say he is ready and waiting at a café table in one of the departure areas. He has already checked in with his bags – all 136 kilos worth of them. So there will be a bit of extra time to talk about Aengus. And we certainly avail of it.

It's a busy morning in Terminal Two as this man, with his American tennis-player's smile (at one point he was ranked professionally, and still plays on the Senior Circuit) launches, for the next three hours into a fluent litany of veneration, even exaltation of Aengus Finucane as he passionately declaims the humanity, charisma, goodness, stature, saintliness – almost godliness – of the person, behaviour, even genius, of this Irish priest.

He leaves no space for questions, really; it is best to sit back and enjoy the ride. Almost right up to the end, he said, he would talk to Aengus about every aspect of his life, his career and the failing health of his parents. 'Little did I know that he would die before Dad did.'

He tears up. 'At 77, Aengus's time had not come. He was not done. He died too early.'

He starts with the first week of his stint in Dhaka when his mentor took him along to a meeting of all the NGOs operating in Bangladesh at the time. They were called in by Abdur Rab Chowdhury, the lawyer and government minister who at the time was bent on putting some sort of shape on the activities of a melee of disparate NGOs:

And Rab said the following, singling out Aengus and Concern: 'Never has an organisation done so much good with such little fuss.'

He repeats it slowly, aiming his words towards the microphone end of the little tape recorder on the café table: '*Never. Has. An. Organisation. Done. So. Much. Good. With. Such. Little. Fuss.*'

Aengus inspired lives by living his own; by his own example. Some people think he was just a friendly Irish priest. He was an artful negotiator and a skilful fundraiser.

I was going home from Bangladesh, he was travelling through Europe and we got together in Germany, where he'd just been meeting with a group and looking for funds. I asked him, 'How did it go?'

'It's much more of a blessing to give than to receive, and I was just giving them the opportunity to be blest!'

Irwin loves that. *Loves* it…. As he chuckles, there might be an opportunity here to insert a couple of questions into the conversation.

(Irwin, there have been a few criticisms here and there about Aengus's style of management. Like, from time to time he might have been a bit autocratic? And do you think, maybe he enjoyed the limeli…)

[Wrong! Wrong! Oh, so, so *wrong*….]

Leaders emerge! They are not selected! [Irwin is now furious.] It was Aengus's innate altruism to be in service that made him become a leader. It was a consequence, not an objective.

He leans forward and again addresses the tape, still mildly turning:

I'll say that again: *It. Was. A. Consequence. Not. An. Objective*! He saw what had to be done and took steps to do it. He was a pioneer, an author, a humanitarian, a colleague and always a friend. And those who say any different, they were confrontational. They'll always be there. They are wrong.

[To tape once more] *They. Are. Wrong!*

Aengus was a visionary. He and Jack were both visionaries. They had the talent and ability to tell it like it is. And you listen. You pay attention. Their demeanours were such because of the spirit of the Fathers. It's one of service to mankind, to God, to themselves. And *that's* what their glow is about, not about anything selfish. *Not* the limelight.

He holds up his hand. Message understood. Time to sit back into the ride.

Aengus found it was his *responsibility* to be in the lime-light to bring attention to our cause, to Concern. If that's what was needed, so be it. Steve Martin [the American film actor and comedian] said: 'I realised a long time ago that I was called to sillyism.' Well Aengus, yes, those pictures of his honorary doctorates, the pictures with Hillary and with Mary Robinson, he did that because he knew it was his *duty*....

Irwin's grandfather, Shlomo Schiller, has been honoured in Israel by having a kibbutz named for him. Irwin went there and took two handfuls of earth, 'some for me and some for Aengus.'

When he got to Dublin, Jack went with him to visit Aengus's grave in Dardistown where Irwin sprinkled the earth from his grandfather's kibbutz over Aengus and recited the Kaddish: 'The praise of God at the time of severe loss.'

He looks at his watch. In this symphony of encomia, the hours have galloped away and he is in danger of missing his flight, although the time needed to extricate his 136 kilograms of luggage from the hold is in his favour.

Throughout this litany of soaring, laudatory epithets about Aengus Finucane, it has been fascinating to watch Irwin's body respond to his passion as if he had an inner drumbeat speeding or slowing with his depth of feeling. His body, it seemed, was too limited to accommodate this store of praise: he leaped to his feet several times when he thought he detected the merest hint of argument or negativity, he squirmed, he glared, but time's up. He stands, but can't resist one more shot across the bows of the nitpickers, however few they are in number and however mild their criticisms:

> Aengus just loved having us, his children, around him.
> And the few fringe people who thought otherwise are
> at the tail end of distribution.

One very sad aspect of all of this is that for Irwin, on the day before he was due to get to Ireland – and Kimmage – to say his final goodbyes to Aengus four years previously, he got the call letting him know that Aengus had died.

As he sprints off to make sure he can get through Homeland Security, it is, however, clear that unless Father Aengus Finucane performs the quantum of recognised miracles necessary to be officially canonised, he will never have another follower as devoted, as sincere, as loving and faithful, or a champion as fervent as Irwin Shorr.

Ciunas Bunworth was one of those women who had hopped to it when it became clear that although he was still at home, the days were running out for Aengus.

> You get a job, and that's your job. His nieces do such
> and such, Ciunas does this ('only Ciunas knows how
> to'), Phena does that, Cleo does the other – and you
> didn't cross over or interfere in anyone else's task.

At one stage, she accused him directly of being manipulative. 'Ah, no,' he responded. 'The true skill of management is to find people who know how to do something, and to allow them to do it!'

Interestingly, Jim Finucane would agree with Irwin Shorr that, at 77 years of age, Aengus's race had not been run. He mourns the fact that his brother, 'didn't get a few more years. When you got to 60 before, you were old, but we talk now of people reaching 80 and 85 as the norm.'

As for Patsy, as soon as she had accepted the inevitability of Aengus's death, like many women, she set about handling her grief by becoming practical, just as the nieces had.

For Susan, Sarah and Kate, clearing out the Seabury apartment was no small task. It was stuffed, as we know, not just with lots of furniture to facilitate gatherings, but with all those awards, artefacts, souvenirs and gewgaws he had received from all quarters.

If, in his presence, you admired an object or photograph (or frequently, even if you didn't) you would be regaled in detail with the story attached. For Aengus, each piece, no matter how rudimentarily potted, carved, painted or written, was equally important because of its provenance.

What to do about all of this? Who now would remember the stories?

Patsy decided that she could help with that at least, and made a deal with Aengus that he would relate all of these stories to her and she would record them for posterity.

The task, she knew, was not going to be easy because of the flow, even flood of visitors passing in and out to pay their respects at Aengus's bedside in the Kimmage nursing home. Everyone knew it was his last terrestrial home and there was a certain time pressure.

The plan was that Sarah, meanwhile, who is a splendid photographer, would photograph 100 or more of these treasures and would publish them in a book. 'So,' says Patsy, 'every morning at eleven o'clock I'd go into his room and try to get him to concentrate on this, and of course he loved to talk.' Nevertheless, the task wasn't easy:

You never saw anything like the number of visitors. It was just as if you rang a bell at the gate and invited all-comers in. And of course if he heard there was a visitor, it'd be: 'Oh, we'll do more on this tomorrow, Patsy.'

She kept at it, however, until at last, with all of Sarah's photographs in the bag, there were perhaps just ten more stories to go:

This was a Monday morning, and as I got out of the car I could see the curtains were drawn over his window ... not good.

We'd had Mass on the day before, the Sunday morning, and he hadn't been well enough to have it in his room.

When she got inside, she dropped into the office of the matron, Regina.

'Is it okay to try to get him to talk?'
'I think it'll be okay ...'.
'If the Pope of Rome comes, don't let anyone into that room until I tell you!'
So I went down and there were people already in the room: Joe, Jack, the old man who lived in Aengus's apartment block. They were all singing 'The Fair Hills of Ireland'.

Bánchnoic Éireann Ó, Donncha Rua Mac Conamara's lament for an exile: *Take a blessing from my heart to the land of my birth....*

Joe knew that I wanted to talk to Aengus, and he shifted people out as quickly as he could. Aengus wasn't a bit pleased.

I was with him for about fifteen minutes when Regina came down, and she said the three Carey sisters have travelled up to see him from Galway.

'Show them in,' said Aengus.
'Don't. Give them tea!' I said.

314

After Regina had left, Aengus said: 'That was a terrible thing to do!' And he started to talk away from the stories in hand:

'That's very strange; I can remember only two Careys. Anne was in such and such a programme; Kathleen was in such a group. But I don't remember a third Carey. Maybe the medication is affecting my memory?'

'Maybe it is, Aengus. Let's get on with this?'

Anyway, I went down to the sitting room and there were the two Careys and Brigid Meagher [handcrafts, warehouses, upcountry in Saidpur, Bangladesh.] Aengus was in the end stage of cancer and on high meds, and yet he could remember not only the names but the programmes they were in in the 1970s! I think it all boiled down to the fact that he loved people.

That was on the Monday. Aengus became unconscious on the Thursday. But not until the material for the book project had been fully gathered by Patsy.

For Patsy and the rest of the family, the completion of the project was bittersweet because it had proved very difficult for them to tell him he mightn't be going home. From Sarah:

He loved all his stuff around him, and it was only in the last week that he said to Jack, 'Yeah, maybe you should let the apartment go.' And that conversation wasn't even final. He didn't know that at that stage we had the whole place cleaned out and ready to go.

Sarah was highly impressed with the quality of care he received in Kimmage:

In the midst of all the bad things, the dignity with which they treat the older men is a lovely thing to see.

While in Kimmage, very close to the end, she ran into Aengus's trusted friend Father Mick Reynolds. He said to her that, while he had been in to see Aengus, his friend had mentioned something he needed to do 'next week.' Sarah advised him of the real situation, and he went in again that night.

'Mick Lally had been in too,' she says:

> They had a whiskey together, and I think it was later that night he had his turn. He did give us all the chance to say goodbye gently.

Just before that final 'turn' that led to coma, Joe Finucane drove fellow Limerick man and pal John Leahy to Kimmage to visit for the last time. Aengus was still conscious that day, but barely.

Leahy found their encounter so moving he can barely articulate it, even though he is talking four and a half years afterwards:

> All along there had been many, many people visiting, and at this stage everyone knew he wanted to see only family and close friends, so it was a privilege to be allowed in.

His guess is that Aengus didn't want 'outsiders' to witness his weakness. 'Joe would be like that too':

> Joe and I have been best friends for forty something years, and I would allow my emotions to show sometimes, but he wouldn't. Or Jim wouldn't. Or Aengus either, or Jack. They'd like to be more in control. They had this pride in who they were: 'We're the Finucanes,' fair play to them. Not snooty, they just had a certain code they adhered to, very strong personalities and very strong characters.

This was one of the most difficult days of my life, but as I say it was a great privilege to be able to go and see him.

When he got into Aengus's room, it was clear that Aengus knew why he was there. 'I could see he knew. We both knew. It was the end.'

John has driven up from Limerick and the interview is being conducted on a Sunday mid-morning in the front lounge of the Radisson Hotel in Stillorgan. It is a sunny day, and outside the formal gardens are in wonderful order. In here, the room, furnished with armchairs and sofas, is humming with delighted tourists, coffee drinkers, small boys in GAA jerseys, Sunday Best little girls and women chatting in small groups as waiters and waitresses bustle between tables. The contrast between this cheeriness and a narration so intimate and harrowing could not be more desolate.

At this table beside the fire we have had to pause several times when tears roll down this man's face. He repeatedly apologises for them, despite reassurances that there is really no need.

There isn't. Apart from Tom Moran, John's grief at the death of a friend whose most prominent qualities he listed as loyalty and being 'a gentleman of the highest quality,' is closest to the surface. When asked what Aengus's last words to him were, he weeps again, then whispers, when he can: 'Goodbye.'

Does he believe Aengus knew it was the real goodbye?

He just looked up at me, raised his hand and looked down again.

With her husband, Eamonn Brehony, Moira Conroy was another of the former Concern volunteers and friends who got in to see him in those final days. As they approached his room, they faltered. 'His sister was feeding him soup. That was a hard blow, seeing the independence gone.'

All that was in early October 2009.

The previous December, Aengus was attending, as he always did, an annual black-tie event in New York. The Winter Ball is a fundraiser organised by the younger generation of Concern supporters in the city. During that night, Siobhan Walsh noticed that he 'wasn't himself.'

Tom Moran gave us his big suite on the thirty-fifth floor of the Mutual building. We had a DJ, we had Santa Claus, Aengus had always loved that night. It was the only night he used to dance. His dance partner was always Vanessa from the office.

But that final year he was complaining about his stomach, he wasn't drinking his whiskey, he wasn't dancing, and I said: 'There's something really wrong here.' A lot of people have said subsequently that he never knew he was dying. I don't believe that.

Almost exactly ten months later, she was at work in New York when she was told that Aengus, whom she knew was in the nursing home, had had a stroke and that the family had now made a decision that from then on it would be 'family only' allowed in to see him.

'I knew I should have gone to see him earlier. I sat down and I started crying, and Dominic said: "Siobhan, you have to go and see him."'

She bought a plane ticket immediately, and as soon as she cleared customs next morning went straight to Kimmage from the airport.

When I got there, I said to Jack: 'I know I'm not supposed to be here, but I really want to see him.'

All the Finucanes were there. I was trying to keep it together in front of them.

After she left the room, she hung around outside and when she saw the family members leave for a cup of coffee, 'I snuck back in for five minutes to sit with him and to hold his hand and to talk to him.'

Did he know she was there?

'I don't think so.'

It's her turn to cry.

Yet it is the way of the world that, officially at any rate, when someone is dying or has died, the grief of close friends, even the closest, like Siobhan, Irwin, Ciunas, Mick Reynolds – and that wide and devoted group of 'Aengus's Irish Colleens' as Mark Malloch Brown affectionately called them – must take second place to that of family members – who, all agree, had been very welcoming until the very end.

Family sorrow on his brother's passing was, everyone says, felt most keenly by Jack. Which makes it especially poignant that, early on Aengus's last morning on earth, Tuesday 6 October, when he actually died, Jack and his twin were stalled in Dublin's rush-hour traffic while on their way back to his bedside.

With the rest of the family, Jack had kept vigil for days and nights since the previous Thursday. On the Monday night, exhausted, he, with Jim and Patsy, had gone home to catch a few hours' sleep, leaving their sister, Mary, and two of the nieces, Avril and Susan, to keep watch.

And so it fell to Susan to make that phone call to Jack and her father.

To her it had been 'a privilege' to be with Aengus as he passed:

I remember the moment. I suppose we didn't really know when to expect it because he was still so huge. I think it was fabulous in a way that he didn't lose his size [or his hair] because he was still like this big bear. The week before you mightn't even have known he was sick, and you'd be in having a sneaky whiskey with him, but I'd been there when Mum died, and you kind of know.

Jack and Jim arrived twenty minutes later.

> Sometimes, when you were growing up, you'd some-
> times hear Jack being annoyed with Aengus going on
> and on. And now you realised, God, he loved him so
> much. So for Jack not to have been there....

At that point, words fail her.

29

'I read about the Good Samaritan and all the other stories in the Bible. I always thought that they were just stories. It was only when I met you that I saw Christianity in action. You are the personification of all that Christ wants to do for us.'

– Army Major Christopher Ejiofor[3]

Aengus Finucane died on the morning of 6 October 2009. Sarah Finucane says she knows that in anticipation of his funeral her uncle would have said to his fourteen nieces and nephews: 'Now all the jobs are done. Make sure ye all look well.' And to the nieces in particular: 'Ye go and get your hair done.'

On the morning of 9 October 2009, Sarah, Susan and their sisters went to get their hair done.

Siobhan Walsh's memory of the funeral is of tears:

> … there were a whole lot of us standing in a row – and every single one of us was crying. At least fifteen of us. How he managed to have so many connections with so many different people … there are lots of extraordinary people in the world, but he was something special.

---

3 Biafran refugee in Gabon, 1970, in a letter to Aengus Finucane.

Tears are, of course, a form of tribute. Who weeps at the loss of someone to whom he is indifferent? And yes, there was a quiet flood of them at that funeral, flowing not only from family and close friends but from a legion of battle-hardened eyes that had borne witness to the most heartbreaking deaths imaginable in lands far away.

Most significant of all was the size of the crowd. They had travelled from all over Ireland, the US, the Far and Middle East and Africa. All were there for Aengus. All were *ad idem* about why they had travelled.

'Ordinary people' understood too what was happening. Mark Malloch Brown flew in from London to attend, and when on his way to Kimmage: 'The taxi man asked where was I going. I told him and he said "there's priests buried every day of the week around here. What was so great about this one?" ' But when given the name, the driver nodded sagely.

From the outside, the basilica-style church with its square campanile sits rather awkwardly within the Spiritans' compound, where Aengus had died three days before. Inside it was choc-a-bloc, but still airy enough to enable appreciation of the plain but elegant architecture, parquet floor, and décor that mixed various shades of cream. That day, there were dozens of priests, including Jack Finucane, crowded into the Boma – the space on the altar to accommodate concelebrants of Mass. Above his own vestments, Jack's face, although under control, betrayed his exhaustion and grief.

As for Mark Malloch Brown's affectionate description of Aengus as 'Jesus-like, with disciples around,' this was borne out by the numbers of Concern staff and former volunteers, ex-volunteers and volunteers whose lives had morphed from volunteerism to staff and hierarchy, older now, crowded into the pews.

There were many who, at considerable personal cost and difficulty, had made the journey to bear witness to the effect Concern, Aengus, Jack and these extraordinary people had had on their lives – people like the man who had travelled all the way from Nigeria with his wife and pictures of his children. Irwin Shorr suspended his global peregrinations, flying in from Copenhagen to deliver from the altar a prayer in Hebrew.

There was a large contingent from the US, as noted by Tom Arnold in one of the three major eulogies from the altar that morning. The emphasis in all three, from Arnold, Jack and Father Mick Reynolds, was that Aengus had been: 'proud to say he had three families: his Finucane family, his Spiritan family and his Concern family.'

Arnold, who was at the time CEO of Concern, went on to say that the NGO was 'immeasurably indebted to Aengus's Spiritan Order for providing Aengus, Jack and a number of other priests over the years' to work with the organisation: 'I want to thank the successive Provincials over forty years who facilitated this.' (Even in his grief, listening to this from the altar, Jack must have felt justified about his conviction that the Spiritans should have run Concern as their own social justice arm.)

'An important part of Concern's identity,' Arnold went on:

> ... was that from its beginning it was a non–denom-inational organisation, supported by people from all religions and from none. But we also had a distinctly Irish approach to being non-denominational; we were led for sixteen years by a remarkable charismatic priest whose values remain central to our vision and purpose.
>
> Aengus's Concern family had many branches. There were his friends from the early days in Biafra, when his Holy Ghost family and his new Concern family commingled. These were heroic days as were recounted so well by Father Tony Byrne as he spoke on radio of Aengus's sheer physical bravery in supervising the night flights to Uli, where he was parish priest ... eventually....

That 'eventually' resulted in a ripple of smiles throughout the congregation. It referred to the well-disseminated

323

anecdote that the Finucanes' mother had been very annoyed that, when he got to Nigeria, Jack, the younger son, was given a parish relatively quickly, before Aengus, the elder, who had been there for years. She had made her annoyance quite clear to her own anointed next time he went home. This, she told him in no uncertain terms, had fallen well short of the plan.

Aengus [Arnold continued] grew to love the Bangladeshi people in all their classes and creeds. Last November I was in Bangladesh, and returned home with two letters to give to him; one from Rab Chowdhury, who had been a powerful figure in the first government of Bangladesh and had worked closely with him to introduce wheat to the country – an achievement of which Aengus was very proud.

The other letter was from Mustafa, the guard, or chowkidar, in the Concern compound. He was the guard when Father Aengus was there, and he is still the guard. He insisted on having his photo taken with me, and got a colleague to write the letter so that he could remain in contact with his friend.

My treasured personal memories of him are of the many evenings we spent together in his apartment over the past fifteen years, just the two of us, talking about Concern past and present, about current political developments, about the next rugby match we were going to watch together. And of being reminded, as I would prepare to leave, that 'these nights will never come again,' and that maybe 'we could have one more small whiskey together?'

And then, from the altar, Tom read one final letter to the attentive and loving members of Aengus's three families. Now part of Concern folklore, it was written, he said, by an American nun, Sister Elizabeth O'Brien, who was in Bangladesh when she was stricken with cancer and whom Aengus invited to spend her remaining months in the Concern house in Dhaka.

> *You seem to crack the hard little shells that hold us in, and say: 'Come alive. Be happy. Not to worry.' This is a wonderful gift, and the mystery becomes a clear reality. It is the mystery of love.*
>
> *I would like to take you like seeds and throw you to the four corners of the earth. It would make a springtime of this old world, and it so badly needs a springtime. But instead your circle of goodness will slowly widen and encompass many people. Thank you so much for making me a part of it. You really are: Believing in Action, Hoping in Action, Love in Action.*
>
> *Each and every one, I love you, Concern.*

She signed it 'Liz', and dated it 14 August 1974.

Tom Arnold concluded:

> Between 14 August 1974 and last Tuesday, 6 October 2009, Aengus continued to widen his circle of goodness and make a springtime of this old world. That is why we are celebrating today a remarkable life; that is why each of us will miss him so much.

For his obituary, Mick Reynolds acknowledged that Aengus had spent himself in the service of others.

He quoted the words of St Paul, never more apt:

> *I have fought the good fight,*
> *I have finished the race*
> *I have kept the faith.*
> *I look forward to the prize that is waiting for me*
> *The prize I have earned....*

As in the other eulogies from Jack and Tom Arnold, Father Reynolds reminded us that Aengus had revered three families, but added a fourth: Limerick.

Every Finucane, every Limerick person, every Concern person, Spiritan, pal, and all who were merely tangentially involved, knew about Aengus's exultation at being granted the freedom of that city. For him it trumped all other awards and honours with which he had been laden during his lifetime. (Jack received the same award that day, something he typically kept close to his chest ever after; so did Ciarán Mac Mathúna. All three were present at the Finucane family hooley afterwards, from where it was reported by several 'amazed' guests that 'Jack *stayed*!')

But from the altar of the church at Kimmage Manor during Aengus's obsequies, Mick Reynolds deflated the Limerick genealogy bubble a little: 'When Aengus traced his family tree, he found that all the roots went back to Clare and Kerry!'

He also raised a chuckle of recognition when he noted that, in the early days, Aengus energetically imposed Spiritan Missionary values on the Concern houses with those edicts about behaviour, hygiene, curfews and so on, leading to some of the volunteers complaining that they were being 'treated like Novices.'

And he lauded, in particular, Aengus's loyalty: to family and friends, to Concern, to the Christian Brothers, 'to whom he felt we all owed so much. And to the Holy Ghost Fathers, who gave him the opportunity and encouragement to live out his dream.'

And Aengus never forgot to pay a tribute to his homeland. In Kimmage just a few days before his death, during a visit from Kevin Byrne, an Aer Lingus pilot friend of his, the two of them were discussing the view of the Irish coastline when an aircraft came in to land from America. Aengus, Byrne told friends afterwards, broke into a poem: 'The Exile's Return' by John Locke:

> *O, Ireland! Isn't it grand you look –*
> *Like a bride in her rich adornin!*
> *With all the pent-up love of my heart*
> *I bid you the top of the morning!*

Mick Reynolds included a story from 1970 when his pal was in Gabon looking after the thousands of refugees and orphans from Biafra and Nigeria itself. There he became friendly with Army Major Christopher Ejiofor, who had been aide-de-camp to the Biafran leader, Ojukwu.

Christopher asked Aengus to officiate at his wedding to Christine, a worker on Aengus's staff, a request to which he agreed with delight. (Rumour has it that he helped the celebration by producing the extra altar wine he had stored away for the occasion, leading to some of the guests comparing it to *The Wedding Feast at Cana!*)

After the wedding, as repatriation of the refugees began, Aengus helped arrange for the couple to go to England – Christopher to take an engineering course, Christine to study nursing.

With resonances of those early stories about the Chicago paediatrician and that MBA student at Notre Dame, forty-seven years later, in 2008, during the year before he died, Aengus was contacted by the pair, now returning to Nigeria on retirement since they had finished work and their English children were well weaned and gone. From the altar that morning, Mick quoted Christopher's letter to his benefactor:

> For many years I have thanked God for sending you into our lives at a time when we were the poor, the downtrodden, the neglected of the world. Over the years I have read my bible, I read about the Good Samaritan and all the other stories. I always thought that they were just stories. It was only when I met you that I saw Christianity in action. You are the personification of all that Christ wants to do for us.

Dominic MacSorley was in the congregation that morning. Listening and watching, he was struck by a number of insights.

During the orations, there had been a lot about the Holy Ghosts' focus on poverty, and of course that's Concern-speak. And then you realise the connection: that the Finucanes, along with their confrère missionaries from their order, took on and lived everything that they were preaching. The only thing left out was soul-saving.

So, as Dominic listened to the heartfelt tributes, the repeated emphases on Aengus's love of his trinity of families, he looked at the blended groups around him and saw that this was not just florid rhetoric, it was very real.

As the Mass ended with that most awful and final of rubrics: the blessing and incensing of the coffin prior to its committal forever to the clay, Jacqueline Duffy, who was sitting beside this author, dug her quickly in the ribs: 'Look! Look!'

We looked. Throughout the ceremonies, it had been cloudy and drizzling outside and the church's stained-glass windows, although nice enough, had been dull. Now, gradually, they were lighting up, drenching the white vestments, the altar, the clothing and hair of the congregation with showers of pastel but ever brightening and deepening colour.

This is going to sound OTT – a flight of fancy arising from the plangent emotion of the occasion – and not least from close proximity to the mysticism that is at the core of Jacqueline Duffy....

Was this really the clouds rolling back from the face of the sun, as they do regularly, even here in Ireland?

Because it did seem that day, just for those few moments, that Heaven was slowly opening its gates.

Dominic had one further insight. He saw that day, probably for the first time, he says, that within the trinity of Aengus's families was a hierarchy. The Finucanes and Concern lived in his heart, but his order owned that heart; since ordination it *was* the heart.

First, last and forever, Aengus was a priest. A Holy Ghost priest. He was part of a bigger family: 'It was their show,' he said.

'And the priests took Aengus home.'

EPILOGUE

'Reaching the poorest of the poor is tough, dirty work.
And when you think you have, you haven't.'

— Aengus Finucane

The following is a piece posted online on Monday 12 October 2009 at 2.11 p.m. by Mike Taibbi, former NBC News Correspondent and Siobhan Walsh's husband. (The original is long and has been edited a little.)

It's been a season of notable deaths – Cronkite, Kennedy, Swayze, Jackson, Fawcett, Hughes, Hewitt, Novak, and other so-called bold-faced names. But there's a great man who died at age 77 in Dublin last Tuesday, Oct. 6 and if Americans knew this Catholic priest who loved their country as well as his Irish homeland, their hearts would be as burdened by grief as are the hearts of thousands around the world.

His name was Aengus Finucane, and for nearly fifty years he roamed the world with a single purpose: to live among and lift up 'the poorest of the poor,' is the descriptive he always used, so they might have at least a chance at the life and prospects seemingly denied them by war, famine or sudden disaster.

He had the full toolkit for that kind of work: a missionary's zeal fuelled at times by righteous anger and sometimes by that peculiarly Irish stubbornness; humour and the right kind of humility, as well as enormous charm and personal charisma; and a wonk's need to know how the often arcane details of assistance programs could be manipulated to serve very simple human needs — food, water, health services, shelter. [A 'wonk' can be sweetly defined as someone who knows a lot about the details of a particular field or subject and talks a lot about it.]

As a young man he looked like a movie star, yet moved naturally among desperate populations who seemed to quickly see him as someone who understood their lives and challenges, and who could find the best route to the nearest solution.

I met Aengus in his role as honorary President of Concern USA, the American affiliate of Concern's Dublin-based worldwide organisation. When he stepped down as Concern's Chief Executive he turned his attention to the US operation, headed by Siobhan Walsh, my wife.

It was my good fortune to have spent a good deal of time with Aengus over the past thirteen years, in New York and in Ireland, and to have come to know him as a person and not just the titular head of an aid organisation. So I know he liked a good joke and good whiskey, Peking Duck and the latest popular movie, and hours of conversation on any subject that triggered his vigorous curiosity.

But here's the thing: at the end of an evening, and though he wasn't the kind of man who revelled in the stories of his work, you were never unaware of what that work was and how that work distinguished him from almost anyone else you were ever likely to meet.

As a missionary priest in the breakaway republic of Biafra, during the famine of civil-war-torn Nigeria in the 1960s, Aengus did whatever he could to bring aid to the neediest caught in the middle of the war. He organised brigades of helpers who raised oil lamps in the middle of the night to form a makeshift airplane runway, so hundreds of aircraft could bring in food and then fly out with the sickest children in the most desperate need of medical care — while Aengus and his team dodged artillery fire from the Nigerian Army.

[With] the relief organisation that came to be known as Concern, [he] began travelling to far corners of the world in the greatest need. To Bangladesh, to Pakistan and Cambodia, Ethiopia, Somalia, Burundi, Uganda, Rwanda just after the genocide; and later to Honduras and Haiti – wherever war or disaster threatened to flatten the most vulnerable and defenceless among us.

A lot of the work was the kind of drudge work news organisations rarely cover except in broad strokes during calamitous events. The work of digging wells, delivering seed to reclaim farmland, grading roadways; getting schools and clinics up and running; providing food, water, medications, shelter kits; fashioning rudimentary sewage treatment systems; teaching Aids patients how to reclaim their self-respect; pioneering micro-finance programs and food-production innovations so that threatened populations could eventually save and sustain themselves. Essentially the long list of projects referred to as 'capacity-building' in the lexicon of the aid community. The primary goal wherever Aengus touched down was to make outside assistance unnecessary as quickly as possible.

But when Aengus would say, 'Mike, will we go out for dinner one night this week?' we might all talk about the latest world crisis, or about whatever scandal seemed to be dominating news coverage at the moment. He liked a good yarn about any subject, and was a captivating raconteur himself. He was just good company, this world traveller who never seemed to be world weary or infected by cynicism, and I was lucky to be among the many he counted as friends. Lucky enough to have him sitting across from me, savouring another bite of duck breast with hoisin sauce.

He was the real deal, a hero priest who for a half century of his journey on this planet spent each day working so that others less fortunate than he could make it to the next day and the days beyond that.

I mourn his loss and will miss him, and though he wasn't a 'bold-faced name' in the way of our celebrity-obsessed society, the world will be the poorer for his having left us.

No matter how long-expected, whether hours, days, weeks or even years, death is always shocking for those left behind. Time has run out.

The dominant, virtually permanent memory is almost always the last time you saw the person, whether it was on a deathbed or, having made arrangements never to be fulfilled, waving goodbye from the front door or your kitchen sink.

So you scrabble for something tangible to cherish, a photograph, a tatty article of well-worn clothing around which lingers the loved one's distinctive smell, a piece of special jewellery, even the dead person's favourite cup or half-finished knitting.

Sarah Finucane's book of photographs, *A place called Home*, with its images of the objects Aengus displayed so proudly in his apartment and explanatory captions collected by Patsy from his bedside, became one such icon for her.

For Jack, it was to be Aengus's writings and historical papers – diligently catalogued but then so cruelly dispatched.

Places are significant too.

For the first three years after his death, Patsy avoided walking past his apartment, hated talking about him, and averted her eyes when passing Concern in Camden Street. Then, belatedly, she began to jot down her thoughts about how she felt:

He was so passionate, so committed, so focused he sometimes exhausted me, but now that I am writing about him, I feel a strength, an indefinable energy.

As she wrote, from her subconscious came yet another of his oft-repeated mottos: *Na Tuirling go Stadadh an Bus* – don't get off until the bus stops.

He certainly didn't get off his bus, dragging himself around Haiti, for instance, until, not too long afterwards, his health problems intruded to such an extent he had to give in. Temporarily, in his own opinion.

Of this, Patsy wrote:

> *Sometimes I found all this 'brave' talk annoying, especially when he was struggling with the side effects of chemotherapy. But he believed what he was saying (preaching!) and he proved it by living it.*

This man's legacy?

Too large to parse.

We use the word 'legacy' these days as a synonym for 'bequest' – to leave something to our descendants. As has been said again and again by interviewees in this book, Aengus has bequeathed to his organisation a treasury of insight, courage, vision, and, to this day, a mission laced with formidable drive for action to alleviate the plight of the wretched of the earth.

We also use 'legacy' in an attempt to describe a tracery of enduring qualities that a person has infused into the way we work, live our own lives or how we leave footprints on the planet. This can be used for good, as in the case of Aengus Finucane, or evil, as in the imposition of the seriously skewed ideas and violence of despots like Hitler or Pol Pot.

The word is derived from the Latin *legatus,* a messenger, ambassador, envoy (as in papal legate; a person who is authorised by a pope to leave his side – *a latere* – as his trusted representative to deliver his message and edict). Where these decrees are concerned the word is also related to *lex,* the Latin word for law.

Starting with his commitment to penny dinners when he was a schoolboy, as Mike Taibbi has noted, throughout his life and work, Aengus delivered a humanitarian message from his heart and soul to millions across the globe: the poorest of the poor do have allies.

Thanks to him, people of his ilk and those he inspired, Concern, its workers, supporters and donors, governments are now a little more enlightened than they were when he started out.

Thanks to him and them, very many 'ordinary' folk have developed consciences about the status of fellow human beings not fortunate enough to have won the birth lottery by being born into a peaceful and stable environment where there is food, shelter, health care – and where, in theory at least, every person is due a measure of equal opportunity.

Thanks to him and them, Concern now deploys 3,000 staff in twenty-eight troubled countries all over the world, and in 2013, the year in which the latest figures are available, responded to thirty-eight emergencies, assisting more than seven million people while working on increasing food security for three million more. It continued to work in very dangerous places such as Syria and no-go areas like North Korea.

And in terms of best practice, Aengus's organisation is very proud that while working with victims of Typhoon Haiyan (fourteen million affected, five million displaced) in the Philippines in November 2013, the UN Deputy Emergency Response Coordinator, John Ging, a powerful international influencer, in dispatches described its work as 'the Gold Standard.'

Now it is Dominic MacSorley who carries this responsibility. Having started his work for Concern under Aengus's aegis, he has not only learned from him: he is imbued with Aengus-isms: 'He always said that reaching the poorest of the poor is tough, dirty work. And when you think you have, you haven't.'

Is Ireland ever going to be the biggest nation in the world? Never! The richest? Never!

Yet our people are everywhere in the world, and what does everyone say about us? That we punch above our weight.

Certainly, the founders of Africa Concern, the Kennedys and O'Loughlins, did just that all those years ago when, without any kind of a road map to guide them, they did what they did. There wasn't even a language for it. Jack would say: 'We didn't know about camps for the displaced, we just knew there were a lot of people in our schools who needed help.'

Just two more stories, similar but supportive of each other, as they illustrate one of the founding principles of Concern's ethos and values.

As we know, Concern does not withhold assistance to victims because rulers or governments are not nice people, or because the recipients themselves may not be morally whiter than white.

In Rwanda, Dominic and Jack went in to check out conditions in 'The Cave', a dungeon under one of the gaols holding those accused of genocide. Some were there for four years. Dominic:

> It was standing room only; the most horrific place I have ever seen. Heat, bodies, thousands and thousands with nowhere to sit. They paid each other for a chance to lie down. One light. And it went off when we were there.

Jack saw a nun in there, and, according to his companion, 'thought she was ministering.' She wasn't. She was a prisoner. The bilateral Rwandan genocide was enough to challenge Jack's belief in humanity; like his brother before him, this evidence of the church's role in Rwanda hit him hard. 'Is there anything I can do? Anything you need?' Jack, says Dominic:

> … worked 24/7 on the phone that night. And the next morning, when I got up, there was a handwritten note, in his very nice handwriting, starting with: *In my thirty years I have never been so ashamed of man's inhumanity to man…*.

And there was another note attached:
'*Dominic, could you get someone to type this up and send it to The Irish Times?*'

'There are great, quiet depths to Jack,' says Dominic.

Jack's letter was published in *The Irish Times*. And Concern people did go into that prison, just as, a little later, Anne O'Mahony went into hers.

Having been responsible for Sierra Leone and Liberia, Anne had transferred to Rwanda in 1997 – and was there when the post-genocide trials were running. She had 350 staff, most of whom, she says, 'were going through their own internal horrors.'

And, in the seven community prisons housing the *génocidaires*, the overcrowding Dominic and Jack had encountered in the dungeon they visited also pertained. 'They had to take it in turns to lie down at night. They could negotiate, for payment, for window views,' Anne says:

> ... but the only food they got was what the relatives brought. These relatives were mainly women who had to look after not just their children and families, but small farms too. Every day they walked as much as twelve kilo-metres each way between their homes and the prisons – so no time to look after the farm, no time to earn. We were looking at this and wondering if we could do the feeding and alleviate this burden on the women.

During the genocide, however, many Concern staff members had been directly affected by the atrocities; many were additionally upset because as relatives of victims they were legally required to attend court while the alleged perpetrators were being tried.

Within the Rwandan office, therefore, the plain and terrible proposition was: *Do you want to be part of an organisation that is feeding your family's killer?*

The debate was anguished: 'But in Concern we've always tended to push the boat out and to do what might be unpopular.' In this specific case, eventually:

> I got permission to go into the prison. Along with one of my female colleagues from the office, I met the governor. The three of us walked forward, and next thing the governor stepped back and the doors closed behind us.
>
> I looked around and he was gone. And there we were, two women in a sea of men, in a yard, jam-packed, no room to move at all.
>
> I had a moment of intense panic: here we are, two women and 8,000 men, and this is probably the first time they've been this close to a woman in all the four years since the genocide ended, and they were locked up. You're processing this very quickly. And then a little path opens and a man steps forward and says: 'Let me show you around.'
>
> It all worked out.

They're great at the understating, these people of Concern. And as an afterthought, could this have been the woman who changed the time on Aengus Finucane's watch so people could go to bed at a reasonable hour?

Don't know. Just saying.

These decisions illustrate perfectly the ethos of Concern and how, in an unbroken chain of similar choices, it has survived for forty-five years. All credit to the founders, the O'Loughlin-Kennedys, to Aengus, Jack and all the others who have preserved it. They have quite a responsibility, these agencies and the donor communities supporting them.

Do ordinary people really care? It seems that despite handy catchphrases like 'charity fatigue', we do. And as the inheritors of the Finucane (and O'Loughlin Kennedy) legacies, Concern will too.

Support from Joe and Mary Soap was somewhat challenged in what Frances O'Keeffe calls 'the charity debacle': the upheaval that in late 2013 and early 2014 engulfed the entire sector in Ireland as a result of weak governance within some charities, and in particular what the media pounced on: overpayments to CEOs and loose controls of donor inputs and of spending.

Concern has survived the groundswell of anti-charity criticism and outrage, not least because of its exceptionally rigorous accounting practices. Imbued with the courage and leadership of Aengus Finucane, since the Tarbett affair the scrupulousness of its accounts has won peer awards, and it is par for the course now that the organisation is utterly transparent about the disposition of donations.

The parade of honour across Concern's annals includes some of the most thoughtful, brave, innovative, and yes, brilliantly odd people ever to have been encountered by this author. Practical Christians too, whether or not they are formally so.

In the very early days of Christianity, from the monasteries of this island, monks and missionaries set out to preach and proselytise. In modern times, however, the spirit finds it hard to survive when the belly is empty and the children dying. So for forty-five years, preaching only hygiene and health, this relatively little agency with the big heart has ministered to the physical, social and psychical needs of its people.

Its workers have pitched their tents in war zones, offered immediate help to victims of floods, famines and pestilences of Biblical order. They have ministered to the dying, cleaned and wrapped the bodies of the dead, taught sex workers about their human and legal rights and how to weave.

They have wept with the relatives of those they could not save and, conversely, have shared the delight of mothers whose babies they have brought back from starvation to health.

All in an effort to give sustenance, respect and dignity to the humanity of the wretched.

They are still doing it, spreading influence and expertise throughout this huge and specialised arena, where one small cohort of the planet's population tries to help the enormous other.

This author is convinced that the public understands the ethos of an organisation whose main ambition is to eliminate global poverty and secure social justice for the poorest of the poor, but can also feed *génocidaires* who have been inhumanely incarcerated.

That could coax Bangladeshi authorities to allow a degree of human comfort and hygiene to professional beggars and prostitutes.

That can admit to being heartbroken at the scale of devastation in a refugee camp ankle-deep in mud (Bentiu, South Sudan) while pulling out all the stops to ward it off.

That in the highlands of Ethiopia can quickly figure out that donkeys do better work than aid trucks. (Or can build Irish bridges so that the trucks can cross through the water of sandy-bottomed rivers.)

That can, in a very violent context, persuade gun-toting crime lords to take a Glencree-style course in peace and reconciliation.

That can come up with ideas as simple as tying mothers and children together with little pieces of string so they won't lose each other in a flash flood of surging humanity more than a million strong.

And that, at the drop of a hat, in very difficult and dangerous situations, is organisationally capable of setting up programmes to alleviate the plight of victims of disasters, both natural and manmade, of such a scale as to be almost unimaginable to those not affected.

A patron of Concern Worldwide, the late Seamus Heaney, paid his own tribute to those who have:

> ... chosen to live at that high level where they are bound to keep facing the challenge – clear, noble and exhausting – that W. B. Yeats formulated as follows: '*to hold in a single thought reality and justice*.'

Now, all worries ceased and striving over, Aengus lies quietly alongside his Spiritan confrères in Dardistown Cemetery, directly under a flight path to and from Dublin Airport, of which he was such a frequent and joyful user.

The organisation he cherished, forever facing new frontiers and challenges, will negotiate them as it always has, with resolution, courage and honesty, prepared to learn from the mistakes it will inevitably make.

And finally: worn-out quotations are worn out because they are so accurately resonant. For, whether he recognised it or not, Aengus took the advice of Ralph Waldo Emerson: '*Do not go where the path may lead, go instead where there is no path and leave a trail.*'

ACKNOWLEDGEMENTS

Organising the material for *Aengus Finucane: In the Heart of Concern*, transcribing interview tapes and then coalescing them into a coherent narrative (I hope) has been, by any standards, a big task, and there are very many people to thank. Some names will appear twice because they were at once facilitators of the project and interviewees.

The initiative for it was Father Jack Finucane's. He supplied the initial list of potential interviewees within his own family, Aengus's priestly colleagues and the family of Concern.

Of course, that initial list expanded exponentially once the interviewing process began, as people suggested others. I simply had to stop at a certain point or the book, as a book, would never have seen a bookshelf. When God made time He made plenty of it, apparently, but not enough to accommodate the publishing schedule for a project like this one, which could potentially have gone on forever.

So to those to whom I did not get around, or who feel that having spoken to me for hours they have been elided in the finished product, may I say that this was because of repetition (only to be expected), all kinds of exigencies too boring to enumerate, and the length of the book overall. To them, I truly apologise.

And to family and friends of Aengus, fellow priests, colleagues, Concern volunteers, staff and council members

– and some outsiders too – whose words are here, thank you all. Many of you welcomed me into your own homes and home places, many travelled to meet me, all much appreciated. Not one person who was approached said 'no'. (Actually there was one, but he went on successfully to meet me anyhow!)

So very sincere gratitude to:

David Andrews, Tom Arnold, Evanna Barry (Schorderet) Giuila Bazziga, David Begg, Ciunas Bunworth, Liam Burke, Donal Byrne.

Joseph Cahalan, Cathy Cicerale (McGann).

Dolores Connolly, Moira Conroy (Brehony), Corinne (Haiti), Howard Dalzell, Jacqueline Duffy, Anita Exantus, Geraldine Farrell, Kevin Farrell, Aine Fay.

Father Jack Finucane, Jim Finucane, Joe Finucane, Mary Finucane, Sister Patsy Finucane, Sarah Finucane, Susan Finucane, Marian Finucane (no relation), Bob Fitzgerald, Eithne Healy.

President Michael D. Higgins, P. J. Howell, Mary Humphreys, Maryellen Johnston, Ed Kenney (Senior and Junior), Father Ciaran Kitching, Michael Lally, Tom Lavin, John Leahy, Michael Lee.

Dominic MacSorley, Mark Malloch Brown, Mary McCauley, Kathy McCauley, Mike McDonagh, Rich McMenamin, Peter McNichol, Jim McShane, Kelly McShane, Tom McSweeney, Patrick Masterson and Brigid Meagher (Ryan).

Tom Moran, Mike Murphy, Jean Linz Najac, Rossa O'Briain, Denis O'Brien, Mary Pat O'Connor, Anne O'Mahony, Phena O'Boyle, Niall O'Dowd, Pat O'Halloran, Frances O'Keeffe, David O Morchoe, Cleo O'Reilly, Father Dick Quinn, Father Mick Reynolds.

Former President Mary Robinson, Ursula Sharpe, Ted Shine, Irwin Shorr, Brian Stockwell, Jean-Frenel Tham and Siobhan Walsh.

Tom Arnold was CEO of Concern when this project was first proposed, and he set it on its way. Similarly, Jim Hynes, Chief Operations Officer, sorted out legal documentation.

Prior to this one, Tony Farmar wrote a wonderfully informative book about Concern: *Believing in Action*. It proved very valuable to me and Tony very generously agreed that I could quote from it.

Along with the tolerance of Director Peter McNichol and the staff of Concern in Haiti, who gave of their time in the midst of very serious work, the patience and steady good humour of Ed Kenney Junior of the New York office while guiding me through the vicissitudes of that sad country was remarkable. Thanks too to Stephanie Dellarocca in the same office for sorting out the rather complex travel arrangements.

At the outset, Aisling Duggan, of the Concern office in Dublin, could not have imagined how much she would find herself having to do. That you to Karen Power, who went the extra mile. Richard Dixon went to some lengths to find information for me. And of course, Dominic MacSorley is now Concern's supreme being and took time out from his peripatetic schedule to watch progress. As for Tom Moran, Chairman of Concern US, it was a genuine pleasure to spend ninety minutes in his company.

James Morrissey facilitated the interview with Denis O'Brien, and Bride Rosney, who continues to work with former President Robinson in the office of The Mary Robinson Foundation – Climate Justice, was of great help too, in organising the interview and securing permission from Mrs Robinson to quote from her own writings.

Thanks to Emmy winner Mike Taibbi of NBC in the US for permission to quote from his eulogy to Aengus. Similarly, Gerry Reynolds was happy to let me quote from his piece on Concern's 40th Anniversary supplement for *The Irish Times*. And George Barker went the extra mile to reminisce for me about Aengus's failures in the ship-launching arena.

Thanks to my RTÉ newsroom colleagues, Valerie Cox, Clodagh Walsh, Caroline Murphy, Fiona Kelly and John S. Doyle, who so kindly covered for me on the occasions when I simply could not be in two places at once. I also owe a debt to fellow writers Rose Doyle, Dermot Bolger and Peter Sheridan for timely advice and help.

Eoin Purcell of New Island took on the publishing of *Aengus Finucane: In the Heart of Concern* with a stout heart and optimistic spirit; editor Justin Corfield was staunch and encouraging and has the tolerance and patience of a saint, and we are indebted to Mariel Deegan for her cover design.

Thank you, dear husband Kevin, for your support and all that traipsing up the stairs with fresh cups of coffee (and removing the ones I forgot to drink!)

There are others to thank: Adrian, Simon, Catherine (and Eve), Declan, Mary P., Larry, Pauline and Mag, Carol and Patricia, Frances, Glynis, Marie and Anne, Mary S. and Mary O'D., Catherine H., Adavin, Brid, Dympna, Treasa, Gill, Mona, Laura, Emer – and Patsy McKeon, who frequently saw me at my most frantic when it seemed nothing could go right. Carmel Milne? You're a brick!

Thanks to all for understanding all the cancellations and excuses for social non-appearances (including you, Eileen Kelly, and my other good neighbours in Mornington, who have to be sick of my disappearing acts and alarmed by the frequent, rather frightening apparitions in a dressing gown at weird times of the day).

Most of all, gratitude is due to the spirit of Aengus Finucane. I knew him hardly at all in life, but do feel I know him now. When all else failed during this marathon, especially when everyone else was asleep, I reached for his most well-known mantra:

Do as much as you can,
as well as you can,
for as many as you can,
for as long as you can.

It's over to him now.

Aengus Finucane

CONCERN CORE VALUES

1. Extreme poverty must be targeted.
2. Respect for people comes first.
3. Gender equality is a prerequisite for development.
4. Development is a process, not a gift.
5. Greater participation leads to greater commitment.
6. All governments have responsibility for poverty elimination.
7. Emergencies call for rapid response.
8. Democracy accelerates development.
9. Environment must be respected.
10. Good stewardship requires good procedures.
11. Experience is the best teacher.

CEOs of (Africa) Concern:

1968–1972:	John O'Loughlin Kennedy
1973–1977:	Father Raymond Kennedy
1977 (June–Sep):	Father Michael Doheny
1977–1981:	Alex Tarbett
1981–1997:	Father Aengus Finucane
1997–2001:	David Begg
2001–2013:	Tom Arnold
2013–	Dominic MacSorley

Countries in which Concern serves:

ASIA
Afghanistan; Bangladesh; Democratic People's Republic of Korea; India; Pakistan; Philippines.

AFRICA
Burundi; Central African Republic; Chad; Democratic Republic of the Congo; Ethiopia; Kenya; Liberia; Malawi; Mozambique; Niger; Rwanda; Sierra Leone; Somalia; Republic of Sudan; South Sudan; Tanzania; Uganda; Zambia; Zimbabwe.

CARIBBEAN
Haiti.

MIDDLE EAST
Lebanon; Syria, Turkey.

INDEX

292, 293, 294, 298, 299, 302,
303, 304, 305, 306, 311, 314,
315, 316, 318, 319, 320, 322,
323, 324, 325, 326, 332, 335,
336, 347, 341, 342
Finucane, Jack Senior 20, 21, 22
Finucane, Jim, 14, 20, 35, 44, 115,
199, 320, 342
Finucane, Marian, 342
Finucane, Mary, 342
Finucane, Professor Paul, 20
Finucane, Sarah, 14, 298, 299,
305, 306, 313, 314, 315, 316,
321, 332, 342
Finucane, Sister Patsy, 14, 342
Finucane, Susan, 271, 286, 342
Finucane, Tom, 20
Fitzgerald, Bob, 342
Fitzgerald, Garret, 46
Flannery, Father Austin, 122
Flatley, Tom, 278, 279, 280, 281
Flynn, Bill, 227, 228, 229
Flynn, Ray, 286
Foley, Ted, 117, 119
Food for Work Programmes, 112
Food Services Institute, 54
France, 49
Frankfurt, 301
Frederick Street, Dublin, 103
Freemason, 46
Friel, Brian, 8, 38
Friendly Sons of St Patrick, 227
Friends in Ireland, 160

GAA, 211, 289, 317
Gabon, 48, 49, 51, 321, 327
Gaelic Football, 6, 282
Gaiety Theatre, 30
Galway, 278, 314
Garcia, Jerry, 231

Gardai, 120
Gardner, Craig, 172, 173
Geneva, 52
Génocidaires, 70, 193, 336, 339
Ghana, 41
Ging, John, 96, 334
Glasgow, 105
Gleeson, Mr Justice, 116
Glencree, 268, 270, 275, 339
Goal, 196, 211
Goma, 158
Good, Father James, 113
Goodman, Mick, 104
Gorta, 80
Grand Ravine, 267, 268, 269,
270, 271, 272, 273
Great South Wall, 32, 306
Grogan, Vincent, 45
Guckian, Mary, 46
Gulf War, The 93

Haiti, vii, 36, 106, 149, 223, 238,
239, 250, 256, 259, 261, 262,
263, 264, 266, 267, 268, 270,
271, 273, 279, 283, 284, 289,
331, 332, 342, 343, 346
Haor District, The 103
Harbo, 141, 142, 146, 284
Harbo refugee camp, 137
Harty, Patricia, 239
Healy, Eithne, 174, 177, 178, 194,
214, 243, 342
Heaney, Seamus, 218, 339
Heart of Darkness, 130
Herbert Park Hotel, Dublin, 163
Higgins, Michael D. (President),
3, 291, 294, 295, 342
Higgins, Sabina, 292
HIV, 73
Hogan, Sean, 113